C000064402

Gestalt Therapy on the World wide web

The Gestalt Therapy Page is the Internet's oldest and most comprehensive web resource for information, resources, and publications relating to the theory and practice of Gestalt therapy.

Visitors can subscribe to *News and Notes*, a free email calendar of conferences, training programs, and other events of interest to the worldwide Gestalt therapy community.

The Gestalt Therapy Page includes an on-line store that offers the most comprehensive collection of books and recordings available – many available nowhere else!

Visit today: www.gestalt.org

The Gestalt Journal Press was founded in 1975 and is currently the leading publisher and distributor of books, journals, and educational recordings relating to the theory and practice of Gestalt therapy. Our list of titles includes new editions of all the classic works by Frederick Perls, Laura Perls, Paul Goodman, Ralph Hefferline, and Jan Christiaan Smuts. Our catalog also includes a wide variety of books by contemporary theoreticians and clinicians including Richard Hycner, Lynne Jacobs, Violet Oaklander, Peter Phillipson, Erving & Miriam Polster, Edward W. L. Smith, and Gary Yontef.

In 1976, we began publication of *The Gestalt Journal* (now the *International Gestalt Journal*), the first professional periodical devoted exclusively to the theory and practice of Gestalt therapy.

Our collection of video and audio recordings features the works of Frederick (Fritz) and Laura Perls, Violet Oaklander, Erving & Miriam Polster, Janie Rhyne, and James Simkin.

The Gestalt Journal Press, in conjunction with the University of California, Santa Barbara, maintains the world's largest archive of Gestalt therapy related materials including original manuscripts and correspondence, published and unpublished, by Gestalt therapy pioneers Frederick & Laura Perls and Paul Goodman. The archives also include more than six thousand hours of audio and video recordings of presentations, panels and interviews dating to early 1961.

A Child's Eye View

Gestalt Therapy
With Children and Adolescents
and Their Families

Ruth Lampert

A PUBLICATION OF THE GESTALT JOURNAL PRESS

Copyright © 2003 by Ruth Lampert

ISBN 0-939266-46-6
ISBN 978-0-939266-46-3

Published by:
      The Gestalt Journal Press, Inc.
      P. O. Box 278
      Gouldsboro, ME 04607

Printed in the United States of America. All rights reserved.
This book or parts thereof may not be reproduced in any
form without the written permission of the publisher.

This book is dedicated to the memory of my father, William Francis Tauber, who died too young but left his family a legacy of love.

AUTHOR'S NOTE

The stories and voices in this book are derived from my clinical and teaching experiences. Names, places and other identifying information have been changed to protect privacy and anonymity; some examples are composites. Therefore, any similarity between any persons described herein and any persons known to readers is inadvertent and purely coincidental.

CONTENTS

VOLUME II

RUTH LAMPERT'S FAMILY THERAPY WORKBOOK

Exercises and Experiments for Working with Children, Adolescents and their Families

FOREWORD

Every so often a book appears for the therapist/counselor that is both professionally enriching and enjoyable to read. *A Child's Eye View: Gestalt Therapy with Children, Adolescents, and Their Families* is just such a work. The author, Ruth Lampert, makes excellent use of her experiences, first as an educator and then as a therapist/counselor, as she explores the innumerable elements involved in assisting troubled children and families in finding the tools they need to bring hope, and sometimes harmony, into their lives.

Lampert also draws upon her skills as an award winning writer to bring a freshness to each case vignette, holding the reader's attention while informing without overwhelming. Trained in Gestalt therapy, the author draws from a wide variety of therapeutic approaches, building on the foundations established by her training at the Gestalt Therapy Institute of Los Angeles. The extraordinary value of Gestalt therapy for working with this population was first established by Violet Oaklander's seminal work, *Windows to Our Children: A Gestalt Approach to Children and Adolescents* first published in 1978. Today, twenty-five years later, Oaklander's book remains one of the preeminent texts used in graduate programs worldwide focusing on child and adolescent therapy and counseling.

Lampert explores areas untouched or given only brief examination in Oaklander's original work including the use of hypnosis as a therapeutic tool and working with the "patient/client" within the context of the family constellation. She also shares her unique use of Frederick (Fritz) Perls's "acting out the dream" with children and adolescents troubled by disturbing and sometimes terrifying dreams.

The author devotes a chapter to adolescent suicide, a topic oft discussed but rarely included in a book offering specific suggestions to the therapist/counselor facing a youth he or she suspects may be suicidal. Her chapter on counseling the abusive parent offers guidance in dealing with these troubled individuals who cause so much pain in the children they abuse.

A Child's Eye View is so well written it deserves two readings — the first to enjoy the author's ability to tell a story full of the interest and excitement that can be found working with developing youth. She shares her own doubts and mistakes as touchstones for learning while letting her wit and self deprecation sparkle through the pages.

A second reading will allow you to focus on the wealth of material here for the child and adolescent therapist — material that includes insights into troubled children and their families coupled with specific approaches and techniques for helping them cope with the diverse variety of problems facing them. It belongs on your bookshelf where you can view it as a trusted colleague — there to be consulted when you find yourself confronted by a therapeutic challenge and could use some advice and counsel.

Joe Wysong
Founder and Editor — *The Gestalt Journal*

ACKNOWLEDGMENTS

To properly thank all the people who have inspired and encouraged me in my work as a therapist and a writer I would need to write a separate volume, and someday I may do just that. For now I will confine my expressions of appreciation to some of the people who contributed specifically to this book.

Of the many teachers and trainers whose influence is reflected in all my work I am especially indebted to Gary Yontef, Laura Perls, Violet Oaklander, Miriam Polster, Jan Rainwater, Stephan Tobin, and the late Arnold Beisser. Many of them are mentioned at different times in the book; all are represented directly or indirectly, and all have my gratitude for their personal regard and support over the years.

Thanks to Jeffrey Hutter, Janet Woznika, and Carl Hoppe who consulted with me frequently and expertly on, respectively, children's dreams, adolescent depression, and resiliency in children.

Ginger Clark, Cara Garcia, Carolyn Giss, Nickie Godfrey, Michele Linden, Vera Reichenfeld-Taylor, and the late Alan Goodman are among many whose personal friendship and professional capability have made the work of practicing and writing about psychotherapy so rewarding.

Typing and other secretarial chores were capably and cheerfully performed by Betsy Dear, my former secretary (and on-going daughter.)

I am grateful to Joe Wysong for including me as a presenter in several *Gestalt Journal* conferences, experiences which were exhilarating in themselves as well as the being the genesis of articles appearing in various publications, including *The Gestalt Journal,* audiotapes, and this book.

Molly Rawle first mentioned the idea of a book almost a decade ago, saying "Folks are hungry for this." Her intelligence, editorial skills, and patience have been impressive and steadfast though delays, revisions, computer collapses, and what might be termed occasional authorial decompensation. Her comments, suggestions and criticisms have (any protestations I may have made at the time notwithstanding) contributed significantly to the usefulness and readability of this book.

And finally, thanks to my husband, Tony Marolda, who continues to love me no matter what.

— Ruth Lampert, M.F.C.C.
Los Angeles, 2003

VOLUME I

GESTALT THERAPY
WITH CHILDREN, ADOLESCENTS
AND THEIR FAMILIES

— INTRODUCTION —

"Make a habit of two things — to help, or at least, to
do no harm."

— Hippocrates

I once took a class in Conversational Italian where many of the students were perfectionistic grammar zealots. The instructor's goal, per the catalog course description, was to prepare the students to speak comfortably and intelligently with Italians. The zealots persisted in asking for explanations of fine points of grammar theory. Finally, in exasperation, the teacher shouted:

"Don't be so picky, or you'll end up knowing all the rules, but you won't be able to speak the language!"

My purpose in writing this book is to help the reader become fluent in the language of therapy and counseling with children. Theory and research have a valued and honored place, but that place is not in this book.

Neither is this a "cookbook," with specific responses designated for specific diagnoses. It is, rather, an "inside-out" approach: first, explore the material; then consider where, with whom, and how the ideas and suggestions will best fit, be most relevant and helpful. Although one size doesn't fit all, I have tried to achieve some universality of efficacy, as well as some specificity.

Some of the chapters deal with specific techniques, such as hypnotherapy, dream work and innovative approaches; others are essentially commentary on general issues, such as self-esteem and resiliency, with suggestions for clinical implementation.

Hippocrates' cautionary edict to practitioners of healing arts to "do no harm" is about as close as I come to a "rule." New jazzy techniques, "wonder drugs," and charismatic gurus regularly appear on the therapeutic horizon, often only to be abandoned when a new "miracle" appears on the scene. I can't imagine any therapist *deliberately* doing harm to a client, but the combination of urgent need and ubiquitous hype can be persuasive and sometimes damaging. I advocate benign skepticism, a "wait and see" attitude.

No one can learn to be a competent therapist just by reading a book; it is through formal training, and careful supervision, that the neophyte learns the general and the specific areas for caution.

Two examples:

When working with children who have been sexually abused, a friendly hug may evoke fear of sexual assault.

With a child who has been the butt of cruel taunts, humor should be used very sparingly, since such a child may feel that all laughter is directed against him/her.

Obviously, the possibilities are many and can be daunting. The single best rule of thumb is to proceed slowly, watchfully, and sensitively.

No matter how seasoned the therapist, peer consultation continues to be a must, not just for the cases we call "difficult" but for those sessions that somehow don't "feel right."

Do not, in this technological age, undervalue your intuition, which usually just means that you have become aware on some sensory level — seeing a tiny flinch, hearing a soft note of sadness, catching a subtle change of subject — that something is amiss.

And don't forget to check with the youngsters themselves. I describe one way to do this in the exercise "A Child's Eye View of Process Notes" in the Workbook.

●

I came to the field of psychotherapy via a lengthy and indirect route. I was at a life passage when almost by accident I came upon a facility for something called "educational therapy" which sounded interesting. I walked in, asked what they did there, was shown around, and learned that the teacher of the pre-primary class for disturbed children was pregnant and would go on maternity leave in six months. I expressed my interest — no formal training, but lots of motivation and previous experience in cooperative nursery schools when my own children were young. I was offered an opportunity: assist the head teacher on a voluntary basis until her leave began, substitute in her absence under supervision of the Director, and, if I did a good job and continued my formal training, be considered for a paying position.

Not to seem overeager, I pretended to think it over for three seconds before I agreed. I loved the work and proved good at it. Head teacher decided to be a stay-at-home Mom. I became the official head teacher, with pay, and continued my long-delayed pursuit of higher degrees and licensure. Working with those autistic, aphasic, and severely emotionally disturbed young kids, and later with older learning disabled youngsters, and their parents, was an amazing, gratifying, often frustrating experience which completely hooked me on the field of counseling with children. I have been involved in one way and another ever since.

My education and training in both Gestalt therapy, with its traditional focus on individual, dyadic and group work, and in family therapy, where systems and multiple interactions are emphasized, has been of great value to me in working with children, who are so individualistic, and so much a reflection of their families, schools, and communities. Indeed, "children" and "families" cannot be separated in our thinking or our practice. Just as the trend in family therapy is toward including younger children, so we need to attend to family and societal dynamics when working with a child individually.

This complexity, so fascinating to some of us, may also be one of the reasons why working with children is not a favorite specialty among therapists. Another reason is that children usually don't express themselves in the linear, verbal, polite style of most adults. The directness of a child's observations may seem rude: "You wear dorky glasses" or "You need to take a breath mint," can be jarring. As Lawrence Diller puts it,

> It takes a special kind of composure to respond with dignity and humor to a young client who says, 'I just farted,' or who shoots a toy slingshot at the therapist's groin and says, 'I got your thing.' To be able to go with the flow requires a delicate balance of flexibility and firmness and requires a deep respect for the child's developmental needs and individuality. (Diller, 1991)

Liking kids is a necessary though not sufficient condition for this work. If you are not drawn to children, working with them in therapy will probably only exacerbate your antipathy. If you are, your affection will likely be enhanced. I love incidents such as the time a six-year-old client was engrossed in constructing a sand scene when apparently out of "nowhere" she said, "So, tell me, have you always liked children?"

Tolerances for messes, a willingness to mop up spills, scrape dried clay, and sweep sand from the floor are other useful attributes for the child therapist.

Humility is crucial. Consider the story of the therapist who in youthful enthusiasm gave lectures on "The Ten Commandments for Parents." After his first child was born, he changed the title to "Ten Suggestions for Parents." After his second child, he changed the title to "Some Thoughts on Parenting." After his third child, he stopped lecturing.

Although I have not stopped lecturing, teaching, and training I definitely have become less dogmatic about my opinions; in fact, I thought about calling this book "Some Thoughts on Gestalt Therapy with Children."

Among the special gratifications of working with children is that progress is usually seen more quickly than with adults. Their resiliency is greater, their willingness to trust is usually not as eroded, their innate creativity more available. Problems have not had as much time to harden.

Not to be overlooked is the opportunity to shop for and use toys, games, and creative materials — check with your accountant about income tax savings!

Another word about toys. The playroom, or office corner, may be one of the few remaining low-tech provinces of our time and place. When kids first explore my play area, they usually ask: "Where are the computer games? Don't you have any _____?" (fill in the current hot techno-gizmo.) The clay, Legos, doll-house, Lincoln Logs, drawing materials, playing cards, board games, and, hands-down favorite, the sand tray, work their projective and challenging magic in short order.

If I needed vindication for my insistence on having classic toys that challenge and stimulate, among the hot items of the 1998 holiday season were Tinkertoys and Yo-Yo's. Can spinning tops be far behind?

One of the most difficult and frustrating aspects of working with children is when in spite of and/or because of good progress, and in spite of and/or because the *child* is eager to continue the work, the *parent* calls a halt, sometimes abruptly. When finances are the issue, it is almost always possible to work something out and have a "tapering off" time. When the issues are parental animosity or jealousy the therapist's best efforts may not prevail, and this situation is one of the most painful to accept. That is why establishing trust and rapport with parents is such a crucial part of child therapy, and why I address it at some length in the chapters: "The Child in the Family/The Family in the Child" and "Working with Parents: The Dialogic Challenge."

Gestalt therapists, like other healing art professionals, are having to make accommodation to managed care (or as some of us call it in snarly moments, "managed chaos.")

I personally don't consider the managed care climate the healthiest for growing creatures, but for most therapists it is a reality which calls for as creative an adjustment as possible. To that end I have focused on interventions which with some modifications will be useful in both short and long term therapy. The latter carries its own hazards — children can become over-therapized. Since they are constantly growing and changing, new issues are constantly emerging — but an "issue" is not necessarily something to be remediated. In the best of all clinical worlds, the experienced, competent therapist can make reasoned judgments about how long therapy should go on, and the wherewithal to provide it will be available; in the real world compromises must be made.

The benefits of an early positive experience go far beyond the immediate. Many adults report that their youthful experience in counseling, the memories of warmth, encouragement and support, made it easier to seek out professional help later in life. Whatever the parameters of time and money, the therapeutic relationship remains the single most important aspect of the experience. I have had former child clients, now in their teens or young adulthood, contact me to give me an update on their lives (and sometimes to ask for advice about becoming a therapist.) If they were very young when we worked together, they often say "I don't really remember exactly what we did, but I do recall feeling happier after our sessions, and I think I am stronger and happier now because of them."

What more can any therapist ask?

—— HEALING HURT CHILDREN ——
A GESTALT APPROACH *

I happened upon Gestalt therapy about fifteen years ago, while working as an educational therapist and doing graduate work in psychology. Using a blend of affective and cognitive approaches with learning and emotionally disabled children, I sometimes incorporated into the sessions fantasy work and playful techniques, such as converting the ruler into a "magic wand" and visualizing improved grades, and giving names and personalities to the many plants, which the children helped to grow and care for. I still remember with fondness Carey Coleus, a plant that (who) required a lot of watering and responded with lushly beautiful growth, and Spider Lady, each of whose many legs required an original story instead of a stocking.

I kept fairly quiet about these activities, since I was unable to give the erudite rationale for their use, which was expected of me as a supervisor. I did mention them in an offhand way to some super-

* Based on a presentation at *The Gestalt's Journal's* Eleventh Annual Conference on the Theory and Practice of Gestalt Therapy May, 1989.

visees, one of whom had to change her time with me to accommodate her therapy sessions, which seemed to be doing her a lot of good. I was looking for a therapist myself, and asked her who she was seeing; that is how I came to know Gary Yontef, and Gestalt therapy.

In those days Gary used various props, and when one day he whipped out a magic wand, bringing vitality to my listless monologue, I knew I had found the orientation that fit for me, personally and professionally. (Gary might flinch at this particular choice of memorable moments, resonating as it does of the circus acts of the 60's; however, as a patient I did not concern myself with theoretical rationale for interventions, I only felt grateful that I felt better.)

Later, during my training for certification at the Gestalt Therapy Institute of Los Angeles, Gary was my consultant and one of my trainers, along with other gifted therapists including Arnold Beisser, Bob Martin, Janette Rainwater, Stephen Tobin and Lolita Sapriel.

Violet Oaklander's workshops, and her supervision at the GTILA Clinic (unfortunately no longer in existence) were extremely helpful to me in understanding how — and why — the Gestalt approach worked with children and adolescents.

What I appreciate most about this approach is that it is such a good fit. Other theoretical approaches seem to be cut-down from adult size to fit a child's form and like any apparel alteration the result may serve the purpose adequately but the look and the feel is somehow not exactly right. While Gestalt therapy was not originally conceptualized with children in mind, it fits wonderfully well, perhaps in large part because of its roots in psychoanalytic theory, and its humanistic, existential flowering.

With children who have suffered severe trauma, such as physical or sexual abuse, this approach goes straight to the heart of their needs.

They are accepted as they are.

There are no expectations of performance or behavior to meet the needs of another.

It is a deeply respectful and non-intrusive method. The goal is not to fix or change, but to facilitate self-healing.

I'll briefly touch on just a few very basic theoretical principles, as they are important and relevant to me in my work with youngsters:

The I-Thou relationship, about which we are hearing so much throughout this conference, is the single most important factor in promoting healing. The following tenets stem from, and contribute to, the I-Thou relationship.

The Paradoxical Theory of Change, so beautifully and succinctly described by Arnold Beisser, permits children to honor their own basic way of being. Certain behavioral adaptations may make it easier and more fulfilling to live in the world as it is. To illustrate the congruence of these notions, following is an exercise I frequently do with kids who tell me they have been brought to therapy because they are "too this" or "not enough that."

Perhaps the complaint is that he is "too slow." When I ask in a surprised tone, "What's wrong with being slow?" he may look at me disbelievingly, and say something like, "Everybody knows you're not supposed to be slow! You've got to get moving if you want to get stuff done."

I suggest an experiment. On a large sheet of paper or chalkboard I draw a line down the center. One side is labeled, "Helps To Be Slow," and the other, "Helps To Be Fast."

"Tell me some times when it's a good idea to be slow," I begin, and after some thought the child may tentatively suggest,

"Well, maybe like when you are chewing your food?"

I agree. We proceed to list other "helpful slows," and I contribute some ideas, such as, when walking through a flower garden. We also list some "helpful fasts," such as getting dressed in the morning, and running races. Then there are activities which are sometimes better done slowly and sometimes better done quickly, such as crossing the street.

The moral of the story for this child — and for his family — is that there is nothing intrinsically wrong with his way of being in the world. The realization that "it will be better for me if I can get dressed faster in the morning" — which doesn't violate his person — has quite a different effect than believing, "The way I am is not a good way to be."

The rage of abusive parents is frequently triggered by just such innocuous behaviors as being slow. As the child gradually takes in the sense that basically she is a good and worthwhile person — no matter what others may have said or done — it is possible to honor other traits, including the defenses developed against experiencing pain.

Awareness in children is manifested differently than in adults. For instance, I never suggest that children do the awareness continuum experiment; they express their awareness through paintings, stories, sand-scenes, and play. With children the task often is to intervene in the attempts of the adult world to blunt their awareness.

The child who has been abused may need to distance himself from the pain in order to survive. To heal, the therapist can gently and in small increments encourage expression of the pain. Work with "messy" materials such as finger paint and wet clay can help the child get safely back in touch with shut-off bodily awareness, and provide a medium for working through trauma.

Organismic self-regulation, (or the self-regulating organism) can be simply described by again using plants as a metaphor. If we brought a plant into this room and placed it on that table, it would, without any instruction from us, extend its leaves toward the window or the flourescent overhead light. If it was planted at one end of a long planter, and we watered the other end, it would send its roots toward the water. The environment must provide light, air, and water; the plant will do the rest. If these commodities are deficient, the plant will do what it can and what it must to survive — it will adapt. Perhaps its leaves will become spindly, or its form distorted. We may not find that pleasing; we might call it "disturbed!" Or, we might marvel at its ability to survive at all, and, if possible, we will enrich the environment, providing opportunities to develop more fully and organismically.

When we tend a garden, we can concentrate on the weeds, uprooting them with grim determination; or, we can focus on the flowers, watering and tending carefully, allowing them to take over as much territory as possible with a minimum of our digging around.

Joseph Zinker has written elegantly about the rich opportunities for creativity in the process of Gestalt therapy. Working with children is tailor-made for enhancing the latent ingenuity in the therapist and the young client. Children express their gift in the way they use art and play as metaphors; the therapist expresses hers in the way she follows these metaphors and creates new opportunities for their emergence.

Children who have experienced severe trauma may mistrust this side of their nature, and become reality-bound as a defense against anxiety and depression. This stance should be respected and honored; the wider repertoire of reactions should be offered gently and in good therapeutic time.

SOME SPECIFIC TECHNIQUES

Play and Art Therapy

Play is what kids do best; it is their area of expertise. I use a structured, non-directive approach. The structure comes from deciding which materials and activities will be available for the child to choose among, depending on individual needs and goals. Rarely if ever do I put out of sight the building blocks, the doll house and its equipment, the sand tray, or the art materials.

The non-directive nature of the play is in my not deciding how the materials will be used, not giving advice or suggestions of "better" ways of playing. Most children believe they are in therapy because of something they've done that adults disapprove of, because they have been "bad." This irrational guilt is especially poignant in children who have been abused. When we give children the freedom to express themselves fully, in their own way, we are helping them to accept themselves as secure, adequate, and worthy.

In art work, I am interested in the *product* only to the degree that it helps me, and the child, understand the child; I care about how "good" the work is only if affords an opportunity for validation. I am vitally interested in everything about the *process*. How does the child hold the scissors? What is the expression on his face? What does she avoid drawing? When making a montage is he relaxed and interested, or is he so painstaking, so perfectionistic, so focused on doing it "right," that the project is neither fun nor complete-able?

The list of materials which can be used in artwork is almost endless. Clay and play-dough are musts, and each has its virtues. The consistency and texture of clay lends itself to projections of all kinds of concerns and interests, including those of bodily functions. It is wonderful for pounding. It is healing, and cleansing — I often remind parents who are dismayed to find their child's fingernails encrusted with clay that when it dries, it is as easy to brush away as sand, a time-honored cleansing agent.

The vivid colors of play-dough are evocative of emotions and creativity. Play-dough is easy to work with, and easily portable. It can be made at home, or purchased anyplace that sells toys.

Other useful and inexpensive equipment includes kitchen tools, such as a garlic press, cheese slicer, and cookie cutters, to use with the clay and play dough; lots of plain paper (newsprint is fine) paste, glue, and scotch tape; crayons and felt pens; and pictures, cut from magazines, displaying a wide variety of situations and feelings.

Also useful are stickers and stars, sequins, pipe-cleaners, finger-paints, buttons, bright bits of cloth — keep your imagination open to the possibilities for all kinds of "found art." I save the side tear-off perforations of computer paper; kids find many uses for it.

Story Telling

As in all activities, I want to validate the child's phenomenology. If a child's stories are full of morbidity, or depression, I will not simply let that stand; my intervention will come from my honest need and wish to suggest other possibilities, other perceptions, rather than to imply that my way is better or smarter. For example, eight-year-old Mary, who six years ago had been kidnaped during a fierce custody battle, told a story of a baby left all alone on a desert island.

"How long did it take for someone to come and help her?" I asked.

"No one ever came," was the response.

I thought about this for a while, and then said, "You know, that makes me feel terrible. That's a very nice baby you told about. Such a nice baby deserves to be cared for. I feel awful to just leave her there all alone." After several minutes of silence, Mary said, "Well, then, let's see . . . how about . . . this nice old lady and nice old man come to take care of her?"

"I feel much better now," was my sincere reply.

We left it there. About a year later, Mary's mother became seriously emotionally disabled and could not provide a stable home; the father, who had once fought so bitterly for custody, now lived in another state with a second family and wasn't willing to take Mary in. Perhaps you are guessing who came to her rescue — her grandparents.

I have often wondered if Mary hadn't picked up clues of her mother's deteriorating mental status long before they became apparent to anyone else, and if her story represented not an expression of a past trauma, but rather the prophecy of a future one . . . . including a realistic resolution. I'll never know for sure.

I often use "Story-Starters," which are simply 8 x 11 sheets of paper with a picture at the top and an opening sentence. You can buy these in school supply stores, or make your own. After the story is told, I frequently ask the child to tell the story again from various points of view, ála Gestalt dream-work.

For example, here is a Story-Starter that shows a dog asleep on a rug. The Starter says: "The dog is sleeping. He is dreaming about something. Tell about his dream." Nine-year-old Sofia had been severely punished by her father for stealing from classmates, although the teacher and principal had tried to persuade him that the stealing was a symptom of emotional distress. Here is Sofia's response to the Starter:

"He is dreaming that he has a bone. When he finished with the bone, he went and chased the cat because he did not have enough food. He found the cat but the cat was too smart and ran up a tree. The dog followed. But when he got the cat he did not eat it because he was stuck. The cat got down but they had to call the firemen to get the dog down. The End."

I asked her to tell the story from the cat's point of view, and she responded:

"I am the cat. A dog chased me up a tree. He tried to eat me but I was a very smart cat. I came down. He didn't eat me because he was stuck. I was very scared. I thought he was going to eat me for real. I got down, the dog was stuck, and I think it serves him right.

To people who don't try to eat me, I am nice. But to people who try to eat me and threaten me, I am mean. The End"

I told Sophia that I was very glad that she — as the cat, of course — was smart and had ways to take care of herself. I also said, "I feel kind of sorry for the dog because he didn't have enough to eat. Maybe dogs are like people — when we don't get enough of what we need, we do things we aren't supposed to do."

Hypnotherapy and Guided Imagery

Requirements for hypnotherapy training vary from place to place and from time to time. My personal conviction is that where children are concerned, the first requirement is to be a skillful child therapist; then, understand the basics of hypnotherapy; in that way you will heed the dictum "Do the patient no harm."

In my tape "An Introduction to Hypnotherapy with Children" I cover some of the basics, including contra-indications. I'll share with you here some ideas you can safely and effectively incorporate into fantasy and imagery work, as well as use in hypnotherapy.

Get to know the child's specific sensory likes and dislikes, such as favorite color; what smells good; what sounds are pleasant; what feels good to touch; what tastes nice.

Weave these into any "imagination games" you play. If you are doing a relaxation exercise, create scenes that you know reflect the youngster's own preferences, and avoid those images associated with fear. That may sound quite obvious, but consider: While most people find the sight and sounds of a peaceful lake pleasant, to someone who experienced drowning they evoke terror. To me, clouds represent softness and serenity, but to my flying-phobic friend they are reminders of the terror associated with airplanes.

When doing a guided imagery or fantasy exercise, be especially careful to use only positive terms. Whether or not the child is officially in a "hypnotic trance," these activities induce a relaxed, and therefore highly suggestible, state.

Sometimes parents will ask me to hypnotize a child so that he will "forget" a traumatic event; I am clear that this is absolutely *not* what should be done. Hypnotherapy *can* help a child heal the effects of trauma, develop greater coping skills, and enhance resiliency.

Sand Scenes

The sand-tray is one of the most used pieces of equipment in my office, and one of my favorite modalities. It affords all the projective advantages of painting and drawing; is reassuring to the "product-conscious" child since the objects already exist; can be used at almost any age after about two and one-half years old, and for most children is engrossing and just plain fun.

My clear plastic shoeboxes are full of objects garnered over many years and from many places. I avoid representations of television or movie characters, with the exception of one "Snoopy" dog. The collection includes twigs, marbles, colored paper clips, stones, and clothespins.

Transference and Counter-transference Issues.

In general, the transference phenomenon in therapy with children is less apparent than in adult therapy, and does not warrant here more than a passing reminder that the child may wish you to be a magical, all-powerful figure, and may be angry when you disappoint him.

Some of the counter-transference issues to be especially watchful for in working with children who have experienced severe trauma are:

The unattractive child. This is the youngster who you feel you *should* like, but whose appearance puts you off. Perhaps she has an unpleasant facial expression; maybe he is very overweight, and that is a sensitive area for you.

A child who reminds you of a child of your own. This may bring the incident too close to home — it could happen to your child. Perhaps you are reminded of your child with whom you are having difficulty, or even a child you loved and lost.

A child who reminds you of yourself as a child. It's easy to "love" — or "hate" — such a child, to the detriment of the treatment.

Any of these and other reactions can, if not illuminated with awareness, distort your reactions. Both positive and negative counter-transference can lead you to a stance of, "Oh, you poor darling — *I'll rescue you!*" Rescuing isn't what we are about. When the child turns to us for comfort, we cannot offer the false promise of "Whatever happens from now on, I'll be there for you." What we can do is reinforce and validate the child's ability to reach out appropriately, and wisely, for comfort and nurturance.

We cannot take these children home with us. We *can* help them to build an internal home that, like the third little piggy's, will withstand the huffing and puffing of a world that is not fair.

Healing Hurt Children — A Case History

Seven-year-old Jonathan was a pale, tow-headed, thin boy with dark circles under very large eyes. His appearance suggested a Dickens like waif, an orphan fending for himself in a cruel and exploitive world.

In fact his extended family included his intelligent and competent mother, Monica; her down-to-earth, youthful mother with whom they lived; and various uncles, aunts, and cousins living nearby. His father had died a year and a half ago. Monica had recently started dating a man she described as "very nice; stable and serious."

I learned this at the initial interview, with both the child and parent/s. I had started by asking Jonathan why he was here today and learned that "She thinks I'm not very happy."

"*Are* you not very happy?" I asked.

He shrugged, said "I'm o.k." and asked if he could use the nearby sand tray.

I assured him and Mom that it was fine for him to do so while we talked, and invited him to join our conversation any time he wanted to.

Monica then described how in the middle of each night he awakened at least twice, screaming, and could be comforted only by going into either Mom's or Grandma's bed.

"All three of are getting worn out," said Monica. "I've told him nothing bad will happen to him, but he says he gets scared."

From the sand-tray a few feet away, Jonathan was heard to murmur, "Well I do get scared and I can't help it."

"It sounds to me as though you are doing the only thing you can think of to help with being scared, Jonathan" I said, and was rewarded with a brief, grateful, glance.

"That's right, all right" he replied.

"When did Dad die?" I asked of the room in general.

The response to this was curious: Jonathan put his thumb in his mouth, and Monica said in a flat voice, "Last year. My mother thinks Jonathan misses him." With no change in tone or expression she continued, "I heard you use hypnosis, do you think you can cure him of being afraid at night?"

I explained that *sometimes* I used hypnotherapy with children, but first I'd like to get to know both Jonathan and her better, and could I meet Grandma, too?

Jonathan agreed that he would like to come back and play with the other toys; mother agreed to come in with grandma; and so we began our work.

Had I done an initial interview with just mother I would have gleaned more facts; however, meeting with child and mother together the first time provided me with an illuminating glance into their process. It was clear that that there was some mystery, or family secret, around the father's death. Mother's flat affect and deflection was surely not lost on Jonathan any more than on me, although she seemed unaware of his instant thumb-to-mouth response.

When I met alone with Mom and Grandma I learned that Jonathan's father had been murdered, in a brutal, drug-related incident. Mother told me this in the most matter-of-fact tone, adding, "I was the one who found his body. I just told Jonathan he had died, and he never asked any more questions, so I thought he was fine. "

"How can he be fine?" demanded Grandma. "That boy knows something bad happened. You have to tell him the truth before he overhears someone else talking about it and then we'll really have a problem."

We agreed that we would explore this further in every-other-week meetings with mother.

At Jonathan's first weekly individual session he went directly to the sand-tray, and working in a careful, well organized way. I commented, "It looks as though you really know just what you want to do here." "Here" could mean "here at the sand-tray" and/or "here in therapy," a kind of no-lose embedded suggestion.

I asked if he would tell me a story about his scene, which I would put on the computer in his private file. "Good, I like telling stories" he said, and produced the following one:

"Once upon a time there was a war between America and Canada and the people in America were the knights and the people from Canada were trained army men. There were two castles. The American one was called 'Knight' and the other one was 'Shelter.' So they all went to war, and some of the army men got shot and stabbed by some knights. The Canada men had weapons that could blow up tanks, and some tried to blow up the American flag, but, pretty soon, all of the Canada men died. The knights won the war, and America was safe."

This scene and story could be understood on many levels. I wondered about the possible double meeting of (k)nights, and made a comment which, if it hit the mark, would be helpful, and if it didn't, would do no harm:

"Boy, the Knights look pretty tough. Maybe the army men think they can hide in their Shelter, but Knights win in the end."

"Right," was his instant response. I was aware of his need to be agreeable, which was again demonstrated when I asked if he wanted to take home the printout of his story or to leave it in his folder.

"Either way is fine," he said. I said either way was fine with me too. He struggled for a few moments, and then said "Print two, and I'll take one home and you can keep one here."

I did, but the first copy had a typographical error, which I corrected for the second copy.

"Keep that one (the corrected copy) here, I'll take the other one home," he said, and I agreed. It seemed clear he needed to do something unambiguously "good" before leaving; he wasn't yet ready to experiment with being assertive.

Toward the end of this first session I touched briefly on the subject of his father's death, and how sad that must be for him. I shared with him my experience of losing my father when I was nine, and how for a long time afterward I dreamed that he was still alive.

His eyes widened with that look of grateful relief felt by a patient, of any age, whose therapist has made true contact, has understood. Holding the gaze, he said in a small voice, "You too?"

We sat quietly together for the remaining moments of the session.

As Jonathan and I got to know each other better and our relationship deepened, his healing processes gradually grew until they were first a match, and then more than a match, for his pain.

At our first session I had let him know indirectly that his strong and well-organized imagination was a valuable asset. Later I stated this more directly, and suggested we try some "special imagining" (hypnotherapy) that would help him to sleep better at night. Drawing on everything I had learned from him about what he liked, what comforted him, what was fun, and what he was good at, I "went on pretend trips" with him" while he "took it easy and sort of day- dreamed." Here is an excerpt from one of those brief interludes where I reminded him of things he already knew.

" . . . and while you are in this special place, which you made, and can never lose . . . look around . . . and see the ocean that you love . . . and hear its soothing sound . . . and you realize that you can think of that sound whenever you want . . . when you go to sleep at night, you can think of it . . . and remember it . . . and the wonderful tree with its green leaves . . . that you call your "sleeping tree" . . . and you can even smell chocolate chip cookies . . . and if you want, you can have someone there with you . . . or Tiger your cat to pet and feel his smooth fur . . . and if you start to feel scared, you can just say "Hey man, it's o.k., everybody's scared sometimes . . . and you remember that you can always turn on your light whenever you want to . . . and it's o.k. to cry . . . and you won't always feel sad . . . you don't always feel sad . . . lots of times you are a happy boy."

As long as the true circumstances of his father's death were withheld from his conscious knowledge, self-comfort for grief was the limited goal of this hypnotheraphy.

As Monica and I developed our relationship, we talked more about her husband's violent death. She said she had been told by friends that she was "avoiding" thinking about it, and I agreed, adding "You probably *had* to avoid really letting yourself think and feel about it, or you wouldn't have been able to go on, to go to work, to be a mother to Jonathan. Just like he does what he most needs to, have you or Grandma comfort him in the middle of the night when he gets scared and lonely and misses his dad."

(Most of the time, parents need the same things their children need: validation, reassurance, comfort, and the expectation of growth and healing.)

After Jonathan's fourth session she said she was ready to be more, if not entirely, truthful with him about his father's death. She wanted to do this in my office, with her mother present.

At that meeting she reminded him of the things he had learned in school about the dangers of drugs. She said his father had not realized those dangers, had used drugs and even sold them, and bad people had killed him to get the money.

Jonathon's reaction was swift and torrential: "Why didn't you tell me before? Why did you lie to me? You lied, you lied, you lied! . . . I suppose you thought you had to . . . .well, maybe you did, a little . . . and Grandma, you lied too . . . and so did you, Ruth . . . well, maybe not exactly *lied* . . . boy . . . *I'm* never going to use drugs, and if I see anybody who does, I'll say, 'Listen stupid, don't do that, I"m telling you, and I know, because if it weren't for drugs my father would still be alive, so take a lesson from me!' With tears now streaming down his face, he continued to pour forth:

"Why did he take drugs in the first place? Did you try to stop him? Why didn't you tell him if he didn't stop you'd get a divorce? Are the people who killed him in jail? Well at least that's something, how long will they be in jail? Did you what-do-you-call it, testimony? Where was I? Why couldn't I be there? Who else knows about this? You didn't take drugs did you, Mom? Boy, what a stupid thing to do. How could he be so stupid? Maybe he wasn't really on drugs, maybe he had some kind of sickness, like we saw on that t.v. show where the man acted nuts but he really had something in his brain that the doctor cut out and then he was o.k.? Why would he do such a thing? Didn't he care what happened to me? I guess really you could say he was sick, huh, because otherwise he wouldn't be so stupid. He probably wanted to stop but couldn't. Gee, I wish he could have got help. Don't cry Mom, we'll be o.k."

There was more, much more, as he raced back and forth through denial, anger, grief, anguish, rationalization, sublimation, and a beginning acceptance, within forty-five minutes.

Mother and grandmother listened with astonished respect, and answered as much as they could.

I couldn't possibly improve on the process. I made a few comments about how impressed I was that Jonathan could ask all those questions and that Mom and Grandma could just hang in with him even though they were hurting too.

That dramatic session marked a turning point, but of course not a resolution of all the issues.

Jonathan needed to do the rest of his grief work (as to an even greater extent did his mother.) Dealing with ambivalent feelings about his mother's new boy-friend was in itself a mighty task. He had lost ground academically, felt ashamed of his lower grades and unsure that he could recoup his former high status.

Play-dough and clay were among his favorite activities. One day I made some little "snowman" figures from play dough and simply placed them on the edge of the board. Jonathan took one of them and placed it in a lying-down position, then made a play-dough blanket and covered it. He placed two more figures near the head of the covered one. His face took on the sorrowing expression which had been so noticeable at the beginning of therapy as, without any words, he removed one of the two "watching" figures.

Silence seemed the best intervention. I put my hand on the table close to his; he touched it; after awhile he said "Well. So. You wanna play a game?"

From that point on he talked quite a bit about his father; what he remembered most, what he missed most, what he had learned from his father that could help him, questions about his murder, things they had done together. We looked at some family photographs and laughed at the ones of Jonathan and his father clowning at the beach.

Scheduled to present a workshop at a conference, I told Jonathan I would be away for a week at a meeting where I would share some ideas with other therapists who work with kids; I asked his advice on which of the many sand-scene slides (of his scenes and of others') would be most helpful to the audience.

He considered and evaluated each one thoughtfully: "That's a good one, you can tell that kid feels sad."

"Leave that out, it's too dark, why waste their time?"

That one's kind of weird. But it's kind of interesting, too."

And so forth.

I wondered if I had gone too far in this consultant-to-therapist activity when one day, talking about the strange but normal feelings people have when someone dies, I told him that, for example, even to this day I sometimes felt mad at my father for dying and leaving me.

His response:

"I think that's perfectly normal, Ruth." I thanked him for his insight, and moved on to a rousing game of "Blockhead."

2

— RELEASING CREATIVITY —
INNOVATIVE INTERVENTIONS

"Against the ruin of the world, there is
only one defense: the creative act."
                              Kenneth Rexroth

Question: How do you carve a walrus?
Answer: Easy. Just cut away everything
that isn't a walrus.
                              Anonymous

One of the original and lasting attractions of Gestalt therapy for me has been the high value placed on the creativity of both therapist and client.

As Joseph Zinker (1973) says,

If Fritz were alive today he would be disappointed to see multitudes of little people parroting his work as if it were the last word in psychotherapy . . . Like all artists he was nourished by the process of his own

creative juices . . . If Gestalt therapy is to survive it
must stand for this kind of integrating growth process,
this kind of creative generosity.

It is as true in therapy as in all else that there is nothing really
new under the sun. Creativity involves taking components from the
known and re-arranging them into fresh variations. All of the ideas
and techniques I'll be discussing have undoubtedly been used before,
either in the same way or in another version. Very often the work
itself has yielded ingenuity, originality, and innovations both effective
and delightful.

The cardinal value of innovations is the energy they release.
Therapy sessions with children and adolescents may be quite calm
and peaceful, or they may be active and animated; in either case, if
they are effective, they are full of energy. In the same way, innovations may be lively, or they may be quiet.

Since I will be using many case histories, I'll sometimes be
making connections between the problem, or diagnosis, and the
intervention. However, I certainly do not intend to imply that these
interventions are limited to the kinds of situations portrayed.

Creative Expression with Computers

Having been dragged kicking and screaming into the computer age, it took me a while to recognize the creative potential
inherent in what I considered my natural enemy.

When the computer first appeared on my desk, kids were
elated. "Do you have Nintendo? No? Well, what games *do* you have?
None? None at all? How's about I bring mine from home next time?"

Necessity once again delivered. I adapted for computer use an
exercise I had been doing for years using chalkboards or 5x7 cards,
and called it "Being Silly With Feeling Words."

First, the child and I generate a long list of "feeling words"
such as:

happy . . . sad . . . embarrassed . . . delighted . . . sleepy . . . thrilled . . . relaxed . . . bored . . . uptight . . . proud . . . bashful . . . powerful . . . tender . . . centered . . . miserable . . . grossed out . . . bummed out . . . and so on and so forth. I print out the list each time, to be used for reference.

Next, I compose a sentence stem, with three or four choices of words to complete it. For example:

"Jason finally got the bike he had been wanting for three years. He felt:

Sleepy

Happy

Miserable

Frustrated

The child then deletes the words that "don't fit," such as "sleepy" "miserable" and "frustrated," so that the sentence now reads, "Jason finally got the bike he had been wanting for three years. He felt happy."

This makes good sense . . . which isn't what we are after! Therefore the next step is to *delete* all logical choices, so that we have a non-sensical, or silly statement. For example,

"Mary wanted to stay overnight at her favorite aunt's house; her aunt invited Mary's older sister instead. Mary felt:

Angry

Disappointed

Jealous

Powerful

The silly statement will read: "Mary wanted to stay overnight at her favorite aunt's house, but her aunt invited her older sister instead. Mary felt powerful."

The next step is for the child to make up a sentence stem, with possible conclusions, for me. Now the youngster can consider various emotions and their good or bad fit to the situation while enjoying watching me struggle, and hearing *me* express concerns that he may have needed to avoid. For example, here are some stems kids have put on the computer for me to complete:

"Steven's parents made him give away his cat because his little sister is supposedly allergic." Steven felt:

Terrific . . . awful . . . bummed out . . . nothing.

"There was this really cute guy and Nicole really liked him and she thought he liked her friend but it turned out he liked her." Nicole felt:

Fantastic . . . lonely . . . frustrated . . . awesome.

Her friend felt:

Happy . . . jealous . . . pissed . . . bored.

Ruth was driving too fast and she got a ticket. She felt:

Proud . . . stupid . . . mad . . . delighted.

Some folks learn very early on that the computer can provide an escape from painful feelings and difficult contact. Seven-year-old Jessica was reported as bright and well-behaved in school, but without friends. The teacher reported that Jessica was spending more and more time in solitary pursuits, including use of the classroom computer whenever possible.

In this case, I decided to utilize her demonstrated interest in reading and writing rather than in the computer, and went back to the original "feeling cards." As we teased out various feeling states, Jessica cut up the cards and printed the words in differing colors.

I gave her the stem:

"Marty was a new kid in class. He didn't have any friends, and that made him feel":

Lonesome . . . wonderful . . . sad . . . embarrassed.

The silly word she chose was "wonderful."

I shared this with her first-grade teacher who adapted the game to the classroom; she reported that this was the first activity in which Jessica seemed to enjoy interacting with other kids, and they with her.

The silliness of this activity provides some needed distance and diffusion of loaded issues while paradoxically focusing on them. It eases discussion of difficult topics, and also helps to identify and refine emotions, which often are lumped together under a few indiscriminate labels such as "fine," "boring," "dumb."

Picturing the Emotion: Another simple computer game is to ask the child to show you how an emotion might *look*, using only non-letter characters on the keyboard. Here is one child's expression of "Sorrow:"

> > > >????}}}}????{{{{????}}}}< < < <

After printing out these expressions, the youngster can draw a picture to go with it, or paste stickers, stars, or whatever on the paper. The only restriction is that nothing be verbally expressed; of course purposefully avoiding the verbal is a paradoxically effective way to highlight it.

With the addition of a mouse to your computer, you can branch out into many artistic renditions. I expect to master the use of the mouse and accompanying programs within the next decade or two.

My lack of expertise with computers, and with mechanical things in general, has been used to advantage.[*]

Eight-year-old Michael was a whiz with all things mechanical, including computers. During my period of learning the basics, I sometimes exaggerated my difficulty, (not easy to do) and Michael — who, in his family, was seen as rather intellectually dull — had an opportunity to shine in glory. In fact, he had such a natural talent that I took him to the computer store with me and introduced him as my consultant. The salesman smiled patronizingly — until Michael engaged him in conversation, demonstrating that he was, indeed, an expert. Michael also repaired my stapler, put new film in my camera, and glued together a broken flowerpot. His parents assured me that

---

[*] In my Child and Adolescent Psychotherapy classes and workshops, I often refer to my diagnosis of SED — Severe Electronic Dyslexia. This allows me to call on someone in the class to operate the audio-visual equipment for me. The more astute students usually recognize this tactic as a cheap trick to avoid overcoming my difficulty.

they were willing to pay *me* for *his* assistance, especially when they saw how his improved self-esteem favorably affected many aspects of his life.

BOARD GAMES AS METAPHORS

Ordinary board games can be used simply to help establish a relationship with a child; they can be used out of desperation when you can't think of *what* to do with a youngster, usually an adolescent, who resists being in counseling; and/or, they can be used creatively to further the therapeutic work.

What I watch for in board games is the opportunity to go beyond the required skill itself into validations and metaphors. For example, checkers is a game that requires several skills, including the ability to think ahead and to use strategy. I watch for and comment on every move that indicates these skills exist or are developing:

"Now that you plan ahead, it's harder for me to win."

"That move showed excellent strategy. I'm really impressed."

Thinking out loud is a good way to model, and to label processes:

"I enjoy this game a lot more now that I know how to play it well."

"I seem to be playing very defensively today — and it seems to be working!"

Both winning, and losing, can be grist for the mill of validation:

"I appreciate that you don't gloat and make me feel stupid when you win; you're a good sport."

"You handle losing very well. How do you do that? Perhaps I could share your method with kids who fall apart when they lose a game."

Or, "I could tell you felt bad losing, but this time you really pulled it together. You sure are learning how to get past those yukky feelings, and keep playing."

Perfection

This game ("Perfection") requires good eye-hand coordination and the ability to withstand the anxiety of a clicking timer and explosive expulsion. I sometimes suggest as a variation that we play it cooperatively instead of competitively. The apparatus has been nick-named "The Nervous Machine" and "The Panic Pusher;" players adopt pseudonyms such as "Trembling Tricia," "Cool Julie," and "Steady Freddie."

Jill and the Pick-Up-Sticks

My favorite example of the treasure of metaphors buried in board games is when Jill and I were playing "Pick-Up-Sticks." At ten-years-old, Jill was tall for her age, with big hands and feet that were forever knocking over lamps and vases in the immaculate, decorator-designed home where she lived with her highly controlled and perfectionistic parents, who were dismayed by their rambunctious, impulsive, ebullient and outspoken daughter.

I noticed that Jill never did well in the game when the sticks fell in an easy-to-get position; however, when they were all snarled and tumbled together, she would carefully, patiently, and successfully extricate them. I commented:

"I notice that when it's easy you just rush right in and mess things up; when it's hard, you really are careful and precise and do just fine."

She blushed and said, "I've heard that before. Only, not the last part — just the first part about rushing in and messing things up."

This awareness was helpful to Jill many times in her struggle to maintain good self-esteem in a family that did not value her kind of personality.

— A CHILD'S EYE VIEW —

Games of Chance

I used to advocate using only games of skill, or the better "therapeutic" games such as "The Ungame," "Imagination," and "The Talking, Feeling and Doing Game," believing that while games of chance provided fun and rapport-building, the same, and more, could be accomplished with games of skill and therapeutic purpose. Work with traumatized children has shown me the effect — often disastrous — that chance has on children. Abused children may blame themselves; they may carry into adulthood a driving need for control to subconsciously make up for the loss of control they had experienced. Games of chance offer a gentle and effective healing metaphor:

"Sometimes a person just has bad luck. You played the game well, but the dice came out wrong. There will be other games and better luck; there will be games where you have more control and more chances to win."

Organic Games

Another variety of games is the "organic" one, grown from the soil of therapeutic issues.

For example, eleven-year-old Carla had the idea of making a game she called "To the Rescue." On a piece of cardboard she drew paths going to and from "scenes of disaster," including a fire, an automobile wreck, and (my office is in Los Angeles) an earthquake. We color coded the markers from another game as green for ambulance, red for police car, and blue for helicopter. Players chose their markers from a hat, and the throw of the dice determined the number of moves to make. Along the route were squares with typical instructions such as "go forward two spaces," "out of gas, go back one space," etc.

The winner was the vehicle first completing the trip to and from the disaster bringing the injured back to "hospital."

Conversation was about the factors of luck, time, available rescuers, and other splendid metaphors.

Some common issues emerging from the therapy which can be utilized are Debt; Moving Day; Dating.

It will quickly become apparent that whether or how often the game is actually played is not as important as the process of creating it.

Other board games and their various uses, such as *Memory* (also called *Concentration*) *Blockhead*, *The Ungame*, and *The Family Squares* game are described in the Chapter: "The Child in the Family — the Family in the Child", and in Volume Two, *Ruth Lampert's Family Therapy Workbook*.

Pencil, Paper and Sand-Tray

Some children, especially in homes where communication is highly valued and therapy is a readily accepted resource, may experience so much urging to be open, to share, to talk about their feelings, that they retreat from this intrusive prodding and become highly defended.

(This is not the only or primary reason children become withdrawn, but it is an often overlooked one.)

Nine-year-old Jeremiah was such a child. His mother and father had been to Marriage Enrichment classes, communication workshops, and various kinds of therapy and counseling including conjoint work with me. They worked and socialized with highly verbal, outgoing people, and their daughter was a vivacious chatterbox. They were sure their reserved and contemplative son was a bundle of neurotic misery, and brought him to me saying, "He won't talk to us, maybe you can 'get him to open up.'"

I decided that what Jeremiah needed most of all was a place where he could simply be who he was. I met frequently with his parents to discuss this approach, which was hard for them to accept. They usually dropped him off with the statement, "Remember, you can talk to Ruth about anything!" (meta message: "And we expect you to!")

I assured Jeremiah that it was OK for him to *not* talk if he didn't want to. I invited him to take paper and crayons, or toys, into the portable tent I keep stashed behind the couch. I would sit outside the tent, and interact only when he wanted me to.

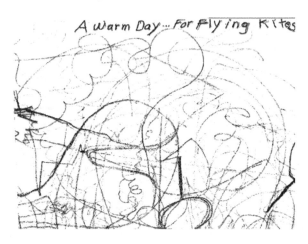

A Warm Day... For Flying Kites

It was the title, not the scribble drawing itself, that revealed the creative spirit of this nine-year-old boy.

One day I asked him if he would like to experiment with our *writing* to each other for a few minutes; that became a favorite activity. Here is what we wrote one day:

Ruth: Your sand scene is still there from last time.
Jeremiah: So it is. Do you like it?
R: Very much. It reminds me of one of my dreams.
J: It does? Well. Was it a nice dream?
R: No. It was scary.
J: It was. Do you like tea?
R: Sometimes. On a cold evening, or when I have a cold. Usually I like coffee best.

J: I couldn't spell coffee, so I wrote tea.

R: Very clever!

J: Have you read any good books lately? I haven't. I think I spelled it wrong.

R: I can understand, even if the spelling isn't perfect. I read a good book called *The Shipping News*.

J: Your cup is falling off the table. This month is my sister's birthday. That's all for now.

A few weeks later, we did another written dialogue, again about the sand tray, which Jeremiah loved to use. This time Jeremiah chose to ask some questions that had to do with him as well as with me, and to directly and indirectly share some of his feelings.

J: My sand picture isn't there this time.

R: That's right.

J: I liked seeing it there last time.

R: Ah. Usually I have to take them apart because other kids use the tray.

J: Ah. Are you hot? I'm not. It's fine in here for me.

R: I'm glad. I am enjoying how peaceful it is. Even the walls seem relaxed to me!

J: HA HA HA! What was my mom talking to you about when she called you yesterday? Or was that Monday?

R: It was yesterday. She says that you think that she doesn't care about you.

J: I don't think that. I know she cares about me. Sometimes I *say* I think she doesn't care about me. It's to get her attention if you know what I mean.

R: Yes, I certainly do know. Seems like it works.

J: Yes. I think I've had enough of this. Can we play checkers?

Over time, Jeremiah did learn some other ways to get his mother's attention, and his parents did relax their efforts to "get him to talk." As they paid more respectful attention to the child he actually was, he was able to relax his vigilance; as he became less guarded and defended his parents found it easier to relate warmly to him.

More Ways with Sand Trays

One day I neglected to clear the sand tray before the next child came in, and before I could say or do anything, she went over to it and began to tell a story about the other child's scene. Now I always ask if the child wants to keep his/her scene in the tray for awhile to let other children see it and talk about it, or if he/she prefers it be cleared away.

(Be sure you phrase this in neutral fashion without weighting one option over the other.)

Seven-year-old James made a battle scene using little toy soldiers to depict a battle, and said he would like me to leave it there. Later seven-year-old Susan walked in, took one look at the tray full of toy soldiers, and with an expression that suggested she had smelled something rotten said "Ick, there was a boy here!"

And indeed, I have seldom seen a little girl use the soldiers in that precise, classical, battle-scene way. I cannot say whether this reflects socialization or an innate impulse.

The sand-tray also serves a useful function in family therapy, as I describe in the chapter, "The Child in the Family and the Family in the Child." For a description of setting up a sand-tray, see the chapter "Play and Art Therapy."

Tape Recording

I frequently tape record, with permission, sessions for use in consultation, self-supervision, and preparation of case studies. Other uses of tape recording are constantly evolving, and I consider my recorder an essential (and simple to operate!) piece of equipment.

Taping interviews of "famous people" is an activity most kids enjoy. I ask the youngster to imagine he is a person famous in some occupation of his choice (sport and entertainment stars are most frequently chosen.) Using a realistic toy "mike," I inquire:

"When did you decide you wanted to be a _____?"

"What did you have to do to prepare for this work?"

"Who helped you along the way?"

"How (did they help you)?"

"What was the most difficult challenge you had to overcome?"

"Would you recommend other youngsters consider going into this field?"

"What special talents are necessary?"

"Knowing what you know now, what would you have done differently to prepare for this career?"

"What is one piece of advice you would give to a youngster preparing for this career?"

Slant your questions to the child's situation. Responses may reflect projections, imagination, biographical information about a real famous person and any or all combinations.

Another version is to reverse the process and have the child interview the therapist. I use this variation as an opportunity to slip in a few "sermonettes," and to selectively self-disclose my own true-life experiences.

For example:

"To become a therapist I had to take a class in statistics, and math was always my worst subject. I didn't think I could pass the class. Two people helped me — my older brother who was good in math, and a tutor. That made all the difference, and, believe it or not, I got an A in the statistics class."

When working with adopted children, I suggest they conduct an interview with their parents, and ask questions such as:

"What was it like for you when you were waiting to get me?"

"What's the first thing you noticed about me?"

"How did you happen to pick my name?"

"What funny things did I do when I was little?"

"How did our relatives react when you told them you were going to adopt a baby? (or child)"

"What did you say when you first saw me?"

If no tape recorder is available this interview can be conducted with pencil and paper; however, a tape provides an especially rich emotional memento for the child to keep and listen to as often as desired.

Another fortuitous use of the tape recorder resulted in "Virtual Group Therapy." I was seeing an eight-year-old boy in my Los Angeles office, another eight-year-old boy in my Sherman Oaks office, and a third eight-year-old boy in a clinic. Coincidentally, all were having trouble learning the multiplication tables. Boy One asked if he could practice them on my tape recorder, which he did. I asked him if I could share this with another boy; he said, "cool." To make a long story short, we ended up with a therapy group composed of three boys who never saw one another, but who shared encouragement and friendship via my peripatetic tape recorder.

I used a version of this activity with two pre-adolescent boys whom I would have grouped except for the cross city logistics. Once again, a problem proved to be an opportunity. Their favorite taping activity was competing as to who could record the most boring story, and they would include such comments as: "This will really put Ruth to sleep" and "Let's talk in code so she can't understand."

I was able to arrange one session where they could meet each other in person. They were quite shy with one another for the first few minutes but soon took over the session completely, playing their favorite games and comparing notes about Ruth, "The Therapist From Hell."

When the therapy work is finished, or a stopping place has been reached, the tape recorder can provide a memento of the final session if the child wishes.

Plants

I consider, and use, plants as metaphor for many things, such as growing, nurturing, organismic self-regulation, the relationship between the organism and its environment, and so forth. Here is a poignant example of how a youngster incorporated the plants in my office into his therapy.

— RELEASING CREATIVITY—

Thirteen-year-old Timothy's mother was a "secret" drinker. That is, she thought it was a secret, but Timothy had realized a few years previously that it was unusual for a mother to go to bed every night at 5:30 and leave father and son to have dinner without her. Mom reappeared every morning for breakfast, and when Timothy questioned her about going to bed so early, she replied with something like: "Everyone in my family needs lots of sleep."

Timothy's father brought him to therapy. He was willing to participate himself, and hoped eventually mother would come with them — and would eventually acknowledge her drinking problem as a first step toward recovery. This did not happen. What did happen was that Timothy took a lot of interest in the plants in my room. It became his job to water them each week, and we made up names for them, such as Crafty Coleus, Phil O. Dendrum, and Charlie the Creep.

He began to use the plants as though they were puppets, having dialogues, creating scenes, and thereby expressing some of his pain and bewilderment, as well as his hopes and aspirations.

One of the most painful occurrences in child therapy is when the parents abruptly terminate treatment. Unfortunately this was the case with Timothy. Father and mother separated, and it was agreed that father would move to his sister's home some sixty miles away, taking Timothy with him.

Timothy arrived at his good-bye session bearing several tightly rolled sheets of colored 8 ½ x 11 construction paper. When unfurled, each sheet was seen to bear the name of one of the plants. He rolled them into cone hats, and soberly placed one on each plant, saying: "This is my good-bye party, and these are my guests."

He spoke to each of them, saying what he had liked about coming here; telling them he hoped they would grow and be strong; telling them he would miss them, and think about them; and assuring them that "Ruth will make sure someone waters you after I've left."

I never saw Timothy again; I hope his resilient spirit continued to persevere through what must have been difficult years ahead.

— A CHILD'S EYE VIEW —

Bibliotherapy

Using books and stories to facilitate emotional healing has a long and honorable history. *Webster's Dictionary of the English Language* defines bibliotherapy as: "a form of psychotherapy utilizing printed material to structure, explain, and universalize problems."

Recommending non fiction which speaks to a particular issue, such as puberty, loss of a parent, learning disabilities, sibling rivalry, etc., is a useful tool in counseling children as well as adults, and I use it frequently and appreciatively.

I suspect fiction and poetry are under-utilized. Try this informal survey among adults: ask which childhood books they remember most fondly, and why they were so cherished. Here are some of the answers I have heard:

"The poetry let me get away from the real world of my childhood which was very painful."

"Reading that book made me feel powerful! I imagined I was the hero, strong and courageous."

"For many years, when in a tough situation, I would ask myself what the heroine would do in such a case."

"Collecting the whole series was like accomplishing something really special — it made *me* feel special."

"She reminded me of myself. In my neighborhood I was considered pretty odd, but at least in my favorite book there was someone like me."

I keep some perennial favorites in my office to read aloud to young children or to read with them. I often recommend that parents read aloud to children as a behavior modification reward, or for the sheer shared pleasure of the activity.

Unfortunately, some wonderful books go out of print; fortunately, new ones are always coming out. Children's librarians, specialized bookstores, and the book review sections of major newspapers are all good sources for new titles.

Recently I started asking my young clients to act as reviewers for me. I have them answer, by dictation or in writing, questions such as:

What was one part you especially liked?

How did this book help you in your own life?

What ages do you think this book is suitable for?

Would you read other books by this author?

Who do you think would *not* like this book?

Did it remind you of your own life, or the life of anyone you know?

If you could only take three books with you on a long trip, would this be one of them?

Book discussion clubs have become very popular; one imaginative youngster conceived the idea of a book club where a group of books would get together, and take turns choosing people to discuss!

At one meeting, "Heidi" chose to discuss the third grade teacher; at another, "Peter Pan" discussed Robin Williams. [*]

Consultants from the Real World

In addition to book reviews, I often solicit opinions on child therapy techniques from the real experts — the children. I explain that I am planning a workshop, or teaching a course, or writing a book for people who do therapy with children, and I want to know what they think has helped them. Or not. An example of this intervention is described in the chapter "Healing Hurt Children."

The Therapist's Creativity

These specific innovative interventions I've discussed are just a very few examples of the fruits of the creative process which is

[*] Thanks to my grand-daughter Alex for this contribution to the field.

fascinating, elusive, and difficult to define categorically. It has been described as the juxtaposition of concepts or ideas that at first don't appear to go together. It appears that people we call "creative" are especially open to their subconscious thoughts and fantasies. It has been suggested that the very process of higher education tends to diminish this ability in favor of so-called "left-brain thinking," which must be vigorously exercised in the pursuit of high test scores and academic degrees.

With this in mind, I often begin training sessions in child and adolescent therapy with the following exercise:

Each person contributes some item on his or her person or in his or her briefcase to a collection in the middle of the floor. The item should not be so intrinsically valuable that the owner will be upset if it becomes scratched or soiled. A typical collection might include: keys . . . a comb . . . a mirror . . . a belt . . . a watch . . . a shoe-string . . . a pencil . . . some paper clips . . . beads . . . a paper cup . . . a pad of paper . . .

I ask for two or three volunteers to imagine they are children in a room where the only playthings are these objects and the furniture. Further, I tell them that although in actual play children often do use objects in a representational way — that is, they will open a door with the key, pretend to write a letter with the paper and pen, and so forth — for the purpose of this experiment, nothing can be used in its actual form. A bracelet cannot be a bracelet; a paper clip cannot be a paper clip.

After a self-conscious start, these students-as-children get into the spirit of the activity, and some wonderful play-times have resulted. Below is a photograph of a game in which a belt is used as a river (with a lipstick barge) that ran through a town of pretend houses made up of paper weights, stones, mints, little cups and paper scraps. At the end of the town is a sandal-cum-magic castle with a fairy princess made from a hair scrunchee and a coffee stirrer. Two dragons — paper cups festooned with hair clips and pencil erasers — guard the entrance, and behind everything is the Magical Mountain — an overturned wastebasket.

— RELEASING CREATIVITY—

Participants report that as they get into the exercise, it's as though some barrier falls away, freeing them to experience playfulness, excitement, silliness — and even naughtiness! Perhaps our need to be serious and purposeful interferes with creativity, because creativity is fun, and we mistakenly believe fun cannot be purposeful.

I (purposefully) use many expressions such as "let's just play with this notion a little" and "let's get into some problem-solving games" when working with adults, as well as children.

If you'd like to play with this idea of developing creativity, here is an exercise you can experiment with by yourself, and/or with your young clients.

Put an ordinary pencil on the table, and see how many uses you can find for it. Don't be concerned with the logic of your ideas, just brainstorm and toss out anything that comes to mind. After you've exhausted the obvious — such as poking a hole in paper — let your mind romp around in different situations and ask yourself: How could I use this object while driving a car? Cooking a meal? Climbing a tree? Just roam through visual scenes in your head, knowing that you aren't going to get a grade on this; no one will judge you. Allow one thought or image to lead to another; play off of other people's ideas; it's just for fun.

Being more creative in your work doesn't rule out learning specific approaches. After all, a novice cook scrupulously follows recipes and learns by observing expert chefs. As the learner becomes more proficient, and adventuresome, different combinations of spices and seasonings are used. Variations are made to suit special diets, to utilize the availability of certain ingredients, or to compensate for scarcities.

Encouraging children's creativity does more than facilitate therapy in the here and now; it also strengthens their abilities in divergent thinking, which involves the production by the thinker of a variety of appropriate ideas.

Richard de Mille (1981) uses the cooking metaphor in his excellent book of children's imagination games, *Put Your Mother on the Ceiling*. He says,

The menu planner has great need for divergent production. When she (sic) sits down, pencil in hand, numerous animal and vegetable thoughts should flow through her mind. Only with a variety of good possibilities will she be able to plan for each day, not *the* good dinner, but *a* good dinner that has not been served recently.

CAPS

When I worked primarily in educational therapy, I developed a technique I call CAPS — Creative Approach to Problem Solving. I find it equally useful in counseling and psychotherapy.

The operative word is "Creative" — letting the mind roam around, experimenting with all kinds of ideas. The corporate world calls it brain-storming; all possible solutions are entertained, including those so ridiculous they really are entertaining. The non-workable ideas are allowed to fade away into the cognitive background (some of them will prove to be useful in other situations) while the more likely possibilities move into the foreground.

Following is an example of an exercise I recommended for working with children with comprehension problems. Little did I know then that years later the hypothetical situation — power outage — would become a reality in Southern California. The instructions are:

Imagine there was a power outage, and all the electricity in the city went off. How would your life be effected?

Some children generate (no pun intended) many responses; some only a few obvious ones such as, "The lights would go out and the TV wouldn't work."

The next step is to stretch divergent thinking with some questions and directions, such as:

"Think about the different rooms in your house, starting with the kitchen. What runs on electricity?" The child begins to picture and name appliances, and then moves to another room, maybe the bathroom, and realizes that her hair dryer is not the battery-operated type. In the bedroom, there is a clock radio; and so on as the list of electricity dependent items grows.

The next step is: "What could you do about all that? You mentioned that the refrigerator and freezer wouldn't work. The food will all spoil if we don't think of something!" (I switch to "we" to form a partnership.) Some common immediate responses are "go out to eat;" my counter-response might be, "we still have all that spoiling food to think about — do we have to throw it all out?" Soon we are cooking as much food as possible to prolong the life of the food — assuming it is a gas stove. If it's electric, the challenge widens, as do the solutions: marinate; barbecue; preserve with salt; and ????

By the time we have finished this exercise, a host of alternative ways-and-means have been listed or discarded (bring it to the neighbor's house . . . oops, it's a city-wide outrage; just throw it all down the garbage disposal . . . oops, that runs on electricity too . . .)

Sometimes I tell the following story:

The Thirsty Sparrow

One day a thirsty little sparrow was out looking for some water to drink. The day was hot, and the sparrow became thirstier and thirstier. "If I don't find something to drink soon," he thought, "I'll get sick. I might even die."

Suddenly he saw on the grass a small pitcher. He looked inside, and at the bottom was just enough water for him. But when he tried to reach it, it was so far down, and he was so small, that he couldn't reach it.

"This is terrible!" he thought. "This is worse than not finding any water — it's so close, but I can't get it!"

But although he was small, and very hot and thirsty and frightened, he was also a smart little bird.

"If it was on the sidewalk, maybe I could knock it over and break it and get a few drops that way," he said to himself thoughtfully. "But there's nothing here except grass and a few pebbles. Aha! Pebbles! That gives me an idea!" He picked up a pebble with his beak and tried dropping it against the pitcher, but the pitcher didn't break.

"What else could I do with pebbles, since that's all I've got to work with?" he thought. "Let's see . . . I could drop one into the pitcher . . . aha! I think I've got it!"

So he dropped a pebble into the pitcher . . . and then another pebble . . . and another . . . and slowly, little by little, the water in the pitcher came up nearer to him. Finally it was close enough that he would drink the water, which he did. He drank it all. It was enough to satisfy his thirst, and it tasted better than any water he'd ever had.

The rest of the day went very well.

In all experimentation, there are some failures, if by failure we mean it didn't have the *expected* result. Unless they cause suffering, failures are simply valuable lessons. Following the fundamental rule of "do no harm" is the best assurance that ignorance or incompetence will not masquerade as creativity.

References

De Mille, Richard. (1981). *Put Your Mother on the Ceiling*. Highland, NY: The Gestalt Journal Press

Zinker, Joseph (1973-4, Winter). "Gestalt Therapy Is Permission To Be Creative: A Sermon in Praise of the Use of Experiment in Gestalt Therapy." *Voices 9 #4*. 75.

3

—— HEALING WITH HYPNOTHERAPY ——

The world of reality has its limits; the
world of imagination is boundless.
— Jean-Jacques Rosseau

One of the gentlest forms of healing is hypnotherapy. The components of relaxation, story-telling, imagery and positive suggestion have been beneficially used throughout history, in all cultures, with all age groups.

A word about terminology. "Hypnosis" is an altered state of consciousness, which may, by itself, have — or not have — therapeutic benefits. "Hypnotherapy," refers to the use of hypnosis as a psychotherapeutic intervention. Although these terms are often used interchangeably, the distinction is important.

Exactly what hypnotherapy is has been the subject of many debates. Most researchers and clinicians agree that it is an altered state of consciousness whereby the patient uses his or her abilities to concentrate and block stimulation that would otherwise be present in the environment. Theoretically, this makes the subject amenable to suggestions.

Everyone has experienced hypnotic states, or trances. For example, remember the times you have driven your car over a familiar route, such as from home to work. You've probably been surprised on occasion to realize that you arrived at your destination without having any memory of the trip. You weren't "unconscious;" you made all the correct turns, stopped for lights, braked when necessary, etc. In fact, you were quite alert, but with a different kind of alertness.

Daydreaming is a trance state. When you are totally engrossed, or "lost," in a television show, movie, a computer game, or book, or when you do a repetitive task in an automatic, "spaced out" way, you are experiencing a state of hypnosis. Contrary to popular misconception, hypnosis does not mean loss of control. In fact, the opposite is true. While theatrical demonstrations may be staged to make it appear that the hypnotist has exceptional power, and some older forms of hypnotherapy were based on authoritarian commands, it can and should be a tool to increase self-direction, self-regulation, and self-mastery.

To these ends I use, and will be describing, the Ericksonian approach, which blends so nicely with Gestalt principles such as "self-responsibility . . . the uniqueness of solutions to life problems, of learning through discovery and experimentation rather than through imitation of others" (Levitsky, 1997, p.112). In both Gestalt therapy and Ericksonian hypnotherapy, the unique experience and sensory perceptions of the client are utilized.

I had been working as a Gestalt therapist for a number of years when I decided to earn a California State certificate in hypnotherapy. A wonderful quote from Milton Erickson will illustrate why I chose to learn the Ericksonian method: "Each person is a unique individual. Hence, psychotherapy should be formulated to meet the uniqueness of the individual's needs, rather than tailoring the person to fit the Procrustean bed of a hypothetical theory of human behavior" (Zeig, 1982, flyleaf).

Hypnosis has a long and interesting history, dating back to pre-historic use by shamans. In the 1700's, Franz Mesmer's work resulted in the word "mesmerized" being added to our language. James Braid, an English physician, in the late 1800's coined the term "hypnosis," and described the susceptibility of the senses to suggestions made under certain conditions. Jean Charcot, the French neurologist, considered hypnosis an abnormal state of hysteria. His countrymen, Auguste Leibeault, and Hippolyte Bernheim, recognized it as a normal phenomenon, and caught the attention of Sigmund Freud who came to recognize the unconscious as a major source of psychopathology through his observations of patients in hypnotic states. With his later rejection of hypnosis in favor of free association and dream interpretation, interest in hypnosis declined and was not renewed until the late 1940's when World War II created a need for faster treatment methods for mentally ill servicemen.

Although research on hypnotherapy with children remained scanty and anecdotal, by the end of the last century students of the field recognized that children were suitable hypnotic subjects; that middle childhood was an especially favorable time for hypnosis, and, perhaps most important, that a wide variety of childhood problems, medical as well as psychological, responded well to hypnotic techniques.

Whether one trains in Ericksonian or some other school of hypnotherapy, the single most important concept for child therapists is this:

Work with your young patient's inherent strengths and abilities. Let your guidance always be with the unique grain and not against it. Join the child's personal world, and honor the trust given you. This is basic to all humanistic psychotherapy and counseling. Hypnotherapy can be used as gimmicky manipulation, but it will not be that in the hands of a competent, ethical therapist.

More important than formal hypnotherapy training is expertise in child therapy. Many child therapists successfully use interventions such as imagery, guided fantasy, and relaxation techniques, which may be quite similar to hypnotherapy. Before being a hypnotherapist, it is imperative to be a competent therapist or counselor; before using hypnotherapy with a child, it is crucial to have training and experience in child therapy or counseling.

While an experienced child therapist can incorporate hypnotherapy adaptively and creatively in work with children without an intensive hypnotherapy background, I'm assuming in this chapter that you already have, or plan to acquire, more theoretical knowledge and supervised experience so that you can bring the highest possible level of expertise to the work.

Different geographical areas and disciplines differ in the requirements for training and practice in hypnotherapy. I personally consider it imperative that anyone wishing to use hypnotherapy experience it personally first. You may find you are uncomfortable with the process, or resistant; in that case, don't attempt to use it in your work with others. Reputable training programs include practicum experience.

Why and When Hypnotherapy is Appropriate for Children

As with many aspects of hypnotherapy, the exact "why" is not known. Empirical evidence, confirmed by many clinicians over long periods of time, indicates that children respond quickly and positively to hypnotherapy. It seems likely that children's love of imaginative play is one factor in their responsiveness. Children often have a surprising capacity for intense concentration and deep involvement in the immediate present. Cognitively, they tend to be literal, even concrete. The openness to and wonder in new experiences is one of the most delightful characteristics of children, and probably is a significant factor in their hynotizability.

Another possible factor is the relative willingness of children — even abused children — to trust adults. Seeking help comes fairly easy to children, and they are usually responsive to "authority figures."

Those of us who have extensive involvement with children are aware of a special quality that is difficult to express clearly, let alone scientifically. It has something to do with being tuned in; in touch with; connected to some basic truths about reality. Perhaps in the process of growing up, most of us "unlearn" those truths, ignore them, forget them. When we meditate, experience hypnosis, or have a spiritual experience we recapture, for a time, that innocent wisdom. Adults in a hypnotic trance have a physical appearance strikingly similar to that of a peacefully sleeping child, and often report a feeling of temporarily returning to a prior state of being. Perhaps children, not having traveled very far from this state, make the return journey more easily.

The concept of mastery is one of the developmental issues that comprise the rationale for using hypnotherapy with children. Gardner and Olness (1981) describe these development themes (pp. 3-6) as:

First: the urge for experience, which begins at birth with the seeking of stimulation by babies and continues through the active sensory and motor exploration of all childhood.

Second: the urge for mastery, of the self and of the environment, expressed by the use of building block toys, through highly abstract concepts. This element is especially vital for abused children, who may feel they have little or no control over their lives.

Third: the urge for social interaction, which is seen from the beginning of life with a newborn's response to the human face (most children, in spite of even severe abuse, retain trust that some relationships are safe).

Fourth: the urge to experience an inner world of imagination. Gardner and Olness raise the intriguing possibility that Western culture's devaluation of fantasy during adolescence may contribute to "some of the conflict and strife typical of that developmental period;" the fact that other cultures have a very different view and experience of adolescence lends weight to this possibility and suggests the potential for more creative uses of hypnotherapy in our culture.

Fifth: the urge for wellness — what Gestalt therapy calls "organismic self-regulation." The physically stressed organism adapts to retain equilibrium, as does the psychologically distressed organism. As noted earlier, the coping devices may be maladaptive, but they always serve a purpose. The Gestalt humanistic position is that since the organism seeks health, maladaptive behavior can be replaced with behavior that serves the same purpose more constructively and with greater fulfillment.

Children have the added advantage of greater flexibility and ego resiliency than adults, and, as noted earlier, are usually more comfortable accepting help. When we use hypnotherapy in a respectful way, we can help nurture these existing healthy attributes.

With young children — up to about nine years — I present hypnotherapy as an "imagination game that many children find helpful and fun." With older kids and adults, I explain that hypnotherapy can be useful in overcoming learning problems, in reducing anxiety, controlling pain, and dealing with the presenting problem, such as nail biting. I make a point of explaining what hypnotherapy is not — it is not doing whatever the therapist tells you to do, it is not giving up control, it is not mysterious or spooky or weird.

The Hypnotic Process

The induction, or beginning part of hypnosis, is not a discrete, separate stage of the process. It is an aid to relaxation, and can be structured in various ways. For example:

"You feel your toes tingling . . . now your knees are all limp and relaxed" etc.; or it can be improvised to match the patient's actual behavior:

"You are sitting there all comfortable and cozy . . . I'd like to tell you a story, if I may . . . your hand on your cheek helps you to relax even more . . . every sigh takes you deeper into that peaceful place . . . " etc.

Just as there is no sharp line between induction and therapy, the coming up, or ending process, is also a gradual, blended process:

"Well, as you start to leave this wonderful place you created for yourself, you look around . . . you know you can come back whenever you want . . . as you slowly and easily come back here, to this room, you bring the lovely warm feelings with you . . . " etc.

Unlike adults, children often change positions, open their eyes, and may even talk, while in a hypnotic state. Incorporate the motions, or comments, into your 'patter' as smoothly as possible. If the child clearly is resistant to the process, you will know; comments like: "Why are you talking in that slow funny way? What are we going to do today?" should let you know it's time to move to some other activity, and maybe try again another time.

An experienced and creative child therapist can incorporate hypnosis into treatment for a wide range of problems and situations, following some basic guidelines.

The first is semantics. Phrase all suggestions for change in positive language. For example:

"You are getting better and better at growing nails the length you want them to be."

"You feel so good, so comfortable waking up in a dry bed."

"Today you discovered some new ways to help yourself."

"You're surprised that there are so many healthy things you can do to comfort yourself."

"You're finding out that its okay to talk about what happened to you."

"More and more you are realizing that you are a good child and deserve to be treated well."

"Little by little, you're learning that bad memories are only memories."

"You know, better than anyone, which memories can help you, and which ones you can be letting go of."

Notice that this language suggests an on-going process; "you are becoming," "you are learning," etc.

Keep in mind that hypnotized persons tend to be quite literal, and children especially so. The phrase "you are a regular lion" could have unfortunate results if taken literally! However, if you tell a story about a lion, or say "It's as though you borrowed some strength from that lion," you draw on the power of the metaphor to accomplish the intended purpose.

Remember that the end doesn't necessarily justify the means. For example, telling a child under hypnosis that her thumb will have a dreadful taste, or smell, might work as far as stopping thumb-sucking, but do you really want a child to perceive any part of her very own body as disgusting? If, instead, you tell a child she is learning new ways to comfort herself, you validate her need for comfort and reinforce her ability to learn acceptable, adaptive ways to provide it for herself.

Utilization of Sensory Stimuli

Many children (like many adults) are not consciously aware of their connection to their senses, although " . . . the deeper layers of affect mobilization are intimately tied to sensory body processes. Alterations and expansion of consciousness go hand in hand with alterations of body activities, body experiences, and inner revelations." (Whitmont, E. and Kaufmann, Y., 1977, p.93).

If I know the child well, I will have some awareness of my own of her orientation to the environment: a child who loves mountain vacations may resonate to pine smells; mention of a beloved pet likely indicates pleasure in stroking fur; the "whoosh" of roller blades is thrilling to an enthusiast; the taste of tofu may be relished by a vegetarian.

Be watchful too for jarring images; the sight, smell, and sound of the ocean are relaxing for most people, but for some conjure images of drowning.

In addition to personalizing the "script," learning about individual reactions helps the therapist to know her client more intimately, and sometimes offers surprises; learning that one "typical" teenager loved classical music provided an unexpected point of contact.

Not least of the benefits of enhancing sensory awareness is the way it makes the individual's universe ever-expanding. As one youngster put it, "I never noticed that I noticed all that."

The Power of the Metaphor

The concept of the therapeutic metaphor is time-honored. Bible parables, Zen Buddhism koans, allegories and fairy tales have for centuries used metaphors to convey ideas indirectly, and powerfully.

When children are engrossed in play they are creating their own metaphors; by identifying with the characters and action of the metaphor, they work through their problems and traumas.

I like best to work from metaphors the child has generated, and, when creating metaphors, to use the child's own preferences, such as favorite color, movies, smells, foods, etc. The process illustrates again that expertise in child therapy is the single most important ingredient in child hypnotherapy. This weaving of hypnotherapy into the fabric of psychotherapy will be discussed more fully later in this chapter; a brief example here will help illustrate the point.

Nine-year-old James was struggling to keep his balance in a chaotic family situation, which involved frequent and histrionic parental separations and reconciliations. During their periods of breaking up, the parents considered James a serious behavior problem, largely responsible for their discord; during the reconciliation periods, he was viewed by his parents as being depressed, "for no reason."

James' favorite material in therapy was the small animals that are part of my sand-tray equipment. A recurring theme was that of the baby animals rescuing the adult animals from various threatening situations such as fires, cattle rustlers, etc. I stayed with his metaphor with comments such as "wow, those baby animals sure have a job taking care of the big folks." When I incorporated hypnotherapy I encouraged James to look for, and find, strong adults who would be supportive of young, growing children. As a child, he could not be in full control of his environment, and his parents at that time were not emotionally available for him. However, he was able to experience mastery in his choice of auxiliary parental figures, and by focusing on his ability to relate to teachers, scoutmasters (and therapist), his self-support strengths were encouraged. Also, I believe, the danger of developing a victim role was mitigated. This approach of using animals as the metaphor for the family is easily adaptable to many situations involving abuse and neglect, and permits the child to disclose information he/she may feel would be disloyal to express directly, or may perceive as simply "the way things are."

The use of self-chosen metaphors represents another bridge between Gestalt therapy and Ericksonian hypnotherapy. Arnold Beisser (1970) eloquently described what he called "the paradoxical theory of change" in Gestalt work, wherein the patient is encouraged to fully experience himself/herself and thus becomes freer to change in healthful ways, as opposed to the therapist causing change.

As Beisser says, "Change occurs when one becomes what he is, not when he tries to become what he is not." Self-chosen metaphors promote this process.

Erickson's development of indirect naturalistic hypnotherapy also utilizes the patient's understanding and behavior a respectful way. He stresses the over-riding importance of honoring the individuals unique phenomenology, as opposed to strict adherence to procedural rituals which may impede or prevent healing.

By staying with the child's metaphor we avoid the intrusiveness of interpretation, which may or may not be accurate. For example, perhaps my understanding of James' work/play with the toy animals was incorrect. If I had said to him, "you feel as though you have to take care of your parents," he might have agreed in order to please me, even if I had been off the mark. Or, I might have been too close to the mark, and prematurely exposed a raw and tender place. By simply commenting on what the animals appeared to me to be experiencing, I left the choice with him as to whether or not to identify with that experience.

In the hypnotherapy session, he was not pushed to agree with my perception of his parents as being unable to provide him with necessary nurturing; he was, instead, given the opportunity to broaden the parameters of his world to include various helpful adults.

Abused Children

The concept of respectful non-intrusiveness is poignantly critical when applied to abused children. Their self-image has been cruelly violated; any habits (defenses) must be respected.

For example, one four-year-old boy who had been sexually abused by a baby-sitter was reported by his mother as masturbating violently and obviously at highly inappropriate times. This kind of behavior, in less severe form, is fairly common in four-year-olds, and is usually effectively dealt with simply by telling the child where and when it is okay to masturbate. In this particular case, however, the child needed extra reassurance that his feelings were valid. As part of the treatment, this hypnotherapy "patter" was included in one session:

". . . and isn't it funny how sometimes grownups just don't understand a kid . . . how they can get all fussed and bothered if they see a little boy playing with his penis . . . well, maybe they just don't know what it's like . . . what that little kid needs . . . he's sure a good kid . . . sometimes he needs to do something to feel better . . . sometimes that's playing with his penis, which all little boys do . . . even big boys . . . and grown men . . . and most of them know how to do it in a way that doesn't hurt or bother anybody . . . and moms and dads can really help a little kid to learn that . . . I know that you have people who are helping you to heal your hurt . . . and you are so good at finding the people who can help you . . . and it's so easy to like you, no wonder there are lots of people who really like you, not just pretend to . . . and isn't it fine that you are finding so many different ways to help heal your hurt."

This youngster was fortunate in that his parents were able and eager to follow through on ways to encourage their son to limit masturbating to certain times and places. Instead of confining the behavior to the boy's bedroom, or bathroom, they said it was okay with them; they understood how strong his feelings were. When company came to the house, or he was out in public, they would remind him, with a hug, that he needed to wait. As the healing process progressed, his urgent need for self-comfort lessened.

An important part of the hypnotherapy approach was the suggestion that most of the adults in his life cared for and loved him, while acknowledging that he had been hurt by one of them.

Here is another example of using the power of the metaphor in hypnotherapy with an abused twelve-year-old girl. The perpetrator was someone known to her and who seemed safe. She did not tell anyone of the abuse, but an alert teacher sensed that she was troubled and talked to her. The abuse was disclosed, the offender was apprehended and jailed, and the girl was referred to therapy. As often happens she blamed herself for the abuse, saying that she was "stupid" to have trusted the abuser.

The therapist incorporated hypnotherapy, explaining that while she was relaxed she could use her own preferences for many things to help herself. She said she liked the color blue; the sound of ocean waves; the smell of popcorn; the feeling of fur; the look of clouds, and the song "I Just Called to Say I Love You." The therapist told the following story as a metaphor, using the name "Mary" for the imaginary heroine.

I'd like to tell you a story . . . you might want to lean back on the couch while you listen . . . maybe lie down . . . you know the ways you help yourself to get most comfortable . . . and it's okay to let your eyes close when they want to . . . and you know you're very much in charge of all this . . . and you can use this little story to help yourself in any way you want . . . well . . . this story starts when Mary was listening to some music . . . and she was just doing what all girls her age like to do, just listening and kind of going along . . . sitting in the chair . . . and she couldn't know that that chair was dangerous . . . it looked just fine . . . no way a kid like her could know that it was broken . . . nothing she could have done about it if she did know . . . she was a great kid and . . . it was just one of those unlucky things . . . the chair tipped over one day in a weird kind of way, and she fell . . . and there was a bad pain in her arm . . . but you know, Mary was a brave girl and she didn't want to complain . . . so she didn't tell anyone for a pretty long time even though it kept hurting . . . and she really didn't want to sit in that chair any more . . . but it looked okay . . . and she thought maybe it was her fault, maybe she had made it tip, or something . . . you know how kids are . . . how they blame themselves for things that aren't their fault . . . so this was all very hurtful for Mary..and then . . . one day . . . her teacher, who liked her a whole lot, noticed that something didn't look right with her arm . . . and just went right ahead and called a doctor . . . the doctor thought Mary was a pretty terrific kid too . . . and said to her . . . I'm so sorry this happened to you . . . we are going to start right away to get you healed . . . and we are going to put that broken chair in the repair shop and keep it there so you won't get hurt again . . . and the doctor took some blue medicine from the cabinet . . . Mary thought it was funny and wonderful that medicine could smell like popcorn . . . and the doctor told Mary's mom to take her to the ocean every week, where the warm sun and sand would help her to heal . . . and Mary noticed from week to week that kids fell down and bruised their knees, and their knees healed . . . and they had colds, and the colds got better . . . and one boy had a broken leg in a cast, and that took longer to heal than a skinned knee, but it did heal . . . and the kids talked about all this . . . they got to be friends . . . and they would stretch out in the warm sand, and watch the ocean . . . and sometimes someone brought a radio and they'd listen to music . . . and they all talked together about things that had hurt them . . . and there were even some grownups who told them about being in car accidents when they were little and how it did still scare them sometimes to be in a car . . . and there was a cute little puppy that made friends with Mary, and she would pet the puppy . . . its fur felt so good . . . and she noticed one day while she was petting the soft fur that her arm felt kind of better . . . and she told her friends about it, and they were soooo glad to hear it . . . it really encouraged some of them who had pretty bad hurts too . . . and you know, Mary got so that she knew which chairs were okay to sit in and which ones weren't . . . and her arm healed up very nicely . . . sometimes, on certain days, it bothered her a little . . . but not a lot . . . and I hope you like that story . . . when your eyes open, in a couple of minutes, you'll feel very good . . . it feels good about now to stretch . . . and smile . . . as you are doing . . . and we can just sit here a few minutes, and be glad we know each other and get to spend some time together."

The Anxious Child

Following is a case history, with partial transcript of a session with an anxious eleven-year-old girl.

Roberta had been referred to me initially by her teacher, who was concerned about recent episodes of crying and "getting hysterical" over minor incidents of being teased by peers, or receiving a poor grade, or even reading a sad story.

Roberta's parents were successful people in the publishing business. They were currently having serious financial and marital problems, which they (mistakenly) believed they had kept hidden from her. During couple and family sessions, Roberta's fears, real and imagined, about potential divorce and perceived loss of a parent and being cared for, were aired. In time, the financial situation eased, and the parents continued to work on their marriage. Roberta made good progress, until one day the family home was burglarized, and Roberta was the one to come home first and discover the torn apart, damaged home. (Quite likely you are aware of what a powerful, negative metaphor this presented.)

Although every possible preventative measure was subsequently taken — alarm systems, double bolts, iron grills, etc. — Roberta's fears increased to the point where she was unable to sleep. She told me that all night she heard strange sounds, and was convinced someone was again trying to break in.

Roberta and I had already established a warm relationship, and we had previously had "imagination sessions," as I called them with her. I acknowledged that indeed there was no way to absolutely guarantee that her home would never again be burglarized, and explained that lots of children, and adults too, had similar fears. I decided to focus first on the disrupted sleeping pattern, and wait until that was regulated, before dealing with the fear of the endangerment of family units.

Here is how part of one hypnotherapy session went.

"Well, here you are, relaxing in just the way you most like . . . stretched out on the little couch . . . knowing that you don't have to keep your eyes open . . . it's okay to let them close if you want to . . . and maybe you'll take a little pretend trip with me now . . . to a lovely place you really like . . . maybe the island of maui . . . warm and sunny . . . the ocean your favorite color of blue . . . you can tell there's a rose garden nearby too, it smells sooo nice . . . and you can hear lots of things, too . . . you can hear a twig snap, ping! As a friendly squirrel plays in the bushes . . . and the waves, what a lovely sound they make, so soothing . . . clouds are drifting overhead . . . there's a gentle breeze . . . the breeze sounds as though it's dancing in the trees, making sweet little swishing sounds . . . it's so wonderful on that beach . . . and you know any time you see, or smell, or hear anything that wouldn't be good for you, you'll know exactly what to do to take good care of yourself . . . and all the wonderful things you see, and feel, and smell, and hear seem even more delightful than usual . . . and right now you've decided to be alone on this private little beach .

. . maybe you will want company after awhile . . . that's easy too, people are right across that little path there, any time you want to see them . . . but right now it's so peaceful . . . restful . . . quiet and comfortable to relax by yourself and think whatever you want to think . . . and you know you can come to this super place any time you want to, it's your special place . . . you can always add anything or anyone to it you want . . . and if you don't like something you can just send it far away . . . you can give yourself any suggestions you like that will make you feel good, and strong . . . my suggestion is that when it's the best time for you to go to sleep at night, you'll have a lovely, healthy, sleep . . . you'll remember whatever it helps to remember about this fantasy trip . . . and pretty soon now you'll be ready to come back here, and open your eyes, and stretch, and feel sooo good . . . when your eyes are ready to open, they will . . . you're probably noticing now how the couch feels under you, and the traffic sounds outside . . . you start to stretch, and yawn . . . and now your eyes are open . . . and you feel refreshed . . . and wide awake . . . and you're feeling great."

As always at this point, I waited quietly until she was ready to talk. Sometimes it's difficult for me to do this, especially when I've noticed pleased smiles, a relaxed body, and I'm curious about the person's experience. But I don't want to disturb that lovely "after-calm" with my need for feedback, and so I gently and slowly follow the youngster's own pace.

There are some specific points about this example.

During parts of this session Roberta's eyes opened; sometimes she moved about on the couch; occasionally she made brief comments, such as "I wish we could go to Maui next week, but Dad says we can't afford it." In adults, this behavior would indicate that the person was not yet in a trance; in children, it is quite common.

I used Roberta's actual, present behavior in both the induction and the coming up; that is, she had stretched out on the couch. Had she put a hand to her cheek, I might have said, "Your hand on your cheek helps you to relax even more;" had she sighed, I could have said "Every sigh takes you deeper into this restful place," etc.

Remember, there is no sharp line between induction and therapy. Even if no suggestions are given during induction, the child will experience the induction in what will hopefully be a positive, therapeutic manner.

I *invited* Roberta to take this trip with me; I said "maybe" it was Maui. I used places, colors, and kinesthetic experiences that I already knew were her preferences. I moved into more direct suggestions, such as "you hear a twig snap, and it's a friendly squirrel," in order to re-frame ordinary sounds from harbingers of disaster to pleasant, ordinary, benign auditory experiences. I wove them in with other pleasant sensory experiences, so as not to over-focus on hearing, and I also noted that she would be aware of, and appropriately react to, anything dangerous, or, as I put it, "anything that wouldn't be good for you." If I had tried to "hypnotize away" the fear of sounds, she would probably have automatically canceled out that suggestion through her subconscious knowledge that some sounds could signal a need for action. It's important to always include this reassurance that the organism will always act wisely and appropriately. Learning to be a safer being includes being " . . . aware of novelty in the environment that is potentially nourishing or toxic. That which is nourishing is assimilated and all else is rejected." (Polster and Polster, 1973, p. 101).

Roberta's response to this session was dramatically positive, and she had no further difficulty sleeping. There was also some apparent carry-over to her overall life situation, in that she came to understand that she could contain her realistic fears about her family situation; she need not deny them, nor be overwhelmed.

The Depressed Child

The mental health field is coming to recognize that depression in children is more widespread than previously thought. Some acting-out behaviors may actually be a reflection of pervasive sadness; tragically, even suicide occurs in children and adolescents.

Christie was a pre-adolescent girl whose depression expressed itself in what was perceived by others to be a "bad attitude." Parents, teachers, family physician, friends all had tried unsuccessfully to persuade Christie that if she would just take a more positive attitude in life — look on the sunny side! — she would have more fun. It was said of her "she's her own worst enemy."

Of course, Christie's initial response to therapy was: "This won't help, talking to you isn't going to change anything." I didn't try to dispute this, but asked her if she would be willing to experiment and to share with me her opinions. I deliberately said "opinions" and not "feelings," because I sensed that discussing feelings would be quite threatening. Sharing opinions, however, gave her permission to voice negative comments, assured her that I respected her reactions and also implied that she would have some positive comments.

After about four sessions of psychotherapy using drawings, poems and just being with her and establishing trust and rapport, I asked if she would be willing to experiment again, this time with hypnotherapy. Naturally, she was quite suspicious at first:

"You mean you're going to rule my mind? You can't do that!"

I assured her that she was quite correct, no one could rule her mind. I explained hypnotherapy as a way to use her excellent imaginative powers in ways she would decide. She reluctantly agreed, and I began using versions of guided imagery exercises. I felt it was best with Christie to have her respond verbally as we went along, to counter her depressive tendencies to move quickly into fantasies of futility and despair. I incorporated here some of the ideas of Joseph Shorr's Psycho-Imagination therapy, in which imagery can be used as an investigative tool, to open action, and allow for experimental problem-solving behavior.

Here is how our third "fantasy journey" went:

"I don't know whether you want to imagine beginning this fantasy journey in a field, or a valley, or a path in the forest ... choose

any beginning you want . . . whichever helps you feel the most comfortable . . . and just do those things you've discovered work best for you, like breathing deeply deeply . . . and I remember that you have figured out your own way to relax your hands and feet . . . you could do that now . . . I'll ask you some questions along the way, so that I understand your journey . . . and I'll make some suggestions to you."

I then began the guided imagery of slowly climbing a mountain, reaching the top and resting, seeing another mountain very close by, jumping over to it, and discovering a cave. This journey continues with the person finding many doors in the cave, one of which has his/her name on it, going inside, describing the room, and then re-arranging it to suit the person's tastes and needs.

Our trip up the mountain followed a fairly typical course, but when I came to *"now jump over the other mountain,"* Christie threw me a curve by saying:

"I've fallen down between the mountains all the way to the bottom and I'm stuck there and can't get out."

I should have known. What to do now? Any direct suggestions, such as "There's a limb over there, grab it" would probably have been met with something like, "the limb breaks and I fall back down again — even further." Besides, even if I could give her the solution, it was much more important that she increase her sense of mastery by solving the problem herself in her own way. Gathering my faith in the process into both hands, I said,

"You'll figure a way out."

"There isn't any way out," said Christie.

"You're looking for the answer," I persisted, "and it's okay if it takes five, or ten, or fifteen minutes to find it" — thus embedding the suggestion that it was only a matter of time; a successful outcome was assumed.

"Remember," I continued, *"in your imagination you can get anything you need . . . or you can ask for help . . . you know lots of*

ways to solve problems . . . I don't know which of all those good ways you know will be the one you choose to use for this problem . . . " (another embedded suggestion.)

After what seemed to me a very long time, Christie suddenly said, "Oh yeah, I see it now, there's a trampoline at the bottom. When I fall on it, it shoots me right back up to the top. Yeah, that's it. No big deal."

Exercising what I considered to be remarkable restraint, I said,

"Well, that's a clever solution all right. Now, do you want to stay on the first mountain or jump over?"

"I'll stay here," she responded, and impressed by the emotional wisdom of her decision, I briefly explored with her that mountain, came back to where we had started, and ended the hypnotherapy session.

Christie's discovery of that creative metaphor was indeed a turning point for her in what proved to be a slow, uneven, and long journey out of chronic depression.

Habit Disorders

The term "habit disorders" refers to a wide variety of behaviors including hair pulling, nailbiting, thumb sucking, facial tics, sleep walking, enuresis and encropesis, sleep walking, some eating disorders, and even drug use. Some habits may initially have carried emotional significance, but that meaning may have been lost by the time treatment begins. Sometimes the habits develop by repeated association with certain situations. The case I will share with you is of an eight-year-old boy whose habit of eye blinking was fortunately addressed quite early. (Any organic etiology had been ruled out.)

Robbie's parents described him as an angry, defiant youngster who fought physically with his younger brother, and often hit adults as well. During the recent summer at camp, he had experienced a great deal of difficulty. For reasons not clear he had become the camp scapegoat and was teased and "bullied." His first response was to fight physically, but his tormentors were older and stronger, and in spite of the camp counselor's interventions, Robbie usually got the worst of any physical confrontation. The counselor's advice to just ignore the other boys wasn't too helpful either.

Although the blinking did provide some secondary gain, in terms of increased attention, his parents were open to other, better ways to give him the attention he needed and deserved.

Robbie himself was quite verbal for his age, and expressed the rage and frustration he felt by saying, "my brain feels like it's about to cry."

I began the work with Robbie with sand-play, which works well as a method of induction with children. Using the tray and the many miniature objects available, his first sand pictures were disorganized and jumbled, as would be expected given his inner turmoil; in a surprisingly short time, the scenes showed clarity and creativity. His focused concentration was actually a light trance state, and my observations were made in slow, rhythmic phrases. For example:

"... *You have made a very* ... *safe* ... *place for your animals to live* ... *you put up a fence* ... *a strong fence* ... *a safe wall for them* ... *I see* ... *a person there* ... (here Robbie told me the person was an animal trainer) ... *such strong, safe, animals* ... *learning to be strong and safe* ... *with their trainer to help them learn* ... "

I was working on the assumption that Robbie was striving to achieve mastery over his own anger and that of other people, and I hypothesized that the blinking was somehow connected with the effort it took to control his rage — and to hold back tears.

After that sand-play session I suggested that he relax on the couch while I told him this story:

"Once upon a time . . . there was a little boy . . . who had a big sister and a baby sister . . . and everybody said to him, my, what a big, brave, boy you are . . . you never cry like your baby sister does when her diapers need changing . . . and you never cry like your big sister does when her friends won't play with her . . . what a brave boy you are . . . and the little boy did not know how to tell them he really needed to cry sometimes . . . it was so hard to hold back the tears . . . sometimes, when his little sister broke his toys . . . or his big sister teased him . . . he thought he wouldn't be able to blink hard enough to hold back the tears . . . Then one day, his Uncle George came to visit . . . now Uncle George was as strong as a bear . . . with a roar like a lion . . . and he loved children . . . even when they got into fights, as he and his sisters sometimes did . . . he loved them so much that one day, while they were watching a TV show about a sick little boy, Robbie noticed that Uncle George . . . had tears in his eyes! Wet, wonderful tears! Plop, plop, they went, down his face. Brave Uncle George was crying! Robbie wanted to help him to stop so he wouldn't be teased, and he whispered, 'quick, Uncle George, quick, blink, and no one will see you crying!' . . . and Uncle George said, 'why, everybody in this family knows that I cry when I'm sad. Your Mom knows, your Dad knows, even your grandma and grandpa . . . I can cry when I'm here with you guys, 'cause you're my family!'"

Robbie thought that was pretty strange. But a few days later, when he fell off his bike and really skinned his knee badly, it was Uncle George who picked him up and carried him into the house . . . and Robbie felt those tears coming, and tried to blink them back . . . until he remembered what Uncle George had said, and decided to let one little tear just ooze out . . . then another . . . and Uncle George didn't tease him . . . and neither did his Mom, or his Dad, and it seemed to the boy that those hurt knees got better faster than any skinned knees ever did before. Uncle George went home soon after that, and everybody remembered how much fun he was . . . and how he laughed when he was happy . . . and cried when he was sad or hurt . . . and how he loved them all . . . and they loved him.

Many indirect and metaphoric approaches can be used in telling a story. With Robbie, I chose this more obvious and direct story, thinking he might respond to it by talking about his own feelings, which in fact he did. In family therapy sessions, his parents reinforced the assurance that he was quite acceptable and lovable to them if he cried when hurt or sad — or even very angry. He commented that he probably did need to control tears around his brothers and classmates. Together, we worked out a system of control: he would clasp his hands tightly when it was really better for him to not cry.

Of course, this is all very hypothetical. I don't know for sure if the blinking was Robbie's way of controlling tears; I do know that he was a nervous, frightened, blustering little boy who needed more nurturing than he was getting, and who also needed to learn more appropriate impulse control. Incorporating some theory and techniques of hypnosis into the psychotherapy was effective. The blinking diminished rapidly and ceased altogether within two months. As is almost always the case, there was no symptom substitution.

About eighteen months later, his maternal aunt was killed in an automobile accident. In the ensuing period of familial shock and grief, Robbie's blinking reappeared. His parents again brought him in, and this time a few sessions of hypnotherapy relaxation, and reassurance, were sufficient to restore his emotional equilibrium.

The power of the I-thou therapeutic relationship is well illustrated here. It seems likely that Robbie felt temporarily cut off from his mother during her period of intense grief, and reached out for renewed contact with a person who had been supportive of him at an earlier time — his therapist. *Relationship* is a major factor in the difference between hypnosis per se, and hypnotherapy.

Parental Attitude

In any therapeutic work with children parental attitude is a vital component. I'm sure every mental health worker reading these words has experienced, to his/her dismay, the parent who brings a child to the consulting room and says, in effect, "This object of mine isn't working right, I want you to fix it." This conceptualization of a human child as a malfunctioning thing may make hypnotherapy especially — but contra-indicatively — appealing. The parent may be shopping for a miracle cure. With abused children, this may be a function of the parents' inability to tolerate the anxiety of seeing their child in pain, and they are actually asking the therapist to magically remove the pain so that they, the parents, will be spared seeing and knowing it. These parents are not "bad" — they need help themselves, and it's crucial that the professional not collude with their misuse of therapy.

On the other hand, some parents are very resistant to use of a method that they may misunderstand and thus fear. Using the term "hypnotic state" rather than "trance" is helpful in this regard. Comparison of the process with everyday parenting is usually reassuring. For example, parents often croon and rock a fretful baby, thus inducing a very relaxed state.

Some therapists show parents videotapes of adults and children in hypnotherapy sessions, or let them watch a session with their child through a one-way mirror, if the child gives permission.

When a parent is either over-sold, or deeply resistant, it is best to postpone or eliminate hypnotherapy from the therapeutic process.

Cautionary Notes and Contra-Indications

Just as there are valuable theoretical bridges between Gestalt therapy and hypnotherapy, there is also a negative similarity between the two modalities, in that both are often mistakenly viewed by the public as "Quick Fixes" or "Magic Cures." *Neither is either*! To be effective, both require the painstaking, careful, honest application by a well-trained mental health professional.

Regardless of the presenting problem, the goal of hypnotherapy is self-mastery, and not the covering up of symptoms. Be careful, for example, not to suggest "You will no longer feel the pain in your stomach." Pain — physical or psychogenic — must always be respectfully viewed as a possible warning of serious problems. Routinely include in your hypnotherapy work some version of the following statement:

"Your body . . . and mind . . . and psyche . . . working together for your highest good . . . will always automatically cancel any suggestion that is not in your best interest."

Many youngsters respond well to the analogy of the "delete" key on computers: "If anyone at all — me, you, anyone — makes a suggestion that wouldn't be good for you, your brain/computer just pushes the delete button, and it's GONE!"

This concept ties in very well with the self-care concept that is so important in preventing abuse, and can be adapted to a variety of situations.

Garnder and Olness (1981) summarize contra-indications according to absolute and relative (pp. 94-98). Some absolute contra-indications are:

One: the danger of physical harm. For example, a teenager might wish to be hypnotized out of necessary fear of dangerous activities.

Two: possible aggravation of emotional problems, such as a request to "forget" a painful occurrence. This is particularly relevant for teenagers and adults who were abused as children. Hypnotherapy can legitimately and effectively be used as part of a psycho-therapeutic working through, but not to develop amnesia.

Three: displacement of a problem, as when a parent might wish to have his/her child treated for what is actually the parent's problem. For example, a parent who has sexuality problems might ask you to treat the child using the rationale of "prevention of sexual abuse."

Four: when the symptom provides significant secondary gain. For example, enuresis is sometimes used to express deep-seated hostility to parents; if an abused child was a bed-wetter before the abuse, be especially alert to family dynamics.

Five: misdiagnosis, such as referral of a child for hypnotherapy for poor attention span, when in fact there is an organic hearing problem.

Relative contraindications are usually based on inappropriate timing, and the therapist may suggest a later time or a different manner from what the parent requests.

Remember always the first rule of the healing arts: "Do no harm."

References

Beisser, A. (1970). "The paradoxical theory of change." In J. Fagan & I. Shepherd (Eds.) *Gestalt Therapy Now*. New York: Harper. (pp.77-80)

Gardner, G.G. and Olness, K. (1981). *Hypnosis and Hypnotherapy with Children*. Orlando, Fla: Grune & Stratton, Inc.

Levitsky, Abraham. (1977). Combining hypnosis with Gestalt therapy. In Smith, Edward W.L. *The Growing Edge of Gestalt Therapy* (p.112). Seacaucus, N.J.

Shorr, J.E. (1983). *Psychotherapy Through Imagery*. (2nd ed.) New York: Thieme-Stratton.

Whitmont, E. and Kaufmann, Y. (1977) Analytical psychology and Gestalt therapy. In Smith, Edward W.L. *The Growing Edge of Gestalt Therapy* (p, 93). Seacaucus, N.J.

Zeig, J. (Ed.). (1982). *Ericksonian Approaches to Hypnosis and Psychotherapy*. (flyleaf) New York: Brunner/Mazel.

—— PLAY AND ART THERAPY ——

"... it is play that is universal, and
that belongs to health."
— D.W. Winnicot

Play and art are the child's natural forms of expression. As
therapeutic techniques, they provide the opportunity to experience
growth and healing under the most natural of conditions.

In play therapy and in art therapy the focus is on the child. As
his/her feelings emerge, they can be faced, dealt with, controlled,
accepted, or abandoned. The child can have the experience of being
accepted as is, and of receiving empathetic understanding, warmth,
and security.

Play
I use a structured, non-directive approach. The structure
comes from my deciding which materials and activities will be
available for the child to choose among, a decision based on my
perception of the child's needs at the time. To be turned loose in a
"child's fairyland" is more likely to promote anxiety than healing.

"Non-directive means that I do not decide unilaterally what materials will be used, or give advice about"better ways of using them. I may take turns choosing activities ("I want to spend some time today playing . . .) or introduce something new as an experiment. ("If you enjoy this, we can do it again.")

Most children, even those who have experienced trauma, believe they are in therapy because of something they've done that adults disapprove of, or because they have been"bad." (This irrational guilt is especially poignant in children who have been abused.) When we give children the freedom to express themselves fully, in their own way, we are helping them to accept themselves as adequate and worthy.

The Class Kiss-Up and The Math Monster — Frannie, an eleven-year-old girl, expresses some of her feelings about school.

If your particular setting provides a minimum of equipment, remember that children can and do make "toys out of everything in the adult world. Left to their own devices, children will transform paper clips into buried treasure, Styrofoam cups into people, tables into forts, and so on.

If you are fortunate enough to be able to create a playroom, the following materials are especially useful:

paper and crayons
clay and/or play-dough with tools
building blocks
sand-tray or box
chalkboard and chalk
dolls, doll houses, clothes, and furniture puppets
toy vehicles
toy animals (including dinosaurs)
rebounding doll (bounces back up when hit)
musical instruments,
tape recorder, tapes
dress-up clothes, costumes, masks
baby bottles
games and puzzles
bubbles and balloons
books
light-weight tent, or cloth to throw over table
large empty packing box
toy kitchen equipment
Play-Skool/Fisher-Price type buildings(airport,
        farm, etc.; any well-built kind.)
box of "junk (odds and ends that look appealing)

There are two schools of thought about toy guns and knives. I don't make them available, but if the child converts blocks or other equipment into weapons, I don't intervene.

The sand-tray is a beautiful and powerful intervention for eliciting drives, wishes, feelings, ideas, aspirations, and conflicts, and it need not be expensive. Ideally, a tray should be about twenty inches long by twenty-six inches wide, and three inches deep. These specifications originally were to allow for interpretation in the classical analytic, or Jungian, way with the child's unconscious being made available to the therapist for interpretation and integration. The size represents the view field at a glance, and is intended to specify limits and contain psychic expression, thereby enhancing the freedom of that expression. Polarities — the best and the worst, the good and the evil — can all be represented in the tray; as symbolic expressions evolve, internal conflict can be resolved.

Another, pragmatic, advantage to this size is that it will fit on the top of a conventional T.V. cart, with room underneath for storage. An oblong plastic dish-pan makes an inexpensive substitute. Use building, not seashore, sand unless you can think of some very therapeutic use for sand fleas!

Having shelves where the objects can be displayed in an uncluttered way is most appealing. It also works quite well to have clear plastic shoe boxes, each one containing objects of a certain category, such as: people, realistic or fantastic; structures, such as houses, churches, barns, schools; animals of all kinds; furniture and other accessories such as clocks, dishes, bathtubs, and so on; vehicles of all kinds; and a box of miscellany which doesn't fit into any category except being imaginative. Avoid television and movie representations, such as Batman, since these tend to limit rather than expand the imagination.

Be open to the use of all kinds of "found objects." I have some wonderful trees and bushes that are nothing more than dried twigs. Popsicle sticks have been used in many ways; a small empty can was pressed into service, upside down, as a launching pad for a helicopter; glass marbles have become buried treasure, as well as buried bombs; a well sharpened pencil was utilized as a rocket. By giving permission to the youngsters to use almost anything in the office that isn't nailed down, their creativity grows and thrives — and so does mine.

A more structured way to use the sand tray is to suggest a construction of a problem the child is struggling with. Note that the suggestion is merely to represent a problem, without specifying what that problem should be. When the scene is finished, you and the child can dialogue about it, and then take a photograph of it. Next, you give a new instruction: "Make the scene the way you wish it would be." This technique may help the child to express his/her longings and frustrations, and/or stimulate problem-solving. This scene is also discussed and then photographed. Keep this photographic record in the child's file. At a later time, perhaps when other problems arise, or at termination, these photographs can be browsed through and discussed in relation to the child's cognitive growth, as well as self-esteem and self-definition. Another way I have used the tray is to ask the child to tell me a story, complete with title, it to go with the sand scene. I put it on the computer as it is dictated, and run off a copy. Then I ask if he or she would like to take a Polaroid picture to go with the story. (Kids love to use the camera, and almost all of them do so carefully, respectfully, and proudly.) The child decides whether to take the picture home or keep it private.

For more uses of the sand tray, see the chapter "Releasing Creativity."

The ideal playroom has a child-sized table and chairs, a rocking chair, large mirror, and bookcases. (My office is not "ideal," but it works very well.

The physical setting, like the therapist, represents a consistency, continuity, and stability, which may be lacking elsewhere. The environment remaining essentially the same from session to session helps the child internalize a sense of stability.

Seven-year-old Karen had gone through many life changes in the two years I had known her. For the first nine months following her parents' divorce they had joint physical custody, and Karen spent alternating weeks in the two homes, which were a mile apart. Then Dad took a job an hour's distance away, and for the next nine months Karen spent weekdays with Mom and weekends with Dad. After Mom remarried and took a job in her new husband's state halfway across the country Karen did a lot of flying back and forth.

I hadn't seen her for almost a year when Dad brought her in for a 'touch base' appointment. She gave me a nonchalant "Hi," stood in the middle of the office with hands on hips, looking slowly and carefully all around. Finally she sighed, smiled, and said, "Well, everything *here* is just the same!" (Emphasis Karen's.)

Why not just let the child play alone? Where does the therapist come into the scene?

You are the critical component in play therapy. While solitary play is therapeutic in its own right, playing with a therapist present allows for validation, acceptance of feelings, clarification, and insight.

When you give the child choices in the playroom you demonstrate faith in her judgment and ability. Comments such as "That's up to you;" "You know what will work best for you;" "You can be in charge of what we do next;" "Where do you suggest we play this game, at the table or on the floor?" tell the child she has responsibility and capacity for healthy functioning and growth.

Here is an example of a child and therapist at work/play.

Four-year-old Jason had been physically abused by his older stepbrother. In this session Jason has set up the dollhouse and play-people with various family members in various rooms. One child figure is up on the roof, near the chimney.

Jason: He's the only one who gots permission to be on the roof. Nobody else can come up unless he says.

Therapist: Who wants to come up?

Jason: Sally (Jason had a sister named Sally.)

Therapist: What happens?

Jason has Sally climb up to the roof and he tells her "O.K. you can stay."

He takes another figure and starts to climb it up.

Therapist: Who is that?

Jason: Mom. But she has to go back down. Get back, you can't come here, kids only, hahaha.

He takes another figure, saying: This one is Michael (the older step-brother who was physically abusive). As "Michael" gets to the roof, Jason's body stiffens, and he hurls "Michael" across the room.

Therapist: You really threw him hard.
Jason: Yeah. He's all smushed and broken his legs.
Therapist: It looks like you are in charge here, and get to decide who can come in.
Jason. Yeah. (He grins.)

In this small episode, the therapist has validated Jason's need to gain mastery, and to be in control somewhere; in imaginative play, he can be powerful. The therapist accepts Jason's rage, and refrains from making comments such as "But if you hurt him, he'll only hurt you more," which, although factually correct, could shut off Jason's expression of intense emotions. Of course reality intervention is needed to protect Jason from Michael, and there is other therapeutic work to be done as well. Here, in this little "game" which *he* invented, Jason healed some of his hurt, was reassured that his rage was not "naughty," and was comforted by the presence of his therapist.

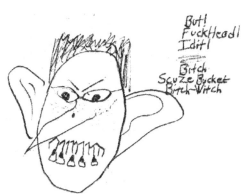

RAGE. Drawing is a good outlet for anger.

Limits are necessary in play therapy as they are in all of a child's life. Limits tell the child that this adult cares about him; they help him build self-esteem and self-control through taking responsibility. Limits give him boundaries he can live within.

The therapist is helped by limits, too. They help her remain accepting and empathetic and completely focused on the child. It's hard to remain accepting and warm if you feel you or your equipment are about to be destroyed.

This intriguing creature lives in my office and has but one purpose in life — to be beaten, twisted, thrown, and otherwise serve as a surrogate recipient of rage. Mr. McFoogle, who loves to be punched in the nose(it squeaks), have his ears and limbs pulled, and generally be a "whipping boy" — he considers it a high compliment.

Although "ventilation" has its limits as a therapeutic tool, this character has helped many youngsters (and some adults) to work off and/or articulate "forbidden" feelings.

Playroom limits should be few, clear, definable, and enforceable. While the global rule may be "you may not hurt me or the things in the office," at times specificity is called for: "I will not let you bite me with the puppet." Usually that kind of statement is sufficient; if not, use a procedure such as:

First infraction: "You may punch the Boppo Boy as much as you want; you may not stab it with the scissors."

Second infraction: "Remember, I said you may not stab the Boppo Boy. If you can't remember the rule, I'll have to put Boppo away."

Third and last infraction: "I'm sorry you can't remember not to stab Boppo, I'll have to put it away for this session. Next time you'll probably remember the rule." The child comes to realize — to really believe — that with you, *some* behaviors are not acceptable, although *all* thoughts and feelings are.

Ideally, his caregivers will be able to take the same stance. If not, the child knows that there is at least one place, and one person, who is consistent and caring. If there is one such person in the world, the child can trust that he/she will find others.

Art

In addition to the "core" materials listed above, there is an almost infinite array of materials which can be used in artwork. Clay and play-dough are musts, and each has its virtues. The consistency and texture of clay lends itself to projections of all kinds of concerns and interests, including those of bodily functions. It is wonderful for pounding. It is healing, and cleansing — I often remind parents who are dismayed to find their child's fingernails encrusted with clay that when it dries, it is as easy to brush away as sand, which is a time-honored cleansing agent.

The vivid colors of play-dough are evocative of emotions and creativity. Play-dough is easy to work with, and easily portable. It can be made at home, or purchased anywhere where toys are sold.

Other useful and inexpensive equipment includes kitchen tools, such as a garlic press, cheese slicer, and cookie cutters, to use with the clay and play dough; plain paper (newsprint is fine) paste, glue, and scotch tape; crayons and felt pens; and pictures from magazines, displaying a wide variety of situations and feelings.

Also helpful are stickers and stars, sequins, pipe-cleaners, finger-paints, buttons and bright bits of cloth.

Keep your imagination open to possibilities inherent in all kinds of "found art."

The simpler and more unstructured the art materials, the greater the likelihood of projection of feelings; the wider the variety of materials, the broader the spectrum of feelings which can be expressed. Finger paints can be messy or neat, evoke disgust or pleasure, be rigid or yielding. Paper goods can be precise or carefree, contain the drawing or scribble or be part of it. Paper can tear, cut, paste, crinkle, and fold, and can evoke feelings of power or submissiveness, anarchy or tyranny, pleasure or pain.

Scribbling helps overcome the awkwardness, stress, and shame of being a "bad" drawer. It provides a stimulus for talking and further projecting. The child can emote, without regard for representation, thus leading the way to awareness at his level.

Unlike art classes, where the goal is the *product*, the goal here is the *process*. I am interested in the product only to the degree that it helps me and the child understand the child; I care about how "good" the work is only if it affords an opportunity for validation. For example,

"Your drawings of cars are very good."

"I like the way you use colors."

"You really made something special here."

I am vitally interested in everything about the *process*.

How does the child hold the scissors? What is the expression on his face? What does she avoid drawing? When making a montage is he relaxed and interested, or is he so painstaking, so perfectionist, so focused on doing it "right," that the project is neither fun nor complete-able?

Many children, like Stevie, learn to guard against criticism and probing by answering "I don't know" to any question. I asked Stevie to draw a picture of what it was like to 'not know;' he drew this picture, with musical accompaniment.

On the following pages (and in other chapters and the appendix) are photos of some of the artwork I particularly cherish. Some examples include my comments, some do not. Listen to *your* reactions and responses. What is this artwork telling *you?*

Ways of Understanding

I am sometimes asked if, as a Gestalt therapist, I ever interpret the child's play/work, as though the choice were between interpretation and silence. Remaining aware of our reactions, sharing them selectively, and owning them is one of the most contactful things we can do. A comment such as "When I look at that picture, I feel comfortable" (or lonely, happy, or any emotion that is appropriate and honest) models open expression of feelings and is free of judgment.

Seven-year-old Sarah, perfectionist and anxious, began her session by drawing this picture.

I prefer to check, explore, and clarify with questions rather than make pronouncements:

"Check me out on this: it looks to me like you're really scared."

"I wonder — are you trying to show me you're really a bad kid? No matter what you do, you'll never convince me!"

"Your face says mad, but your body says scared. Are you both?"

It's wise to be mindful of the uniqueness of symbolism.

Different materials mean different things to different children at different times and in different places.

To one child, sand, clay, clothespins and water may symbolize bad memories; to another child, pleasant ones. I make note of what are considered 'universal' symbols (such as a tree symbolizing human development) but do so with qualification.

Sometimes children say little or nothing while playing; sometimes they say a lot. Listen to them with your eyes as well as your ears.

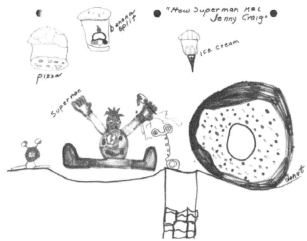

Twelve-year-old Peter struggled with a weight problem.

What is she communicating as she plays with the doll house? Does she mutter things about the garage or bedroom? Or angels in the sky? Does he use the crayon or paint-brush as a weapon, attacking the drawing he just made?

Keep good contact with facial expressions and body language. Listen to intonations, volume, the particular words chosen. Is he active, deliberate, slow, awkward, distractible, aggressive, serene, clumsy, ill at ease, comfortable, rigid, flexible, constricted, open? Is he/she self-accepting during the activity? Has he/she been trying to impress you, or gain your approval? Does he want you to join the activity, or does he prefer to "go it alone?"

Alex's story: "A married couple just got married and moved in after their honeymoon and he carried her over the threshold. It is their dream house. It was built 'specially for them on a hill in a deserted area. They like living on their own. They are going to live there forever. They are going to have three girls and three boys. One will be a pair of boy and girl twins. She likes to garden and that is why there are all sorts of tulips in the garden. They have a little puppy named Jim. The carpet inside is peach, just like the house. They have armchairs. Out in the back they have a swing, and a hammock. And all sorts of birds, like bluejays come to the house because the woman feeds them. The End."

As you stay with the child's process — guiding, facilitating, and mirroring — you can "hear" the messages he/she is sending, such as telling you about anxiety by a frenetic scrambling around the room, jumping from one activity to another. Destruction of materials may be the language of fear, guilt, or anger.

A favorite example of how an interpretation can miss the mark was told to me by a counselor in training at a pre-school.

Lance's regular teacher was out sick, and the counselor took over for the day. She was struck by a picture Lance painted of a figure dressed totally in black, complete to back-pack. Aware that excessive use of black could be a signal of depression, she asked Lance to tell her about the picture.

"It's me," he replied, "I'm yucky." And he smiled sweetly. Now the counselor added "inappropriate affect" to her concerns. When Mom came to pick him she took her aside showed her the picture, repeated his comment, and asked if he might be troubled about something.

Mom looked puzzled, and then smiled. (*More* innaproriate affect? Genetic or learned?)

Taking the picture over to where Lance was waiting, she asked him:

"What's your name?"

"You know! It's Yance" he replied with a happy grin. "Are you a lucky boy, Lance?" asked Mom "Oh, boy, am I yucky"

"How come?"

"Cause I get to help buy my clothes and can wear any color I want!"

The teacher noted with a relieved smile that Lance (AKA "Yance") was indeed wearing a black t-shirt and black tennis shoes; further conversation revealed that his teen-age brother and sister wore almost nothing but the fashionable black dictated by their time, place, and peers. "I've held out on the shorts and back-pack so far," said Mom.

A few words about cleaning up: my position is "I get to do it!" The child may hesitate to be fully expressive if in the back of his head the bee of "clean up your mess" is buzzing around. In other places clean-up is appropriately the child's responsibility, but in therapy it is the therapist's. (This may help explain the dearth of child therapists.)

Every rule has its exceptions. Sometimes cleaning up serves the child's needs. For example, putting the toys away, containing and controlling those fears may comfort the anxious child who has strewn his fears all over the room. Another example is the over-indulged child who has been cheated out of the good feelings of task completion and closure.

CLOWNS FROM OUTER SPACE AND THEIR PETS
"Their little pets can easily get bad guys by turning their hair into prickly spines, or fighting with their powerful antennas. The clowns can do that too, but they have no hair."

(A creative and imaginative little boy who used these strengths to help him through a painful period of parental separation and divorce.)

Children seek approval and acceptance. By honoring *their* world view as they project it in their art and play, by following their lead rather than forcing them down our path, we are telling them they are worthy and valuable in their own right.

— DREAMS —
BUMPS AND SWEETS IN THE NIGHT

From ghoulies and ghosties and long-leggety beasties
and things that go bump in the night,
> Good Lord, deliver us!
>> — *Anonymous*

People who dream when they sleep at night know of
a special kind of happiness which the world of the day
holds not, a placid ecstasy, and ease of heart, that are
like honey on the tongue.
> — *Isak Dinesen* (1985)

Like snowflakes, every dream is unique, created from finite materials into infinite varieties.

The meaning of dreams has been a source of fascination for shamans, scholars, scientists, and philosophers in every culture and every time. Theories include biochemical explanations, spiritual and metaphysical understandings, psychoanalytical interpretations, and, of course, the Gestalt approach. The terrible and wonderful thing about all this is that while none can be proven "correct," neither can any be totally disproved.

With that caveat established, following is how my understanding and utilization of dream work with children has evolved. As in all psychotherapeutic work, the maxim "do no harm" has been adhered to.

"I agree that dreaming is a guardian of one's existence because the content of dreams is always found to be related to one's survival, well-being, and growth" (Thompson & Rudolph, 1988, p.92).

Putting it in the child's language, I say that I think dreaming is something we do to help ourselves in some way. Maybe it's a way of giving ourselves messages or directions "in code." Maybe it's our way of "working off" bad feelings, in the same way that we feel better after running or playing vigorously. That's why even bad dreams can be useful, and why I talk about "Necessary Nightmares."

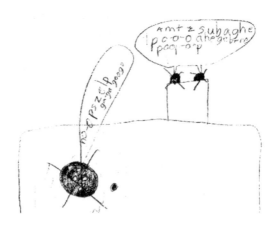

Six-year-old Adam had many fears; one of them was that during the night the dryer would come alive for some horrible purpose. (Stephen Speilberg has talked of similar childhood fears of nocturnal wanderings of malevolent furniture.)

And of course it is the bad dreams, or nightmares, which are usually brought to the therapy session, either by the parent or the child.

Patricia Garfield (1994) has usefully classified children's bad dreams (the reader will recognize that they are also familiar themes of adult nightmares) as follows:

Chase or attack dreams. The child is caught, harmed, eaten, or killed.

A sense of something scary. The dreamer is not actually threatened or harmed, but senses that ghosts, monsters, actual persons who have died, are nearby.

Dreams where something the child owns, rather than the child himself, is attacked. Clothing, the home, school materials, etc. may be harmed, destroyed, lost or stolen.

Dreams of being lost, with accompanying feelings of desperation. See below for a personal example.

Dreams of frustration where the child is thwarted by some obstacle.

Paralysis dreams, where the child is trapped and unable to move, perhaps unable to scream.

Falling dreams, where the child may actually fall from the bed. In the dream, she may or may not strike the ground.

Examination anxiety dreams, with many versions such as inability to find the right room, the sudden dreadful realization of having neglected to study, panic of not passing the class, etc.

Disaster dreams, natural or man-made, such as floods, fires, earthquakes and wars.

Out-of-control vehicles, with various circumstances such as the car going off the cliff, or crashing into something or someone. The dreamer may either be the driver or passenger, and may or may not attempt to regain control. See below for a personal example.

Being nude or scantily clad in public places, with an accompanying sense of shame.

Being kidnaped. The attempt may or may not be successful. The dreamer may identify with the stolen child.

After hearing about the nightmare and sharing my view that all dreams including nightmares can be useful, I ask,

"What message do you think you were trying to give yourself?" and together we briefly consider the possibilities. A comment to the effect that "Sometimes we don't get the message right away, and we keep dreaming our dream over and over until we come to a place where we get it," is reassuring and normalizing. The embedded suggestion is that recurrent nightmares are part of the process, and tell us we are on the way.

I may give an example from my own dream-life, such as the recurring nightmare of my childhood and young adulthood of being lost. In this dream, I was always searching for my home which wasn't where it was supposed to be. I would turn a street thinking I'd find it, only to be disappointed and dismayed. The time was always twilight, and the approaching darkness frightened me; I felt hungry, and alone, and miserable.

I think now that a "necessary" message might have been that it has always been important to me to have family nearby. I love being strong and self-reliant; *and* I need to own and honor the part of me that is dependent, gets lost, isn't always tough. When that "came to me," not only did the nightmares diminish and then cease, but twilight changed from a hated time of day to a well-loved one — which may also be a message for me now about my "twilight years."

The cloud that saves him

I told Mike about my dream of driving over the edge of a mountain. "I had one like that once," he said and drew this picture. He said the message might be "Don't panic, help might be nearby."

Another dream had a message that I understood while dreaming. It was during a period of life when a family crisis seemed unresolvable, and financial disaster appeared to be imminent. In the dream I was driving along a mountain road when suddenly my car went over the edge. As in cartoons, instead of an immediate plunge downward the car continued to move forward for awhile through the air. As it began to drop, I had the loud and clear thought: "If I keep my head and don't panic, I can land on my feet."

I heeded the message, and did indeed land on my feet — not without some painful bruises, but intact and ready to move on.

With older children, and adolescents, the suggestion of an important message may be the only intervention needed. With younger children (under 10 years) I only touch on the "message" part at this point because the first order of business is to help the child gain some control over nightmares of terrifying intensity. Some of that terror is de-fused by the notion that something good can come of these scary experiences, and having noted that, I say:

"Let's think of ways you can help yourself."

Following are some of the ways:

Changing the Channel

Continuing the process of de-mystifying the nightmares and empowering the child, I may reframe the dreams as "television programs in your head." From this stating point, a recurring nightmare can be portrayed as a frightening television show that keeps being replayed; the obvious strategy is to change the channel.

I begin by helping the youngster create some good alternative "shows." For example, he can "program" an episode of going to Disneyland; or playing baseball; or buying new clothes at the mall — any activity pleasing to him.

I suggest: "When the nightmare begins, change the channel to one of those better programs."

Although this is usually met initially with disbelief, follow-up reports indicate a high percentage of success.

Sometimes, however, the child will say she tried it, and it *didn't* work. Then I recommend: "Maybe you need a remote control. Try that, it usually works."

And usually it does. One youngster said at this point:

"The remote control didn't work either, but I figured out it was the VCR that was broken! I got a new one, it works fine."

If that doesn't happen, I simply say in as reassuring a tone as possible that different things work for different people.

Drake, Fifteen, was the 'perfect child' until he stole $50.00 from his mother's purse. His parents recognized the theft as a cry for help. In therapy he drew this picture of a dream and described his reactions:

> **"The tip of the car makes it look closed in, unable to be free, regulated as who what it can do. The motorcycle looks open, free, unlimited as to abilities. It's about safety and restricted vs. free and independent. Something like my parents."**

Drawing the Dream

One of the "different things that work" is to draw the nightmare. This brings it under the child's control and opens up creative avenues for continuing discovery.

James, 8, was indeed a creative and imaginative youngster — so much so that negative, as well as positive, thoughts and fantasies were quickly transformed into stories and games. The good imaginings were wonderful; the bad ones were horrible, as the following nightmare illustrates:

"I was coming home kinda late one afternoon, and I was kinda worried because I had missed the bus. I walked home, and cheez, you know how mad Mom gets when I'm late. It was dark by the time I got home and when I opened the door there were these two HUGE STARING EYES COMING AT ME OUT OF THE DARK! It was the TV set except it wasn't, you know how it is in dreams, I thought it must be the knobs of the TV set, and then I went into the kitchen and all the knobs of the stove were like staring eyes too, and now when I get up at night, and I mean really, not dreaming, it looks like staring eyes are all over the place."

James drew pictures of the staring eyes in every room in his house. Room by room, he outlined them, incorporated them into furniture, embellished them. We chatted about what a mixed blessing a vivid imagination could be, and how drawing was one of the ways to ensure more pleasure than pain.

We also did some "change the channel" work; after several sessions the nightmares diminished and James' nights were generally peaceful. Reports from school were good and his teacher obviously liked and appreciated him; family and peer relationships seemed healthy. Although I didn't know what had triggered the nightmares originally, I felt that his respecting his process of dramatic reactions and creative solutions had been achieved. We agreed to discontinue with the understanding that we could meet again "if things get hairy, or if you just think it would be a good idea."

At our last session, we looked at the pictures he had drawn, and I asked: "What would you like to do with them now?" His quick response: "Put them in that folder there where you keep my stuff. Maybe I'll want to look at them sometime. Or maybe I'll just let you keep them."

"Don't you think you'll need them anymore?" I asked.

He sighed and shook his head, as if bewildered by my denseness. "Why would I *need* them? I said I might want to *look* at them. Like I sometimes look at the pictures I drew in kindergarten."

About a year later I was giving a talk at a local library and James and his mother were in the audience. They came up afterward to chat with me, and tell me that things were going well. James asked if I still had his pictures. I assured him I did, and on a hunch, asked if he might like to have them now.

"Way cool," he responded, and so I sent them to him.

Active Dreaming

Some children report lucid dreaming, that is, they know they are dreaming while they are dreaming. David Chlubna (1992) recommends the technique of "active dreaming" as especially useful with these children.

The first step is to gather data about the dream. What was the weather like? Who was in the dream? What did each person look like? What time was it? What other details are remembered?

Next, help the youngster develop a "rescuer." If you have worked with the child for a while you probably already know her preferences and dislikes, fears and wishes, strengths and weaknesses; if not, the time you spend getting this information is part of the relationship building as well as part of the dream work.

The rescue character can be real or imaginary; he/she/it needs to be both powerful and benevolent. It might be a trusted person such as a favorite teacher, family friend or relative — or therapist; a favorite hero/heroine from fiction, TV, or the movies, or a being created by the child. If the child has difficulty choosing a character, your knowledge of him will guide you in making useful suggestions.

The child calls up this rescuer with special words or gestures when the frightening situation in the dream occurs. He decides whether the rescuer will remove him from danger, or take away the power of the threatening character/s. Making this choice empowers the child, and helps you to understand, and honor, his usual coping strategies.

Eight-year-old Sam loved to draw cartoon characters, and his favorite was "Sam-Man." It was an easy step for him to incorporate Sam-Man as the rescuer of his dream world.

During one session, Sam suddenly became very grave, very serious. Fixing his brown eyes on me with an earnest gaze, he said,

"There is something I want you to promise you won't tell anyone else. Not even my parents."

Oh Lord, I thought, this child has been abused and I never picked up a clue.

"I can't promise to keep your secret if you are in some kind of danger. I *can* promise to do only what I think will help you."

"Don't worry, I'm not in danger," he replied. "I want you to promise not to tell anyone,   *ever* (volume up) — that I AM SAM-MAN!!!"

And I never did. I asked him if I could tell his story if I used different names, and he agreed.

Two cautions with this intervention: A child with issues of trust may fear being abandoned by the rescuer, or of having his/her call ignored; a child with insufficient regard for the rights of others may escalate the damage done to enemies.

Playing the Parts "á la Perls"

Fritz Perls said:

> . . . (the dream) is a message of yourself to yourself . . . (it) is possibly the most spontaneous expression of the human being, a piece of art we chisel out of our lives. And every part, every situation in the dream is a creation of the dreamer . . . Every aspect is a part . . . that to some extent is disowned and projected onto other objects. (Fagan and Shepherd, 1970, p.27)

The classical Gestalt intervention of telling the dream from points of view of all persons and objects in the dream can be adapted to work with children. I do this by suggesting that each of us choose one perspective. This permits me to focus on an area that I consider important, and also gives the child a goodly portion of control. I find that pursuing this intervention much further with youngsters below about age sixteen is inappropriate and frustrating to them.

Eleven-year-old Ginny was the "good child" in her family. Her fourteen-year-old brother Glenn had always been difficult; her mother said: "When I discovered I was pregnant for the second time I was dismayed, thinking I would have another hellion like Glenn. But Ginny was a pleasure right from the start, never gave me a moment's trouble. That's why I was so shocked when her teacher told me she caught her stealing things from a classmate's backpack."

This is a fairly common scenario of the "too good to be true" child who suppresses all "naughty" (child-like) and aggressive (normal) impulses. One day Ginny shared this dream with me:

"There was this scary horrible old witch and she had a broom that had a giant stamper kind of thing on the end of it. She went around Smush!! stamping out stuff, and then all of a sudden my brother was in the dream and she went Smush!! stamping on him and that's when I woke up. She looked like my mother. I think she was my mother. I guess my mother would like to stamp out Glenn."

Her interpretation was almost too pat — just as she was almost too good — to be true. I asked her to tell the dream from another point of view, and she said:

"I'm Glenn and in the dream my mother the witch is trying to stamp me out and I guess I'd better start obeying my parents more so they aren't so mad at me."

Hmmm.

"Now tell the dream from the broom/stamper's point of view," I said, and she laughed and proceeded with:

"I'm a broom but I'm really a stamper. I'm stamping on Glenn so he will learn to behave."

"Tell me more about yourself and what you do, broom/stamper," I continued.

"Well. I don't just stamp *Glenn*. I stamp lots of people. In fact . . . I even stamp on good children . . . well no, not really."

It wasn't far from that point to Ginny's acknowledging that she was very frightened of her mother's rage toward Glenn and feared that if she wasn't super good, she would "get it" (be stamped) too.

A significant part of the work with this family was helping Mom to free Ginny from her constricting role of the good child in the family. (Not to mention the large task of dealing with an acting out teenager.)

I may base my choice of a part to play based on non-sensical, or peculiar aspects, such as a car that has no steering wheel, or a river that runs backwards. As in dream work with adults, I find that these "weird parts" are unusually rich in meaning for the dreamer. I might say:

"A car without a steering wheel! I'd like to know more about that!" or, "I'm intrigued by your river that runs backwards. Be that river and tell the dream."

CAPS

CAPS is an acronym for Creative Approach to Problem Solving. It is described more fully in the chapter "Releasing Creativity: Innovative Interventions."

The operative word is "Creative" — letting the mind roam around experimenting with all kinds of ideas. As in the brain-storming technique, all possible solutions are entertained — including the ones that are so ridiculous they really are entertaining. The non-workable ideas are allowed to fade away into the cognitive background (some of them will prove to be useful in other situations) while the more likely possibilities move into the foreground.

Applying this intervention to nightmares, I ask:

"If you were to dream this again how could you solve the problem?"

Some of the solutions generated might be:

"Instead of wandering around lost, I could ask someone for directions."

"When I realize I forgot to study for the test, maybe I could ask to take it a different day" (read "take an incomplete" for college students)

"When I find I can't move a muscle to get out of the way of the train, maybe I could lay down between the rails."

It's fine to make suggestions of your own for the child's consideration:

"What do you think of this idea?"

"Could it work to _____?"

"Would it be worth trying _____?"

In dream work as in everything else, nothing works all the time; since it is always useful to develop problem-solving skills, this intervention is a no-lose activity.

Bibliotherapy

Among the most charming of children's books in the nightmare genre are *Where the Wild Things Are* (Sendak, 1963) and *There's a Nightmare in my Closet* (Mayer, 1968).

Ira Sleeps Over (Waber, 1972) is specifically and delightfully about a child's first experience spending the night with a friend: I like to read it to kids who find anything about going to sleep disturbing.

Two well-liked books which indirectly reframe ghostly fears are *Georgie and The Noisy Ghost* (Bright, 1971) and *Gus and the Baby Ghost* (Thayer, 1972).

Unfortunately, many wonderful children's books go out of print; fortunately, new ones are always being written; browse around in your library, book store, or thrift shop.

Sweets in the Night

Dinesen (1985) tells us that:

> . . . the real glory of dreams lies in their atmosphere of unlimited freedom . . . Great landscapes create themselves, long splendid views, rich and delicate

colors, roads, houses, which he (the dreamer) has never seen or heard of. The ideas of flight and pursuit recurrent in dreams are equally enrapturing. Excellent witty things are said by everybody. (p.91)

Therapists usually hear only about the bad dreams, while parents are more likely to hear the spontaneous reporting of good dreams. One memorable dream was shared with me by thirteen-year-old Joy:

"My dad always says 'sweet dreams' when he tells me good night. Last night I had a really sweet one that I'll always remember.

"I call it 'The Circus in the Sea.' One of the neat things about it was that it was in color, and I don't remember ever dreaming in color before. And was this color fantastic! I never saw such bright colors before, not even in the movies!"

"I had gone to the beach, just like I do all the time in the summer, but this time I was by myself for some reason or other. When I got there, what I saw was this fantastic circus — all of it in the shallow water at the edge of the sand. There was a merry-go-round; there were clowns; there were trapeze acts — I don't remember what else — and a whole bunch of little kids playing in the water, you know how little kids do."

"All I could do was stand there and look at it, thinking, this must be the most magical thing that has ever happened to me. And I kind of knew it was a dream, you know? And I said, I'm going to call this 'The Circus in the Sea' and I'm never going to forget it. And that's true, it's always going to be there for me."

Shame on any therapist who tries to "interpret" this wonderful experience, or in any clinical way detract from its magical quality.

Garfield (1994) has categorized the themes of pleasant dreams as follows:

Superkid; Desirable Possession; Pleasant Activity; Outstanding Performance; Being Important; Flying; Delicious Food; Being Loved; Adventure: and Animal or Supernatural Friends.

As children share these nighttime sweets, you get a glimpse into their evolving needs and wishes, personal sources of delight, and imaginative strengths. I like to join with the child by making comments such as:

"I'm sure you *will* always remember that dream. You might think about it at times you are a little sad . . . or remember it when you are happy . . . whenever you want to."

"What an adventure you had!"

"If I dreamed that, I'd really feel special."

"Don't you just love it when you have that kind of dream?"

For our own understanding, it can help to look at the themes from various points of view. For example, the super-hero or super-heroine very likely represents the child's need for control. No one can tell Superboy what to wear; the Magic Mermaid goes to bed when and if she wants to.

Do Dreams Foretell the Future?

I frequently recommend that parents listen to Jeffrey Hutter's audiotape, "Understanding Children's Dreams, Pre-Schoolers to Adolescents." (1990). Much of the information is also useful for mental health professionals, such as his explanation to children of the difference between every-day reality, and "psychological truth:"

> Dreams . . . are not real in the same way that you and I are real. I'm still here if you go into the their room or go to sleep. I can still watch over you, protect you . . . what you see in your dreams stops as soon as you wake up or end the dream. We can learn a lot about what we like and don't like from our dreams but just because we dream something doesn't mean it is going to happen. The other day I dreamed that I was flying around without an airplane, but that doesn't mean I'll ever be able to fly around like that except in my dreams.

Working with associations, from the child's point of view, is a simplistic but useful adaptation of psychoanalytic free association, and can help the child "de-code" the message. In the following example, the code may have been only partially cracked.

Fifteen-year-old Ben was dealing with the impact of his parents' divorce. One day he told me he had a dream about a man with a wooden leg. He couldn't remember anything else about it but it made him feel "sort of scared, you know? Like kind of sad?"

Two weeks previously, I had met with Ben's father, who told me about some of the losses in his life, including that of his father who had died six months ago, two years after the amputation of a cancerous leg.

He said, "I guess the fact that the older I get the more I look like him makes me especially aware of my own mortality. I don't want to spend what years I have left in a miserable marriage."

With that information in mind, I decided to begin the dream work with Ben by asking,

"Who does that man with the wooden leg remind you of?"

"Grandpa Steve!" was the response.

"Who looks like Grandpa Steve?" I asked.

Again a quick response: "My Dad."

Then we talked about how Ben could never see Grandpa Steve again, that he had left — forever — when he died. I suggested that Ben's father's leaving the house might feel almost the same, but in fact, he wasn't dead, and Ben would continue to see him.

A happy resolution — so it seemed. Ben's therapy ended shortly after. About a year later, his mother called asking me to see Ben again. It seems his father had re-married, moved away, and cut off all ties to his first family.

I had been wrong. Ben did not continue to see his father any more than he continued to see his dead grandfather.

Although the explanation of the dream seemed so obvious, and did indeed provide immediate reassurance, I wished that I had spent more time in acknowledging and being with Ben in his sadness and fear.

In retrospect I wonder if Ben may have translated into narrative form a sense that his father, in spite of verbal protestations of love, could not be trusted to stay with him. And I wonder about the possible metaphor of "cutting off."

As with "instincts," I think dreams may be telling us something for which we have no pragmatic frame of reference; thus, we 'know' something without being able to express our knowledge in conventional terms.

Can dreams ever be literally prophetic in the 'extra sensory perception sense'? I don't know.

In the examples I have given either the youngster or the parent had brought the dream to my attention. Sometimes I will "jump-start" dream work by weaving it into a conversation. "That picture reminds me of a dream I once had," I might say, or "I just read something interesting about dreams and I'd like your opinion." I am likely to do this if a youngster is reluctant to use project-ive/expressive techniques, or if something in the session (or the back of my mind) suggests it.

So much of the work we do with children is helping them achieve mastery in a world which often is experienced as beset with powerful forces of pain and terror.

As David Chlubna (1991) says " . . . The astonishment shown by many children following the mastery of their nightmares is often perceived by them as evidence of an esteem-building accomplishment from which they can continue to profit throughout later childhood."

In fact the benefits of early mastery do not end in later childhood; they are reaped throughout the life span.

References

Bright, R. (1971) *Georgie and the Noisy Ghost.* New York: Scholastic Book Services.

Chlubna, D. (1991, November-December). Children's nightmares: treatment techniques for the mental health professional – Part 1. *The Advocate. P.8.*

Chlubna, D. (1992, January). Children's Nightmares — Treatment Techniques — Part 2. *The Advocate*. P.10.

Dinesen, I. (1985) *Out of Africa*. New York: First Vintage Books Edition.

Fagan, J. & Shepherd, I.L. (Eds.) (1970). *Gestalt Therapy Now*. New York: Harper & Row.

Garfield, P. (1994) *Your Child's Dreams*. New York: Ballantine Books.

Hutter, J. (Author). (1990). *Understanding Children's Dreams, Pre-schoolers to Adolescents* . [Cassette Recording] Seattle, WA: The MaxSound Tape CO.

Mayer, M. (1968) *There's a Nightmare in My Closet*. New York: The Dial Press.

Sendak, M. (1963) *Where the Wild Things Are*. New York: Harper & Row.

Thayer, J. (1972). *Gus and the Baby Ghost*. New York: William Morrow & Company.

Thompson, C.L. & Rudolph, L.B. (1988). *Counseling Children*. (2nd ed.) Pacific Grove, CA: Brooks-Cole Publishing Company.

Waber, B. (1972). *Ira Sleeps Over* . Boston: Houghton Mifflin Company.

6

—— THE CHILD IN THE FAMILY ——
THE FAMILY IN THE CHILD

Eight-year-old Alexandra was quietly playing in
one room while her mother and grandmother in the next
room discussed matters they considered inappropriate
for young ears. Concerned they might be overheard,
Grandma called out: "Can you hear us talking in here
honey?" The reply: "Only when you whisper."

The Carter family was in therapy at the recommendation of
the school counselor who was concerned at the drop in grades of
14-year-old Eric. While mother, father, and Eric and I sat and talked
on the couches and chairs in the "grown-up section" of my office,
six-year-old Sean was happily engrossed in his sand scene. When he
heard Eric say how Sean really pissed him off sometimes, he was
heard to murmur, "Man, you are telling the truth there." Later, when

mother was describing her conflict with her mother-in-law, the sand scene artist softly commented, "I never knew Grandma hurt your feelings. That's too bad." And when Dad described his philosophy of stern discipline, Sean interjected over the dinosaur scene he was making, "Yeah, but you sure let *me* get away with lots more stuff than Eric, ha ha!"

In this case, including the younger child in a format comfortable for him helped move the family therapy along and gave Sean a sense of importance in this family where the focus was almost unremittingly on the older "problem" child.

Judd was a thin, nervous, nail-biting, nine-year-old. I began his therapy with my customary family meeting; however, his father called just before the meeting to say he was unavoidably detained and would get there as soon as possible, which turned out to be five minutes before the end of the session. Mother went through a laundry list of Judd's misbehaviors, which included lying, not doing his homework, disobeying at home and school, and in general "making things miserable for everyone, and I'm expecting a baby soon so he is just going to have to learn to shape up."

Judd spoke very little through all this except for periodic comments such as "Well you lie too, and then you lie and say you don't;" "I hate that school and I hate the teachers and I hate the kids and everyone hates me and you know it so why can't I go to public school?"

In this case it seemed abundantly clear that Judd needed some time, place, and contact that was all for him. He needed a safe place to express his evident anger at his mother; he needed someone who accepted and liked him as he was; he needed an advocate; he needed a buffer against the coming displacement by a new baby sister.

I recommended individual therapy for Judd for five weeks, with family sessions to be interwoven after the birth of the baby.

The Ruth Office

Stephanie was an angry, defiant, depressed fifteen-year-old. She had not made any suicide attempts but did acknowledge thoughts of death. As I usually do with this age group, I first met with her alone; adolescents need to know that they are respected for themselves, and that although the therapist is an adult like her parents, counseling is not a lineup of the parental generation against hers. After gaining trust and confidence, I asked her how she would feel about some family sessions to help find ways for her and her parents to get along better.

Her first response was adamant refusal. After about six sessions I raised the possibility again, saying "I think if your parents had a better understanding of what you are all about, they would go a little easier on you. And since I'm closer to their age than to yours, they would probably accept some notions from me that they would shoot down if they came from you."

She thought that made sense and agreed to give it a try. We thoroughly clarified the issues of confidentiality, and I asked her if there were some things, which *would* be O.K. for me to share in the family session. There were — such as her feeling that no matter how good she was at anything, it would not be good enough to satisfy them.

At the family meeting it became quite evident that there was serious marital discord and that Stephanie had the truest insight of what was going on, illustrated when she lashed out with "If you two would get your own act together, you wouldn't always be picking on me! The only thing you agree on is that I'm a pain in the ass!"

"Looks like she's got the real skinny," I commented.

Since by this time Stephanie trusted me, I decided to interrupt one of her snarling episodes with "Stephanie, has anyone ever told you you've got an attitude?" — at which all three of them laughed and nodded vigorously in the affirmative.

From this point on the focus moved more and more to family therapy, at Stephanie's request.

Integrating Individual and Family Therapy

I am not a purist in my approach. Probably few therapists in actual practice are, regardless of whether their training was primarily with individual children or in family systems. However, there is often some resistance to integrating the two approaches.

All theoretical misgivings aside for the moment, I believe that the single most compelling obstacle is the feeling of being incompetent outside one's area of expertise. Many therapists skilled at working with adults feel at a loss when it comes to children under the age of about twelve or thirteen; the prospect of having them present in sessions can be quite daunting. For a therapist accustomed to working on a one-to-one basis, the need to interact with so many people at the same time, without a cotherapist, may be equally daunting.

A therapist who is firmly vested in being a child's advocate may in fact be prejudiced against parents, seeing them as the root of all trouble, and thus be unable or unwilling to accord them the same regard and understanding so readily given to children.

And/or, young therapists may believe, sometimes correctly, that parents discount them because of their youth, especially when the age gap is considerable. For a therapist of any age who is still struggling with unresolved issues with his/her own parents, the countertransference issues can be especially intense in family therapy. That's what consultation and personal therapy are for.

Let's assume you have worked through your own issues to the point where they do not impede your work. Let's further assume that you agree with me that 1) not every problem a child experiences is purely a manifestation of family dysfunction, and 2) some degree of parental and perhaps sibling involvement is beneficial and important.

What then about those cases where the parents are highly resistant if not firmly opposed to becoming involved? Do you make their involvement a condition of your seeing the child?

I rarely do, since refusing to see the child will almost always mean a deprivation of sorely needed emotional support. I continue the individual work, while also continuing to be on the watch for ways and means to win over the parents to some family work.

One of the ways I do this is to invite them to leave a message on my voice mail each week about the progress and issues of my work with their child. If they do this a few times (and usually they do) I return a message saying, "Thank you so much for your input, it helps a lot. When you think it would be helpful to you (or both of you) to come in for a meeting with me, please let me know." Frequently they do.

Sometimes they don't. They may be relieved to have someone else take over: "I'm busy now sweetheart, why don't you talk to Ruth about that?" (To themselves they may add: "That's what we pay her for.")

They may have such deep-seated fear or dislike of the counseling process that they will bring their child in only as a desperate "last chance," or in compliance with a legal, educational, or medical order.

Individual therapy *can* be successful with only minimal family involvement. An anxious child may learn adaptive ways to lessen the anxiety. A child consumed with jealously over the new baby may profit enormously by having her true and valid feelings of displacement honored and understood by a counselor. Somewhat similarly, a child in pain over parental divorce may be best helped by having a place where the real feelings of anger and loss can be expressed to someone whose feelings won't be hurt no matter what is said.

Whatever the format of your interaction with parents, the purpose is not to reprimand or lecture, but to establish rapport so that you and they can be members of a team. This may seem self-evident, but is not so easy to do when

1) you are painfully aware of how their parenting is counter-productive to the child's well-being;

2) they keep asking you "so what should we do?";

3) they insist that the problem resides totally in the child;

4) they maintain there really isn't a problem at all, it's just the school, or child welfare, or the probation department, who thinks there is, or;

5) all of the above.

Five-year-old Josh had a "meltdown" when Mom and Dad went out at night. Here is how he expressed his feelings to his parents. They got the message.

Your anger at parental lack of appreciation of a child whom you find delightful may be mitigated when you consider the mismatch factor.

In "Not Seen and Not Heard," (*Family Therapy Networker*, 1991) Lawrence Diller quotes Stella Chess, Alexander Thomas, and Herbert Birch who conducted a 30-year study of aspects of temperament. They describe "goodness of fit" between parent and child as:

> ... a kind of harmony between the needs, desires and understanding of the parents — always defined by the values and demands of a given culture or socioeconomic group — and the personality of the baby . . . Adaptable parents learn techniques and skills for picking up and responding to what the child needs . . .

The counselor's office may be the best, if not only, place to help parents learn this adaptability. I tell parents, and sometimes kids, my tale of the stork flying overhead with a baby intended for the Jones family. Tired after a long day's work, he accidentally drops the baby over the Smith household. As the baby floats down, the stork is heard to apologize, "Sorry about that everyone. Good luck in therapy."

I may assign as homework a read-together of *The Ugly Duckling*, that penultimate tale of mis-matching.

I reassure the parents that having certain expectations is "normal;" their challenge is equal acceptance of the normalcy of a child's not meeting these expectations.

Family Therapy: The Ultimate Dual Relationship

The concept of dual relationships is currently under the fire of professional ethicality. Paradoxically, to effectively serve the family the family therapist *must* serve many masters.

Toward that end I am willing to be manipulative, and never more so than when working with adolescents and their families. As with Stephanie, I might say to a teenager, "You know, I can probably get Mom to see your point of view better than you can — after all, I'm old enough to be *her* mother!"

To the parents I may say, "Kids really do appreciate your values and opinions, but they need to save face. By seeing an older adult like myself, they can transfer their respect to me while keeping up their stance of 'Boy, my parents know nothing at all, they're pathetic.' You'll probably hear them repeat some of my words of wisdom and think, 'But that's exactly what I've been saying for months!' It's a good thing you've got a sense of humor."

Probably all these statements are effective because they are all true.

Once the session is underway, the ability to stand in another's shoes is vital. This ability comes easier to some therapists than to others. The best way I know to enhance it is through role-playing. If you find yourself going into family work with gaps in your training, begin the filling in process by role playing with colleagues as many situations as you can imagine, as well as those actually experienced.

If the child you are seeing has an obsessive-compulsive parent, role play that parent and feel what it is like to be a perfectionist whose child has a bedroom deserving of condemnation by the health department. Feel what it is like to be a father raised in a culture where physical punishment is the response of choice when a son is cutting school and hanging out with a bad crowd. Be the single mother, working long hours to stay off welfare, who is reported for child neglect. Be the young attorney whose firm demands extremely long hours and weekend work, and who is being urged by the school — and you — to attend school events and counseling for the sake of his/her child.

Be the therapist who has a disturbed child.

Family therapy requires kaleidoscopic utilization and blending from many life styles and belief systems. The open-ended nature of Gestalt work, with its appreciation of creativity and experimentation, is well suited to accomplish this. Although Gestalt techniques (most notably the "empty chair") are often incorporated into and other therapy modalities, it is the spirit of Gestalt therapy that gives the work its life and vitality.

Although we work with content, it is our awareness of the process that inspires us to suggest creative experiments to the family, so that the tool of their awareness can be sharpened. Young children are often the most aware members; structuring the session so they can be heard, rather than be "shushed," encourages the organism that is the family unit to thrive.

When young children are included in family therapy — really included, respectfully, as opposed to simply being present in the room — we see the I-Thou concept at work.

Cross Cultural Differences

Every family is cross cultural in some ways. Besides the obvious religious, racial, and national origin differences, there are differences in age and gender, life experiences, level and kind of education, political beliefs, etc. etc.

An example is the M. family. They left South America ten years ago; twelve-year-old Manuel was born there; six-year-old Eva is a native of Los Angeles., as is Roger, the Dad. Maria, the Mom, is a registered nurse; the couple met when Dad was in her country as an exchange student, and they lived there for two years. Three of Maria's five sisters have also moved to California. I speak almost no Spanish; fortunately they all are fluent in English.

Flowing with diversity presented a special challenge with this family, as I turned my swivel chair in different directions, walked back and forth to where the kids were playing, and paid attention to a variety of verbal and bodily nuances of expression.

During one session, the theme was Maria's younger sister Elena who was undergoing cancer treatment in a nearby city. As the oldest sister, Maria accepted the major responsibility for Elena's care, and commuted back and forth while juggling her family and her job. To her I said, "Your sister's demands on you during this hospitalization must have you feeling overwhelmed and fragmented." To

Manuel, "Gee, I guess it's tough when Mom can't go on any of your class field trips. Ever get a little mad at Tia Elena?" To Eva, "So, you really missed Mommy yesterday, huh? It's O.K. to tell her." And to Roger, "I wonder if you ever want to say to Maria, 'Hey, honey, I married you, not your sister.'"

All the while I was mindful that while my profession frowned upon what the literature calls "enmeshment," this woman's culture placed a high value on family connection. She was intellectually and emotionally available for exploration of boundary issues. I needed to eschew any insulting "corrections."

Roger needed support for his resentful feelings.

The children needed acknowledgment of what Mom's frequent absences meant to them.

Modeling

Modeling appropriate parental behavior is an effective alternative to lecturing and scolding. It can be overt or subtle; to be useful, it must be respectful.

An example is the question of when in family life it is, and is not, appropriate for a child to make choices (read also "have authority," "be in charge," "take control," "be the boss," etc.)

You can start this exercise by saying something like, *"I'd* like you all to sit around this table. *Mom,* you will need to decide who sits where, or else we may run out of time. *Marlu and Davie,* you can decide what color crayons you want to use, there are lots to choose from. *Dad,* how far apart do you think the kids should sit so everyone can enjoy this? Now, *each of you* choose a sheet of paper from this stack, and *I'll* give the directions for the first picture."

What Goes on in Here is What Goes on out There

The maxim "what goes on in here is what goes on out there" is usually true for family therapy — but be careful. We may decide, on the basis of what we observe in the consulting room, that interven-tion, via modeling or some other activity, is called for to impact what we see as "dysfunctional" parental behavior, when in fact what we are seeing may be strictly consulting room behavior. The parent who as a matter of course puts a stop to destructive behavior at home may, in the presence of the therapist, become paralyzed to act, wildly wondering, "If I make Steven stop pounding Playdough into the rug, will SHE think I am repressing him? Should I be firm, or try to reason? This is a test of me, I know it, and I think I'm going to fail."

That kind of parental reaction does indeed indicate something worth noting, but it does not necessarily say that the therapist must leap in with an intervention. Remember how you felt the first time you were asked to role play, or present a case, in the presence of THE SUPERVISOR?

Similarly, a parent who sternly stops the two-year-old from touching the plants may not, in fact, be restricting at home. Perhaps there is a cultural imperative to be especially polite away from home.

Certainly if you observe abusive behavior in your office you must assume this is not an isolated example. And just because parents are sweetly reasonable in your office doesn't mean they are that way when not on best behavior. Wait and see. As parents get to know and trust you, and relax, you can more safely assume that "What goes on in here goes on out there."

The First Session

I like the first session of therapy to be with the whole family, and nothing indicates "child friendly" better than the sight of available toys, some child sized furniture, bright colors, and the absence of priceless, breakable objects.

I begin the session by exploring with the youngsters the play materials they can use "while the grownups talk," and inviting them to join the conversation at any time. I make it plain to the parents that this is not just permitted, but encouraged. I remove in advance materials that could be dangerous to very young children, as well as activities that could be noisily disruptive.

As noted in the chapter "The Resilient Child," this practice provides an opportunity for legitimate and healthy distancing during emotionally laden discussions. The young child who is forced to "sit and listen" will urgently need to pee, or get a drink, or do whatever necessary to escape the tension. In the case of six-year-old Sean at the beginning of this chapter, he was able to be a fully participating family member while engrossed in sand tray work.

Drawing is another wonderful way for the child to participate while simultaneously being otherwise engaged. Seven-year-old Molly remained at the table quietly drawing throughout most of the first session while her mother and father discussed their concern about her new school placement. Periodically I addressed a question to her, such as "Do you agree with that?" or "Do you know what that word means?" She answered briefly and politely. After forty minutes she brought all her pictures over and gave them to me. There were pictures of her parents sitting on the couch, and me sitting in my chair. They were carefully drawn, and quite flattering. There was also a picture of her, sticking out her tongue at her teacher, who was portrayed as an evil witch, and me hitting the teacher with a baseball bat. Worth a thousand words . . .

In another case, the two-year-old in the family kept "interrupting" by offering me imaginary cups of coffee. Of course I accepted, while wondering why he only offered this gift to me. The mystery was solved when Mom said she had coached him to give cookies to grandma whenever she came to visit, so he wouldn't think that nice things only came *from* grandma. I thought that was quite lovely, and it bore out my sense that it is much too easy to interpret children's "interruptions" as just wanting attention. (As if there were something wrong with wanting attention.)

In general, the Gestalt therapy concept of avoiding intellectual interpretation is highly germane to family work. You may need to discourage parents from asking the child questions such as "What does your sand scene mean?" Once again, modeling is the intervention of choice, as you comment on the child's process ("You seemed to know just what you needed to finish your scene,") and your responses to the metaphors you observe ("The bad guys are bigger, but there are more of the good guys.")

It is an easy segue at the end of this first session to ask the child, "How about next time just you come; you'll have more time to use these things, and you and I can get better acquainted."

Almost always this meets with pleased agreement. With a very young, or very shy, child the plan may be altered to having Mom or Dad "join us for at least part of the time."

The only instance I can recall of complete, adamant refusal was with a highly gifted and very troubled nine-year-old who proclaimed "It would be a waste of time for just me to be here, because in case you haven't already figured it out, this *family* needs the therapy!" Of course he was right, and I did require family therapy in this case.

Board Games as Metaphors

The concept of board games as metaphors is covered in the chapter "Releasing Creativity." I'll mention here some I find particularly good for use with families.

Memory (also called *Concentration*) is a must for sessions with young children, who enjoy it and are usually better at it than adults.

Blockhead can lighten things up; sometimes I change the name and some of the rules for families given to insulting one another at any opportunity.

Perfection is useful to demonstrate how progress can be measured in terms of one's personal best, and/or family achievement.

The *Ungame* is a natural for families, with or without the special "Family" cards. The therapist can model openness; self-permission to *not* reveal; respectful listening and acceptance, among many other things.

The *Family Squares Game* which requires at least four family members to play is rich in potential for discussion and awareness. (See Workbook).

I have been talking here about including family sessions in child therapy; the eminent family therapist Nathan Ackerman was discussing including young children in family therapy when he wrote,

> . . . if they feel protected here (the family session) and fairly dealt with, their sense of personal impor-tance is gratifying . . . fundamentally, the child's drive for self-expression is a constructive and healing influence for the parents as well. It opens a path for a new way of relating, not only between parents and children, but also between the parents. What is involved is a movement toward a deeper and more appropriate kind of emotional honesty among the family members.

Whichever edge of the sword you start with — the family or the individual child — the impact is therapeutically powerful.

References

Diller, L. '"Not Seen and Not Heard." *Family Therapy Net-worker*. July/August 1991, pp. 18-27; 66.

Zilbach, Joan, M.D. (1986) *Young Children in Family Therapy*. New York: Brunner/Mazel, Inc.

7

—— CHILDREN AND DIVORCE ——

Adults see divorce as the remedy; children see divorce as the problem.

Judith Wallerstein (1995)

The interesting thing about Dr. Wallerstein's comment is that it refers to the *perceptions* of divorce. Although realities may be different, presenting problems frequently reflect how reality is viewed.

This helps explain why, according to Wallerstein and the anecdotal observations of clinicians, the child's initial response is a poor predictor of how he/she will fare emotionally in the long run.

For example, the child who perceives the divorce as abandonment and reacts with panic, or withdrawal, may rather quickly "come around" once it is clear that he/she still has loving parents to depend on.

The child who screams "I hate you!" sobs, or otherwise "acts out" may be displaying reactions that in the long run are highly adaptive.

On the other hand, the youngster who responds with no outward sign of distress may pay the emotional piper later in life.

Although the years preceding and following divorce have profound effects, often you, the therapist will be unable to directly impact either past or future. You are with the child now, and many of the factors which help children cope with life's difficulties are within your province. (See the chapter "The Resilient Child.")

As in all work with children, an understanding of developmental factors is important. Here are some rough guidelines of children's reactions to loss of a parent.

Up to about eight years, children can be expected to be depressed, and to nurture fantasies of their parents being reunited. Between nine and twelve, anger is a common response. The child may be angry with both parents for divorcing, or single out one to blame.

Adolescents may mask their depression and grief with rebellious behavior. (Keep in mind that the concept of masked depression has probably been overused.) Loss of the parental unit may also mean loss of neighborhood, school, and friends, all intensely important in the teen years; the added component of puberty's sexual turmoil makes it an especially vulnerable age.

•

Before proceeding further — here, and in the therapy — some thorny realities must be confronted. Take the common scenario where one parent brings the child in with the stated purpose of helping him/her through a difficult period.

This is certainly a laudable goal, and as therapists it goes against our grain to meet clients with anything other than trust and openness. Nevertheless, a healthy skepticism is called for here. It is important to ascertain custodial arrangements, including whose permission is required for the child to be in therapy. If you have any doubts or concerns, you will do well to consult an attorney specializing in family law.

Unfortunately, enlisting you as a child therapist may be part of a hidden agenda, such as securing a potential expert witness for a custody battle. In other words, there may be an attempt to buy you.

Experience has taught me to routinely ask each parent, regardless of how friendly and civilized the divorce appears to be, to sign the following document:

I (we) the undersigned agree that my (our) child_____ will be seeing you for psychotherapy. In order for this experience to be the most beneficial for him/her, I (we) agree that at no time will I (we) ask, or subpoena, you to make recommendations regarding child custody issues, either in writing, by telephone, deposition, or court appearance.

SIGNED   DATE

This waiver does not prevent me from testifying should I judge it to be in the child's best interest. Nor does it guarantee that I won't be pulled unwillingly into a suit, but it does mitigate against that unpleasant possibility.

If parents choose not to sign such a document, we proceed no further, and at least we are assured the child (and therapist) will be spared the pain of premature termination after the therapeutic bond has been formed.

When parents indicate understanding and willingness to honor the therapeutic purpose, we are off to a good start.

I find two things to be of value in therapeutic work with all the children and adolescents of divorcing families with whom I have worked:

1) Therapy is a place where all feelings may be openly expressed, free of fear of hurting either parent, and free of the temptation to manipulate.

The youngster has permission to wish their parents would not/did not divorce, regardless of the "reality" of the need for it, and permission to grieve for the lost family regardless of how that family "really" was.

2) Therapy fosters a true and integrated understanding that the divorce was not because of something the child did, or is. Many children of psychologically aware parents have heard the statement "It isn't your fault" and can repeat it by rote; not so many really believe it.

I address these issues very early on with comments such as:

"A lot of kids I know feel they have to take care of their parents when they get divorced . . . not say anything to hurt their feelings. That's one reason parents bring their kids here, because you won't hurt my feelings no matter what you say."

"I've noticed that even though kids know up here in their head that they didn't cause the divorce, here in their heart maybe they aren't all that convinced . . . "

Sometimes the reaction is a relieved, "Yeah, me too!" Sometimes it is a determined "Well it's not like that for me!" to which I respond with a simple, respectful "I see." I might add, "Perhaps you'll tell me how it is for you."

Feelings have been named and normalized; individuality has been respected.

Metaphors and Board Games

Be generous with metaphors; slant them to the youngster's age and situation. In addition to realistic family doll figures, provide plenty of animal "families" for very young kids. Watch for the enactment in sand scenes and dramatic play of such themes as smaller animals taking care of older, bigger ones; baby animals being left alone in one corner; groupings that are entirely harmonious and cooperative, as well as those with ominous overtones. Here are the kinds of comments I frequently hear myself say:

"That baby elephant keeps having to rescue the grown-ups."
"I wonder if those big horses realize the little colt is all alone over there."
"Isn't it miraculous the way they always all get along together and never once have an argument! It's almost too good to be true."
"That giraffe sleeping under the tree: is he tired, or bored, or sad?"

Board games, so useful with kids who resist both talking and projective activities, can be mined for their relevant metaphors. A favorite strategy of mine in the game *Othello*, is to gain the corners, from which position: "No one can pull any surprises on me here!" This game is notable for its quick switches from imminent winning to imminent losing, prompting comments (embedded suggestions) such as "Everything changes so fast in this game I have to really keep my cool or I'll get discouraged."

With young children the classic board game *Memory*, which consists of pairs of pictures of ordinary objects which are placed face down on the table and matched by remembering their locations, can be extended to storytelling (see Workbook) with the therapist telling stories slanted to the youngster's particular situation.

The wonderful *Talking, Feeling, and Doing Game* where players move around a board following instructions to pick and respond to either "Talking," "Feeling," or "Doing" cards, evoked this response from a youngster who drew the card: "What is the worst thing a child can say to a parent?" She responded immediately and gleefully: "I hate you and I'm going to live with my Dad!"

Useful directed projective techniques include *cinquains* (structured five-line poems) and story starters (pictures with one or two sentences to be completed to make a story.) These techniques are described more fully in the Workbook. In each, there is a "menu" of topic choices including, but not limited to issues of divorce, separation, marriage, family, custody, and so on. Some examples are in the "Appendix."

Genograms and family trees (especially useful for the highly guarded youngster who appreciates the structure of school-like exercises) can illustrate the potential benefit of the extended family with discussions about which members are or are not "easy to talk to," "have good advice," "remember what it's like to be a kid," etc. etc. etc.

For the same reason I frequently arrange family therapy sessions with as many extended family members as possible.

Group therapy is a wonderful adjunct to individual therapy and often the modality of choice. Since my private practice doesn't always lend itself to the logistical or chronological demands of forming a group, I keep alert for schools, churches, YMCA's, family service agencies, and colleagues to whom I can make referrals.

Books and the Media

There are excellent books for young kids on changing families — and some pretty dreadful ones. My favorite for young children, *Divorce is a Grown Up Business* by Janet Sinberg, is unfortunately out of print, but can be found in some public libraries or the out-of-print book services. Part of the enjoyment is the illustrations with the now old-fashioned clothing and hairstyles; imagine, the feelings were so similar in the olden days of the 70's!

Families, by Meredith Tax, is a charming and reassuring book, delightfully illustrated by Marilin Hafter, about the many forms families can and do take.

Jill Krementz' *How it Feels When Parents Divorce* is a collection of straightforward accounts in the youngsters' own words. (In the same format by this talented writer are *When a Parent Dies, How it Feels to be Adopted,* and *How it Feels to Live With a Physical Disability.)*

Among the many books by the prolific and popular Judy Blume, one that is excellent for both adults and young teenagers is *Letters to Judy — What Your Kids Wish They Could Tell You.*

Check out bookstores for stories that are not polemics, that for young children are brief and have good illustrations, and that you would enjoy reading.

Try collaborating with your young clients on book reviews; ask such questions as "What age do you think this book is best for?" "Do you think kids in certain life styles/geographical areas/specific ethnic groups/etc. would like it more than others?" If they didn't like it, why not?

This activity is described more fully in the chapter, "Releasing Creativity." As with the tape recording activity also described in "Releasing Creativity," this sharing provides some of the benefits of group therapy even though the "members" may never meet face to face.

I discuss movies (current, and older ones available on videotape) and TV shows, watching for appropriate themes, sharing my reactions and soliciting theirs. Chatting about techniques of directing, special effects, acting skill, etc. can be an opening with youngsters who are guarded about their personal experiences.

I recommended the film *Irreconcilable Differences* to twelve-year-old Heather, whose ambition is to become a film writer. Like the young girl in the film, she is used as a reluctant conduit between her divorced, still battling, parents. I said I found the film overdone in many ways, and the acting so-so, "but still, it does have its moments."

After viewing it, Heather said: "Well, it won't win any Oscars, but I like seeing other kids in a situation like mine, and knowing I'm not the only one who goes through these things."

The film *Hope Floats* evokes the humiliation and isolation some divorced moms experience, and carries a message of renewal, of starting over. It is appropriate for teenagers.

The farcical *Mrs. Doubtfire* looks at divorce from the perspective of a loving and creative, if blundering, non-custodial father. It's fun for all ages, and a good discussion starter.

By contrast, the father in *Stepmom* is little more than an ineffectual background figure. The twelve-year-old daughter is realistically nasty, agonizingly rude, and generally hateful to her Dad's young live-in girlfriend (eventually the stepmom) who struggles heroically to make good in a difficult role.

The younger brother, also realistically, is torn between affection for the girlfriend and loyalty to his mom ("If you want me to hate her, I will.")

Mom has her own heroic struggle reconciling her resentment and bitterness at having been displaced by a younger woman with her urgent need to ensure the best for her children — another scenario familiar to family therapists, as is the issue of the obvious sexual attraction between Dad and his new love. Tragedy makes them an extended family, with a "happy ending" laid on with a shovel wrapped in five hankies.

There are rich opportunities here for discussion, especially with adolescent or adult groups. A good opening question is:

"Would there have been the same resolution to the problems if there had been no tragedy?"

With period pieces such as *Sense and Sensibility* we'll talk about the costumes and the acting, and I might remark,

"Those ladies sure didn't have much of a choice of guys, did they — and if they made the wrong choice, they couldn't get out of it."

I was surprised to discover that several teenagers count the TV show *Frasier* among their favorites (it's also one of mine.) Besides chuckling over the witty dialogue and great comedic acting, I sometimes note that Frasier's son who lives in a distant city with his mother, the redoubtable Lillith, is seldom referred to or seen. Hmmm. Why is that? I wonder out loud.

And then there's television's *The Simpsons*, which some parents — and other adults — thoroughly disapprove of but which I find an irreverently funny portrayal of a family with human flaws made functional by basic and abiding affection.

— CHILDREN AND DIVORCE —

Being with the Parents

Parents sincerely wishing to meet their children's needs may be too stressed and preoccupied by their own emotional upheaval to adequately do so. I frame seeking counseling as an example, not an evasion, of exercising parental responsibility. I spend time reassuring and supporting parents in their ability to be "good enough" parents.

On-going contact with each parent, focused on what each can do to facilitate the child's working through the crisis, is ideal — and in my experience, only occasionally achieved. Anger, hurt, resentment, guilt, sorrow — these and a host of other emotions muddy the waters of sessions intended to be educative.

Not all questions are asked in good faith: sometimes an accusation is thinly disguised as a question, such as:

"What do you advise me to do when Johnny asks me why his mother has a different man sleeping in her bed every night?"

At this point you probably don't know if Mom is indeed being sexually inappropriate, or if Dad is irrationally jealous. The best bet in these kinds of situations is to first recommend that the parent "Encourage Johnny to talk directly to his Mom about things that concern him," and then note "You may well have issues yourself about your ex's sex life (or whatever) — do talk to your therapist about that." This conforms with my policy of strongly recommending that each parent have some individual therapy — and not with me. My role with divorcing parents is strictly educational; blurring that boundary inevitably leads to trouble.

There is no formula to determine when one parent's complaints about the other are so legitimately serious as to require therapeutic or even legal intervention. Explain to each parent that unwarranted accusations can backfire, affecting the long-term relationship with the child, and/or having legal consequences; explain the difference between unwise parenting and actual abuse; guard against being infected with a parent's prejudices; remind yourself, and the parent, that there are limits to your influence, and that you do your best to be effective within those limits.

Neither is it necessary or wise to go to the other extreme, encouraging the pretense of warm feelings for the ex-spouse when the truth is quite opposite. It's true that the second fondest wish of most children of divorce is for their parents to be friends (the first being the reconciliation fantasy) and when this occurs it is wonderful. Fortunately it is not a necessary condition for successful co-parenting — what Constance Ahron calls "bi-nuclear families." (Ahron, 1994). It is encouraging for parents to hear that the minimum requirement of their relationship with each other is to be partners in the business of raising their children; as in business, it is quite possible to put aside personal animosities when negotiating important matters. This is reasonable and reassuring and in fact sometimes smooths the road toward a truly friendly association, as members of the same family.

I explain that in the early stage of divorce some youngsters seem driven to make sense of their internal chaos by applying labels of "good parent" and "bad parent." ("Splitting," as we call it in the trade). In their therapy children are helped to develop other ways to adapt; the emotional distress of the parent labeled "bad" (or the diabolical glee of the one labeled "good") is best handled in his/her individual therapy. Our parent education work is focused on understanding the dynamic and keeping a realistic perspective.

I note to parents as well as to children that sometimes good people bring out the worst in each other. When it rings true, this concept helps free everyone from the burden of trying to determine "Whose fault was it?"

It is rare that the decision to divorce is entirely mutual. The person who leaves has a very dissimilar experience than the one who is left; responses to the new challenge of single parenting will reflect these and other differences.

An especially poignant and potentially destructive situation is when the father (occasionally the mother) is so devastated by what has happened that he considers simply abandoning the children on the grounds that "they will be better off without me; they won't have to go back and forth between their mother and me; they can all just start over." I am not talking here about those fathers who abandon their children to avoid paying support, but about those who sincerely love their children and truly believe that their absence won't be harmful.

I see my role in these cases as crisis intervention, and adopt a highly directive posture. I firmly and authoritatively (and compassionately, I hope) state the facts: to abandon children is extremely harmful to them, they will probably never get over it, they need contact with Dad, the wish to flee is understandable but I will do everything possible to thwart that impulse. I also will do everything possible to get that father into individual therapy.

Language is a powerful tool. I never use the terms "Mom's house" and "Dad's house," or even "visitation." I point out to parents that in non-divorced families, a child doesn't say "I am going to Mom's and Dad's house," he says "I am going home," or "to my house." Cumbersome though it may be, I recommend "Will you be with Mom or with Dad?" or "This is your weekend to be at yours and Dad's home," or sometimes, "Which lucky parent will you be with?"

Views of the long-term effects of divorce on children have changed over the last several decades. In the fifties, it was assumed that the effect was anything from difficult to disastrous. In the more permissive climate of the sixties and seventies, it was thought that the natural resilience of children protected them from more than transitory ill effects. Research of the eighties and nineties suggests the latter view was too sanguine, that children and adolescents do in fact experience emotional damage that may be long lasting, depending on many variables.

Each stage of the way, the current view is considered "enlightened" — which means whatever we want it to mean. There is no pure, unbiased research; politics and the Zeitgeist are always operating. As clinicians we base our interventions more on these exigencies than we like to acknowledge, and couple counseling is surely affected by these changing attitudes.

As child therapists our goal remains less fickle. We work to heal. And whatever interventions we use, it helps to remember the curative effects of the tincture of time.

References

Ahron, C. (1994). *The Good Divorce*. New York: HarperCollins Publishers, Inc.

Blume, J. (1986). *Letters to Judy — What Your Kids Wish They Could Tell You*. New York: G.P. Putnam Sons.

Krementz, J. (1984). *How It Feels When Parents Divorce*. New York: Alfred A. Knopf.

Sinberg, J. (1978). *Divorce is a Grown-up Business*. New York: Avon Books.

Tax, M. (1981). *Families*. Boston: Little, Brown and Company.

Wallerstein, J. and Blakeslee, S. (1995). *Second Chances: Men, Women, and Children, a Decade After Divorce*. New York: Houghton Mifflin Co.

Wallerstein, J. and Kelly, J.B. (1980). *Surviving the Breakup* . New York: Basic Books.

8

— SELF ESTEEM —

A CONCEPT IN NEED OF CLARIFICATION

If self-esteem were easy to impart, everyone would have it.
– *Fred G. Gorman*

The *Oxford English Dictionary* defines self-esteem as "Favorable appreciation or opinion of oneself." Although that has a nice ring to it, the concept has been polluted, trivialized, and banalized into one more buzzword, one more instance of "therapy-speak." A definition I like and will be using here is the one attributed to Stevenson et al. (1990) by Katz (1993): " . . . an enduring and affective sense of personal value based on accurate self-perceptions."

How can we promote this? Coopersmith (1981) [Cited in Hillemann and Schumacher 1990] identifies the primary factors contributing to self-esteem as:

> The amount of respectful, accepting, concerned treatment that an individual receives from significant others; the history of successes, status and position one holds in the world; the way in which experiences

are interpreted and modified in accord with the individual's values and aspirations; and the individual's manner of responding to devaluation. (p. 33 of Hillemann and Schumacher)

Key concepts are accuracy and reality. To ignore them is to inadvertently and paradoxically promote narcissism, which, by definition, precludes healthy self-esteem.

There are other factors to consider, such as morality, culture, discipline, and ego-defenses. We do our young clients a disservice if our response to a presenting problem of "poor self-esteem" is to confuse respect and regard with indiscriminate praise and acceptance.

I think youngsters understand this instinctively; it is we adults who sometimes feel compelled to sanitize reality. Thus, when with well intentioned zeal we proclaim "You are really a *fine* student and should be proud of yourself!" the unhappy youngster looking at a report card full of D's and C minuses thinks, "Yeah, right. Well I may not be a genius but I know bullshit when I hear it." Equally misguided though well intentioned is the notion that faith in the impossible is the same as inspiration.

A personal example: I take yoga classes. My spinal structure is such that many postures will always be beyond my ability. If my yoga teacher said "You can do it if you just try hard enough! I have faith in you!" I'd feel like a failure, I'd feel like I had let her down and since I am an adult with adult privileges, I would simply drop the class. (Kids have their own ways of dropping out.) But when I hear "it's the process of stretching to your edge that gives the benefit," and "those hamstrings are starting to loosen up a bit, aren't they? You need to practice more between classes" I know that I'm neither a star nor a miserable failure, and I'm encouraged to continue.

The once cherished belief that neither performance nor conduct could be improved unless and until self-esteem improved seems fortunately to be on the wane. These truisms bear repeating.

> Improved performance enhances self-esteem and vice- versa.

> Behavior and emotions interact.

It is not necessary to be trained in educational therapy per se to effectively intervene with those many children who come into therapy via the school's recommendation. You'll often hear something like: "Johnny is really very bright, but low self-esteem prevents him from getting good grades."

First of all, Johnny may or may not be "very bright." Counseling can be effective across a wide span of "cognitive ability." Working with parents, and often teachers, is essential to encourage, facilitate, inspire, and guide the child to achieving *success commensurate with ability.* My first response to a youngster who has received a "bad" report card is to say honestly,

"This must make you feel pretty rotten."

We'll spend a little time acknowledging that sick feeling of shame, and then move to: "What ideas do you have for getting a better handle on math?" — or whatever seems to be a problem area, so long as it is not the most intractable one. Save that for later in the process, after some successes have been achieved.

This kind of response changes the perspective from "I'm really stupid and it's no use," or "the teacher hates me," or "I don't care anyway," to a creative approach to problem solving (or CAP — see the chapter "Releasing Creativity.")

The youngster's first response to the question of what he or she can do toward improvement is usually "I don't know." Gentle exploration of possibilities will elicit *something*, if only "have my Mom help me more." Although this is not the solution of choice, a legitimate reframing, such as "so you think some tutoring would help . . . that's worth considering. What other things have you ever done to help yourself learn the things you are good at now?" sets the stage for self-responsibility and its companions, power and control.

Learning to tie one's own shoelace, something that is expected of everyone, deserves congratulations but not lavish praise. For the child with fine-motor difficulty, a well-targeted comment such as "that was hard for you, but you didn't give up until you could do it" is honest, transferable to many tasks and skills, and serves as a motivator to proceed to another level of mastery.

As for the child's areas of strengths, keep expectations high. One of the highlights of my training with the late Arnold Beisser of the Gestalt Therapy Institute of Los Angeles took place when he criticized a piece of work I did in the training group. One of the other trainees was appalled. "Ruth must feel devastated being criticized in front of all of us!" he lamented.

Arnie's response was typically succinct: "I know she is competent and mature enough to accept and utilize the criticism. Correct me if I'm wrong, Ruth." My fervent "You're right, you're right!" prompted another member to comment wistfully, "Now I'm jealous. You never criticize *me.*"

Praise can be a sugary non-solution, or it can be steam to push through difficult, but possible, tasks.

Criticism can be a form of commendation.

Self-Esteem and Morality

A similar and disturbing aspect of the self-esteem band-wagon is the notion that *feeling* good about oneself is more important than *being good.*

Rabbi Neil Kurshan (1987) asks parents to pay attention to moral dimensions in order to raise a "mensch," which he defines as a decent, responsible, caring person. He's a rabbi, so talking about morals is obviously appropriate; is it appropriate for therapists to think and speak in such terms? It *must* be if we are presumptuous enough to think of ourselves as members of a "helping" or "healing" profession. We need take no specific political or religious stance in order to encourage decency, responsibility, and caring.

A basic tenet of work with children is the acceptance of *feelings,* even when the *behavior* is unacceptable. There is no conflict between honoring a child's feeling of hatred for his new baby brother and helping him to learn acceptable vs. destructive ways of expressing it, as in the time honored "I won't let you hurt the baby; draw me a picture showing how you feel."

An angry child who refrains from hitting a sibling and/or expresses the rage in art or stories deserves praise and reinforcement. (A small baby doll has been buried in the sand-tray in my office on more than one occasion.) It is also within our province to encourage coexisting loving and protective feelings. When I asked nine-year-old Tim to tell me two good things about his "nerdy" eight-year-old brother, he thought long and hard before replying:

"He doesn't like chocolate, that's one, and two is that he gives his chocolate trick-or-treats to me." Technically that's probably only *one* thing, but I accepted it anyway.

Altruism is a recognized attribute and benefit of group therapy. Knowing that our experiences and understandings help others also helps us to feel good about ourselves, whether we are the therapist or the client. I use this concept in individual work when I ask a youngster for permission to share their CAPS results with other youngsters struggling with similar problems. Some "how-to" titles are:

"Terry's Tips For Losing Weight and Keeping Fit,"

"Marianne's Strategies for Finishing Homework Assignments on Time,"

"How Michael Stops Himself From Losing His Cool,"

"You Too Can Make Friends."

Board games are, among many uses, vehicles for modeling and teaching fair play. I always acknowledge that I enjoy winning a lot more than losing, but what is even more important to me is being a fair and honest person who can lose as well as win gracefully.

I once ran into trouble with this approach when a child said, "My father told me the only thing that matters is winning." I could only respond, "I guess your father and I disagree on that."

Gestalt therapy notes the concept of *"looking* good rather than *being* good." Our *Zeitgeist* seems to be in large measure a narcissistic obsession with marketing image and style over substance. It may appear to be going against the national norm to suggest that it is more important to be and do good than to look good, but there is nothing new about therapists taking the iconoclastic view in service of a worthwhile goal.

Self-Esteem and Culture

Our increasingly diverse culture demands awareness of the cultural implications of theories we may assume to be universal. An example relating directly to self-esteem is that although Asian children actually perform better in math than American children, their *conceptions* of their mathematical abilities are less positive. Researchers such as Stevenson, et al. (1990) attribute this to the fact that in Asian and other non-Western countries, restraint and modesty are attributes of self-esteem, while pride in accomplishment is considered gloating — a very different view of what constitutes feeling good about oneself than the Western one.

What may in fact be damaging is the interpretation of behavior. Lack of eye contact — considered by most Western therapists an indicator of interpersonal isolation — is in some cultures a sign of good breeding and courtesy. To be branded emotionally impaired by teachers and/or counselors for a behavior well-regarded elsewhere is a harbinger of cognitive and affective dissonance.

Another example comes from my friend and colleague Vera Reichenfeld-Taylor, a senior school psychologist in the Los Angeles Unified School District. She points out (personal communication, August 3, 1999) that in many Latino families self-esteem is linked to the success of the extended family. A well-intentioned teacher who praises a youngster for receiving a good test grade may be bewildered by the apparent lack of prideful response. Vera suggests: "say to that child, 'you have a wonderful mama who can raise such a well-behaved and smart child' and you will hit the mark."

Self-Esteem and Discipline

Parents are as likely to ask for your help in matters of discipline as in matters of self-esteem; don't overlook the vital connection between the two.

Mussen, Janeway, Kagan, and Huston (1984) present evidence suggesting that authoritative parenting, as opposed to authoritarian or permissive, has impressive short and long-term results:

> Authoritative parents are described as: warm, loving, supportive, and conscientious . . . . at the same time they were controlling, and demanded mature behavior from their children. Although they respected their youngsters' independence and decisions, they generally held firm in their own positions, being clear and explicit about the reasons for their directives. (p. 386)

By contrast, "authoritarian" parents, described as "exercising high use of control and power, discouraging disagreement with parents, and providing little warmth," rated lower on maturity and competence in their children (p. 386).

The children of "permissive" parents — described as "non-disciplinarian, warm, non-demanding in terms of self-reliance," rated even lower on maturity and competence in their children (p. 386).

In other words, the authoritative parent does not get caught up in an either-or position, but rather steers a moderate course of acceptance and expectations, of patience and discipline. Helping parents steer this moderate course of discipline is part of the work of fostering feelings of self-worth in the children.

A world without discipline is a world without limits, a confusing and scary place where adults have no better judgment than kids and therefore cannot be counted on when the going gets rough. Learning everything by trial and error can work, but the price in anxiety and risk of serious consequences is high.

There are important differences between punishment and discipline. Punishment means pain and deprivation. While pain *can* be an effective teacher, the lessons may inculcate hostility and damaged self-esteem.

Discipline means learning, molding, correcting. It leads to growth, self-discipline, mastery — and hence to self-esteem. It's like having a good coach. When you hold your tennis racket at the wrong angle, a good coach doesn't smack you, or humiliate you, or let you play ten losing games before you catch on. A good coach says, "Try holding your racket at this angle."

You can effectively coach parents in many workable discipline methods, such as:

 1) ignoring behavior that is not harmful or seriously irritating to others;

2) catching the child "being good" and praising him/her;

3) suspension of privileges with the suspension matching the action as closely as possible;

4) invoking logical consequences;

5) being creative in taking preventative action to eliminate the cause of problems;

6) using reasonable fines and work details to "work off" infractions and

7) modeling the behavior you want to promote. These methods are spelled out in more detail in my audiotape (1988) *Parenting in the 90's.*

The Seven-Letter "F" Word

Failure. Few other words evoke such a sense of shame. Failing a test or a grade, a failed business or a failed marriage — these can be synonymous with disgrace.

They can also be one step on a road to achievement. As Seligman (1996) points out, " . . . Failure, in itself, is not a catastrophe. It may deflate self-esteem for a while, but it is *the interpretation your child makes of the failure that can be more harmful"*(Italics mine) (p.14). Avoidance is one way to deal with failure, and at times it is the healthiest, most sensible response. Failure to complete school assignments obviously is not one of those times; extracurricular activities may be. As Michael Lewis (1999) says, " . . . finishing what you started is a useful course of action only if what you started is worth finishing." Not every game or skill needs to be mastered. Fortunately, everyone, even young ones, can make some choices among non-mandatory activities.

Quitting school or avoiding difficult subjects are not acceptable responses for school-age youngsters. Young children must attend school (public, private, or via home schooling) for a specified period of time, and there are classes they must take. Even adolescents who choose not to complete high school must master certain material if they want to pass the high school equivalency exam.

Some educators have attempted to avoid failure by manipulating the curriculum so that the child experiences only success, but as Seligman's (1975) research indicates, "exposure to repeated success in which failure is avoided or glossed over leaves the child helpless, or makes him more so" (p. 157).

The pendulum seems to be swinging the other way now, at least in the time and place (California) where I am writing. The accelerating demand for more and more testing, the increasing tendency to judge schools, teachers, and students almost entirely on the basis of scores, means more and more youngsters will be experiencing failure. This is not the place to examine this trend; I am among those who consider it extreme and shortsighted. I console myself and my clients with Seligman's later comments (1996): " . . . for your child to experience mastery, it is *necessary* (italics mine) for him to fail, to feel bad, and to try again repeatedly until success occurs . . . Failure and feeling bad are necessary building blocks for feeling good" (p.44) .

It's worth remembering that high risk takers in the arts, sciences, and sports virtually always experience many failures. They also achieve more than the usual number of successes, and it's the latter, that the world remembers. Einstein's early math failure is legendary. Steven Spielberg's academic record was so undistinguished that he failed to win admission into any of the prestigious film schools to which he applied. Alexander Graham Bell is said to have been attempting to develop a hearing aid for his deaf son when by mistake he invented the telephone. Michael Jordan's response to being kicked off his high school basketball team was heightened determination to succeed. Legend has it that a prize winning chocolate cake in a national contest was the result of the applicant accidentally adding the frosting to the batter; rather than throw it out as a failure, she took a chance and baked it, and the rest is gustatory history. There are countless other examples in which failures were strands in the fabric of success, even genius. As a writer, I'm especially fond of the stories of authors whose manuscripts were rejected by dozens of publishers before finally being accepted, and in some case, becoming best sellers.

A caveat is in order here: Failure can have serious, even fatal, results. To keep from becoming too sanguine, ask yourself how you would feel about a surgeon who said, "Sure, I make mistakes, but hey, no one is perfect."

To help our youngsters deal with the initial humiliation of failure and move on to the pride of mastery, we need to help them re-frame the concept from "*I* am a failure" to "I failed this time; what should I do differently?" As Gary Yontef, author of *Awareness, Dialogue and Process,* says, "The Captain whose ship has run aground knows where the shallows lie."

Self-Esteem, Abuse, and Depression

It is redundant to discuss the issues of abuse and depression separately from self-esteem, and there are chapters on each elsewhere in this book. Here I will just note that guilt and shame, those constant companions of damaged self-esteem, may be defenses against facing the lack of parental love ("they wouldn't have done it if I didn't deserve it; it was for my own good; they acted out of love for me and I am the bad one") and facing life's uncertainties ("if it was my fault I am in control and therefore can prevent it from happening again"). In all therapeutic work defenses deserve our respect and gentle exploration, and certainly never more so than with the abused child. Polster & Polster (1974) remind us that a defense is "not just a dumb barrier to be removed but a creative force for managing a difficult world" (p. 52) It may be hard for the adult therapist to see self blame as part of a child's creative adjustment, until the perceived alternatives of being unloved by parents, of being totally out of control, are considered. Part of the healing process is understanding that there are other alternatives; with their discovery, self-esteem can be restored.

A Final Caveat

Unmet narcissistic needs often cloud parents' vision and expectations. Therapists also do well to develop and keep their view of the child as uncolored as possible by personal needs. Does our self-esteem require that the children we work with emerge from therapy fashioned in our own cherished image of mental health? Do we need parents to acknowledge their gratitude for our miracle working?

We can't successfully "work through" all our own garbage, and we don't need to. We do need to be keenly aware of when it is getting in the way.

References

Cole, K.C. (1998, September 10) "If at first you don't succeed — all the better." *The Los Angeles Times.*

Coopersmith, S. (1981). *The Antecedents of Self-esteem.* Palo Alto, CA:Consulting Psychologists Press, Inc.

Hillemann, E. and Schumacher, L. (1990). *The Relationship Between Disciplinary Strategies and Self-esteem in Children.* Unpublished master's thesis, University of Los California: os Angeles, CA.

Katz, L.G. (1993). *Distinctions Between Self-esteem and Narcissism: Implications for Practice.* (Perspectives from ERIC/EECE: A Monograph Series, No. 5). University of Illinois: Urbana, IL .

Kurshan, N. (1987). *Raising Your Child to be a Mensch.* New York: Athenum-Macmillia

Lampert, R. (Speaker). (1988) *Parenting in the 90's.* [Cassette Recording No. MS 85]. Seattle: MaxSound Tape Co.

Lewis, M. (1999, September 5). "The joy of quitting." The *New York Times Magazine.*

Mussen, P.H., Conger, J.J., Kagan, J., Huston, A.C. *Child Ddevelopment and Personality.* (1984). (6th ed.) New York: Harper and Row.

Polster, E. and Polster, M. (1974). *Gestalt Therapy Integrated.* New York:Random House Inc. (paperback edition).

Seligman, M. (1975). *Helplessness*. San Francisco: W.H.Freeman and Company

Seligman, M. (1995). *The Optimistic Child*. Boston: Houghton Mifflin Company. (First HarperPerrenial edition (paper back) New York 1996)

Stevenson, H.W., Lee, S., Chen, C., Lummis, M., Stigler, J.W., Fan, L. & Ge, F. (1990). "Mathematics Achievement of Children in China and the United States." *Child Development*, 61(4): 1053-1066, EJ 417114

Stevenson, H. W., Lee, S., Chen, C. Stigler, J.W., Hsu,C. and Kitamura, S. (1990). *Contents of Achievement*. Monograph of the Society for Research in Child Development, serial 221, vol. 55, nos. 1-2. Chicago: University of Chicago Press EJ 407444

9

— UNDERSTANDING ADOLESCENT — DEPRESSION AND SUICIDE

This chapter is an updated version of an audiotape published in 1986 by MaxSound Tape Co. There have been advances in our understanding since then: in this updated version I have tried to reflect, or at least note, societal and statistical differences.

You don't have to suffer to be a poet. Adolescence is enough suffering for anyone.
– John Ciardi

In this strange labyrinth how shall I turn?
– Mary Sidney Wroth

Introduction

The death of a young person is one of the most tragic events of the human condition. We find the deliberate seeking of death by the young not only tragic, but also frightening and bewildering.

"Why?" we ask. With everything ahead, in full possession of the sparkling gift of youth, what kind of desperation leads to forfeiting the future, abandoning existence?

Regrettably, these questions are being asked of and by mental health professionals in increasing numbers. Between 1950 and 1993, suicide rates among adolescents quadrupled. (Stepp, 1993) The need for understanding and insight into the problem has never been greater.

Myths about suicide are dangerously numerous. For example:

Kids who threaten suicide won't actually do it.

If they do make an attempt and fail, they'll be so scared by the experience they'll never try again.

When a depressed youngster becomes cheerful, the crisis is over and we can relax.

A depression so deep that it leads to suicide must be caused by psychosis.

Once the decision to commit suicide has been made, no one can do anything to reverse it.

The tendency to suicide is purely a genetic trait.

Rich kids are at greater risk for suicide than poor kids.

Or:

Poor kids are at greater risk than rich kids.

Those are myths. Here is reality:

Although especially severe in developed countries such as the United States, the problem is world-wide. While not all, or even most, depression leads to suicide, most youngsters who threaten, attempt, and commit suicide have been deeply depressed for a significant period of time.

Most suicidal persons are *not* psychotic.

Threats of suicide often are cries for help, which if ignored *may* be followed by suicide.

Most persons who kill themselves have made previous attempts.

— ADOLESCENT DEPRESSION AND SUICIDE —

The period immediately following a depressive episode is *especially* dangerous.

Most suicidal individuals are ambivalent, wavering bet-ween life affirmation and death wishes, up to the last moment.

Many deaths registered as accidents may in fact be suicide, and self-destructive behavior such as reckless driving and substance abuse may be indirectly suicidal.

More male youngsters complete suicide than females; more young females *attempt* suicide.

Most young males who kill themselves do so with guns and explosives; young females are more likely to use pills and poisons.

Most young persons of either gender who attempt suicide without fatal results take pills or poisons, methods allowing time for rescue; the more violent methods usually do culminate in death. However, it is dangerously unwise to make fine distinctions between intentions; chance may be the determining factor. Some survive the most lethal means, and some, perhaps less determined to die, do so by an accident of timing or place.

Recognizing the Signs of Depression

The classical signs of depression, such as eating and sleeping disturbances, loss of sexual energy, psychomotor retardation, and withdrawal may be masked in adolescents with conduct disorders, acting out behavior, and deterioration of school performance. A frenetic life style, or physical ailments of a psychosomatic nature, should be regarded as possible indications of depression. It is almost axiomatic that the younger the individ-ual, the less likely it is that the classical symptoms will be evident.

Whether a youngster presents as sad and dejected, or frenetic, the common underlying emotional experience of the potentially suicidal youngster is hopelessness, helplessness, and worthlessness. He/she feels helpless to change the self, and is convinced that the world, and his/her relationship to it, is now and forever unbearably bleak.

Most depressed youngsters are not clinically psychotic;*some* are. The practitioner is well advised to review the literature on such disorders as bipolar/affective disorder and schizophrenia, and to utilize consultation with a psychiatrist who can prescribe medication.

Risk Factors for Suicide

Deep depression presents the most obvious risk factor for suicide. Although awareness of youth suicide has risen in the past decades, there may be a hesitancy to discuss it with teenage clients. This reluctance may stem from the mistaken idea that such discussion will itself plant the idea, or from the therapist's out-of-awareness need to avoid this profoundly disturbing phenomenon.

Avoidance of the topic can confirm the adolescent's belief that no one knows — or more importantly, cares — about the depth of his/her despair. Bringing the subject into the open is both realistic and reassuring.

I typically ask a few simple, frank questions: "Do you ever feel so bad you wish you were dead?" If the answer is yes, I ask "Do you mean sometimes you think it would be nice to just not wake up, or do you mean you would really rather be dead and have a plan to kill yourself?" If it is the first alternative, I discuss in a general way the universality of *sometimes* feeling this way, of not really wanting to be dead but wanting the pain to end. I ask for (and have always gotten) a promise, (written is best but verbal is acceptable) that if the feeling of wanting to be dead becomes strong, he/she will call me. I note that if the motive is to punish others, especially parents, suicide is indeed effective and I describe the lifelong anguish suffered by family members and close friends in its aftermath. Perhaps paradoxically, this discourages rather than encourages the act. "And besides," I sometimes add, "you don't have to do it *now* — procrastinate! We'll talk more about it." If there is a definite plan including ways and means to carry it out, hospitalization must be arranged. If that happens, dealing with the anger at "betrayal" will be a therapeutic issue.

Some of the indicators of at risk youngsters are: poor inter-personal relationships; a history of school difficulties; recent suicide of a family member or close friend; perception of failure at a cherished ambition; any significant loss of love object. Suicidal despair is inextricably bound with parent and family interactions, and will be explored further in another section of this chapter.

The suicidal youngster who doesn't present classical symptoms of depression or doesn't acknowledge suicidal thoughts usually does give signs and cues, sometimes subtle, of the intent.

One is when the period following a severe depression is marked by an energy spurt and unusual cheerfulness. This seeming paradox can be understood as the manifestation of a sense of relief when the decision to suicide has been made, and there is "nothing to worry about any more — I'll soon be out of all this." It is a cruel irony that, quite understandably, those involved with the youngster may think they can now breathe easy, that all is well, when actually the need for vigilance is critical.

Another red flag is preoccupation with talking about, reading about, listening to music about, suicide. While it is not uncommon for adolescents to examine and even be fascinated with the dark side of life, if this involvement with death literature, imagery, and music occupies a disproportionate space in the youngster's life, we should be on alert.

A sudden change in social behavior often precedes suicidal behavior. Ending friendships for various overt reasons may in fact be an act of farewell. The giving away of treasured possessions, such as CD collections or prized jewelry, can be the equivalent of the adult's drawing up a final testament and getting affairs in order when death appears imminent.

As noted earlier, deteriorating school performance, acting-out behavior such as promiscuity (or sudden loss of interest in sex) and a frenetic life style may be indicators of depression preceding suicidal behavior. The family physician is in an excellent position to intervene with youngsters who present psychosomatically. Kenneth Schonberg (1984) estimates that half the young people who attempt suicide had seen a physician within two months before making the attempt. Schonberg suggests that the symptoms, brought on by depression, were seen by the youngsters as a way of getting to a doctor in hopes that their distress would be recognized.

Developmental Issues

It is almost axiomatic to characterize adolescence as a stormy and difficult period of life. An understanding of developmental issues is helpful in sorting out what has been called "normal craziness" from behavior clinically labeled "disturbed." "Normal craziness" includes a vitality and vigor of spirit that does much to counterbalance the problems; it is the very lack of these qualities that we note in depressed youngsters.

Developmental psychologist Erik Erickson defined the primary task of the teen years as construction of a sense of personal identity. It is a time of bringing together the various facets of the self into a working whole that includes continuity with the past and direction for the future. By the teen years the individual has accumulated roles and traits, including those of being son, daughter, student; being quiet or outgoing, laid-back or high-strung, and so forth, with specific likes and dislikes and political and social attitudes.

Developmental learning theorist Jean Piaget postulated that in adolescence the ability he termed "formal operations" is developing, with comprehension of abstract subjects like philosophy and algebra, and appreciation of metaphors and similes (and puns). This cognitive ability to reach beyond concrete reality is also manifested in such normal, (though often to adults maddening) traits as criticalness, argumentativeness, self-consciousness, and self-centeredness.

— ADOLESCENT DEPRESSION AND SUICIDE —

Extensive biological changes are accompanied by concerns, often urgent, regarding the body. In developed countries, the 1900's saw earlier onset of puberty in girls and boys, with corresponding impact on emotional and social problems.

Just prior to puberty, in the pre-adolescent stage (about nine to twelve) earlier conflicts may be reactivated. Re-emerging from the infantile stage is an egotistical, demanding, clinging child. The sloppiness, stubbornness, and greediness associated with the toddler stages may reappear temporarily in the adolescent. The pre-schooler is often an expansive showoff, a competitor, a seducer, and these qualities reappear in adolescence, often to the dismay of parents who believed "all that" was a thing of the past.

We see a rapid growth in the ego, or organizing, functions of the individual. Verbal expression tends to increase. The ego is more realistic, more self-critical. The pre-adolescent is becoming less dependent on the environment and this increasing self-support bolsters self-esteem. As he/she invests more in peers, the distance from parents begins to grow, along with an increased awareness of the self as self-sustaining and self-governing.

In early adolescence (roughly twelve to fourteen) biological changes include onset of menstruation for girls and emission of semen for boys. This is the stage when the pulling away from the primary love objects of parents, and the forming of intense, close, and idealized friendships, becomes evident.

The years from about fifteen to seventeen represent middle adolescence. This can be a particularly poignant stage, as the young person making a final break with childhood love objects may experience painful aloneness. A disappointing love affair often compounds this loneliness, and self-preoccupation, fantasies, and daydreams increase. There may be sharp mood swings from grandiosity to self-abnegation, and/or grave, almost obsessive concerns about his/her physical condition.

In late adolescence — about seventeen to twenty years — a period of consolidation brings continuity and more stable identity from this turbulence. If things have gone pretty well, the young man/woman is ready for personal intimacy and social integration.

This developmental process as described is, of course, only a model. Its application is most appropriate in industrialized Western cultures, within which many traditional supports, rites of passage, accepted customs, and societal stabilities, have given way and as yet have not been fully replaced.

Intrapsychic and Environmental Issues

Stress

One of the hardest concepts for adults to accept is that youth is a stressful time — especially contemporary youth. The younger generation seems to have everything, especially that magical commodity so earnestly sought by the older generations — youth itself. I hear a lot of angry adult protestations, such as:

"I had it ten times harder when I was growing up!"

"Talk about stress — all he has to do is go to school. *I* have to earn the money to keep him there, until he gets through college — at least."

"Her biggest stress is that the malls don't open until 10:00 a.m. I should have it so bad."

Is that envy I hear? Understandable envy, for a time of life, which, viewed from adulthood, seems to be all loveliness of face and form, and glittering future possibilities. No wonder that the deliberate discarding of this prize — youthful life — arouses not only grief and guilt, but also outrage.

And yet: surely few if any generations of American students of all ages have been subjected to the kind of academic pressure currently being applied in the name of "standards" and access to higher education. (Two or three hours of homework for first-graders? What can we be thinking of? I have heard that at the beginning of the 20th century there was a movement to abolish home work for children on the grounds that it constituted child abuse, and in too many cases I know of, it seems that way now.)

An informal survey of middle and high school students and their parents indicates that many high school students spend between three and five hours nightly on homework. Add extracurricular activities such as sports, music, and drama, which often require substantial practice time, and jobs, and it's no surprise that six hours sleep is a high average.

Not to mention the pressure on teenage girls to starve themselves into fashionable thinness. Adolescence a walk in the park? I don't think so.

I point all this out not as a paean to an imagined better past, but rather to illustrate the paradoxical adult laments of every generation:

"Boy, have you got it easy these days!" — and —"Boy, those were the good old days!"

Former generations had more illusions, which in the long run are poor defenses but offer immediate protection against some kinds of stress. For example, those of us in America who were teens during World War II (the generation which Tom Brokow (1999) over-generously calls "The Greatest") endured the stress of potential loss of loved ones in combat; young people growing up in countries under siege suffered far more. Most believed, however, that when the war was over (THE War, that is) life would be peaceful and productive for all, forever. The promise of a future without war was a powerful antidote to the immediate stress of war. That promise was not fulfilled, and although the present generation of teenagers did not grow up with the threat of nuclear extinction graphically present in daily life, as did their parents, (the "boomers") television images bombard them with the ever-present reality of war. Perhaps this accounts in some measure for the fascination with violent movies and computer games (a counter-phobic "we aren't helpless against these monsters") and perhaps it also accounts in some measure for the sense of despair about life.

Marriage probably never held as much real promise of personal fulfillment and security as was claimed for it, but in earlier times the illusion sustained many a lonely teenager whose counterpart today knows only too well that marriage is precarious, and no panacea. This is perhaps ultimately a more realistic view, but also a colder one.

Violent death in American schools is not a recent phenomenon; there have always been some neighborhoods in our cities where kids and teachers attended at their peril, but since no one except the people who lived and worked there paid much attention little publicity was given to the situation. Although statistically school is still far and away the safest place to be *(The Los Angeles Times* notes that "Children are twice as likely to be struck by lightening as they are to be killed at school" (July 11, 2000)) it is perceived as among the most dangerous places. This illusion obviously brings the opposite of a sense of security, and while I know of no statistics that link it directly to youth suicide, I have a hunch it plays a part in the overall feeling of despair and pessimism. Surveys such as those by Stepp (1993) reveal that a majority of twelve to seventeen-year-old American youths are pessimistic about the future of the country, feel disconnected from social institutions and support systems and powerless to make a difference.

War, violent death, and parental divorce are events over which teenagers realistically have no control. The first two symbolize potential loss of everything; the third represents loss of the family that was, or was idealized. In the hierarchy of stresses, loss is the penultimate.

Sometimes a young child who loses a parent appears to make a "good adjustment," only to have the reaction erupt later, in adolescence. The compliant, "good" child (in my experience more typically a girl) may keep rage at being abandoned out of awareness by turning it against herself, as in the following illustration.

Mandi's father died when she was eight and her sister thirteen. Mandi doesn't remember much of that period, except that for some reason she was terribly tired and didn't want to do anything except sleep, while her sister took it upon herself to scrub and clean the family home, do the laundry and help Mom with shopping and cooking.

Ten years later, her sister still reacts to stress by stepped up activity, usually of the "helping" kind. Mandi at eighteen is going through the throes of a love affair that ended painfully, and she can scarcely move, study, or even keep herself neat and clean. Thanks to people close to her who recognized her behavior as depression, she is in therapy. She is beginning to let herself feel her rage toward the lover who chose someone else — and toward her father, who also left her.

Some combinations of losses are particularly traumatic. A family move to a different neighborhood, or city, may herald improved material comforts and social status, yet to the adolescent who must leave friends it can be experienced as an overwhelming loss. Adults may offer well-meant assurances that new friends will easily be made and old friends can visit; they are speaking from their adult experience, appreciation of which is not a noteworthy teen attribute. Depending on other circumstances of school, family, health, etc etc, the move may well be incorporated into life's fullness of experience. If it follows on the heels of a major loss of a loved one by death or divorce, the impact will be far more severe.

Changes in the status of family members represent loss of the familiar and known, and may include realistic fears for the future. For example, parental problems with the law; the marriage or pregnancy of a sibling; a parent's loss of job, or retirement, all represent present or potential loss of the order of things as the adolescent knows them.

All these losses are connected in some way to the adolescent's role in the family. While parental death and divorce impact strongly on the emotions, clinical observation and research tell us that alienation from parents, whether or not divorce has occurred, is the single most devastating condition, and the one most strongly correlated with suicide and suicide attempts.

Joseph Sabbath (1969) used the term "expendable child" to describe the depressed, difficult youngster who is so disruptive that parents overtly and/or covertly express their wish that the child were out of the family, and may ignore suicide threats and gestures.

Woznica and Shapiro (1998) have validated this concept. Their investigations also indicate that:

> ... adolescents have a higher rate of suicidal ideation and attempts than parents recognize.
>
> ... parents were unaware of the extent of significant losses experienced by their teens.
>
> ... It is crucial for parents to develop a greater understanding and awareness of adolescents' depressive and suicidal feelings and for teens to feel a greater sense of comfort disclosing these feelings with trusted adults. Increased mutual understanding between parents and teens is critical in order for teens to receive essential familial support and appropriate professional help when needed. (pp. 5-6)

Teicher and Jacobs (1966) describe a process of escalation of problems between child and parent during adolescence: The parents have tried to contain their ambivalent feelings and control the child's behavior. Now these efforts begin to fail. They feel shut out by the teenager's provocative behavior, rapidly changing moods, and secretiveness. As this rift grows, the covert wish of the parents to be rid of the child becomes more apparent.

Sometimes parents give mixed messages: stay here/but on my terms. Stay here/but only as the person I want/need you to be, not as the person you are.

In our rightful concern for the youngsters, we professionals often become angry with the parents for "not knowing better," forgetting that they too suffered in their earlier years, and are suffering now. In the following section on therapeutic approaches,

I'll talk about family therapy, which avoids censure and focuses on the family system, providing an effective way to stay out of the blame-the-parents trap (see the chapter: "Working with Parents: The Dialogic Challenge").

Another illustration from my work: Nina had been the "thorn in the family side" since her infancy. Mother had a fairly good relationship with the two sons, but she and Nina seemed to have missed some essential bonding experience, and there was never much closeness or warmth between them. Father was concerned about Nina but hesitant about expressing affection to her, since his wife insisted he was simply spoiling the girl.

Nina's older brothers were high achieving, well liked youngsters, who were always close to one another but either ignored or condescended to their troublesome little sister.

She had no really close friends, which she said was because the kids she knew were stupid and shallow. She did have one important thing going for her — she was a gifted writer. Her main solace was in fantasies of become a famous novelist, thus "showing them," and being loved and admired around the world.

As the children grew older the long-standing parental discord worsened, and when the boys were in college and Nina in her last year of high school, they separated. Nina had submitted a short story to a national contest, and at about the time the separation finalized as divorce she received word that her story had not won any prize; this followed close on the heels of the rejection of two manuscripts she had submitted to magazines. Her English teacher reassured her that beginning writers always face much disappointment, but for Nina the rejection of her work was the last straw. This is how she explains her suicide attempt by aspirin overdose:

"I knew that at seventeen I was a complete failure. My mother hated me and my father was too much of a wimp to stand up to her. My brothers are O.K. I guess, but they were always buddies to each other and didn't have much use for me. I was too fat to have any boyfriends, and my one "sort-of" friend had suddenly gotten popular and was always off on dates. I've always known that my one chance in life was to be a great writer — and I mean a *great* writer, like Toni Morrison, or Eudora Welty. And I failed at that, too. So why live?"

The family became involved in the therapy process. Mother, happier now in her own life, was able to be a little more accepting of Nina, though never really loving. Dad, free of the tension with his wife over Tina, allowed himself to express his warm affection for her. Slowly, she began to develop some self-confidence and hope for the future. When her oldest brother married, she found an unexpected ally and friend in her sister-in-law.

She stayed in individual therapy for four years, and a close, trusting alliance was forged. She is not famous — at least, not yet — but writing is still her passion and she is a whole and relatively happy human being.

Drugs, Media, Music

What about these powerful extra familial influences? Klagsbrun (1981) points out that drug use, which includes alcohol, is a kind of chipping away at life, and that some youngsters alternate between drug abuse and suicide attempts, and some combine the two.

Schonberg (1984) believes that depression not only leads to suicide, but also to substance abuse, rather than substance abuse leading to depression and suicide. I agree that attempting to lay responsibility for suicide on drugs is simplistic, and an easy way out — I also believe that minimizing their impact is shortsighted.

It is probably true that a well-integrated, optimally functioning, emotionally and physically sound individual can absorb enormous stresses, disruptions, and negative influences without serious damage; it is also true that few of us at any age can claim that degree of health and strength. We are vulnerable. So are our children.

Similarly, I don't believe that today's popular music *causes* suicide, but it often lends highly emotional support to the consideration of, if not preoccupation with, violence including self-destruction. Television music stations routinely combine music with self, and other, destructive acts with strong sensory stimulation.

As Charlotte Ross notes (1985) the lyrics of popular songs sometimes explicitly discuss "(1) the method, (2) the act of suicide, (3) the anticipation of immortality, (4) the anticipated grief reaction of survivors, and (5) the expression of a 'cry for help'" (p. 157).

Whether and/or how the media should be monitored is a subject beyond the scope of this chapter, but it seems clear that while we need to be cognizant of all the influences on all of us, attempts to prohibit information seldom result in its suppression. As Ross points out, added to the allure of the forbidden is the presumption that if the information were not important, it would not be withheld; attempts to do so may, in fact, give rise to a covert network of information.

Therapeutic Approaches

The favored modality used to work with any patient population depends to some degree on the preference and expertise of the therapist. My own training and professional approach is Gestalt therapy, and this orientation underlies all my therapy and training work — including this chapter. I especially appreciate the adaptability of Gestalt principles to a wide range of modalities — individual therapy, family therapy, group therapy, parent education, and work in classrooms and hospital settings.

The depressed and/or suicidal youngster urgently needs a deep, personal, validating relationship. The one-to-one alliance with a therapist able and willing to be there to help face the lonely, ashamed, frightened, angry feelings is arguably the single most powerful intervention.

Family therapy, either ongoing concurrently with individual therapy or as a periodic adjunct, is effective and germane. Without a change in the existing family system, the burden on the adolescent to learn more adaptive ways to live in that system is often cruelly heavy.

An important feature of the family therapy approach is that it eliminates the notion of the youngster as "identified patient," and looks at the family system as both the problem and the most potent healing force. While it is difficult not to initially view a youngster who has attempted suicide as the I.P., in on-going family therapy the focus does in fact change as the process of interactions becomes clearer to all members. In family therapy, everyone has the potential to be a healing agent for all others.

An example of this is the progress that Linda, now thirteen, made over several years of therapy. I began seeing her on the recommendation of her teacher who reported that Linda worked so slowly and made so many corrections and changes in her work that she never completed a task, and thus received poor grades. The teacher correctly suspected anxiety and/or depression were factors in keeping Linda from performing at her potential.

At first Linda's parents were committed to the "we pay- you fix" mode, and strenuously resisted further personal involvement. After a year of psycho-educational therapy, which produced measurable academic progress, they trusted me and the process enough to come in for a few sessions of their own. Father acknowledged his history of depression, which he had endured without professional help. ("It's my problem, and I can handle it.") Mother was pleasant and likeable in a detached way. Satisfied that Linda had achieved the stated goal, her therapy terminated, or, as I framed it, "came to a stopping point."

Two years later, Dad called to say Linda was very depressed, had made some suicidal comments, and he wondered if the whole family could come in.

During a subsequent session, Dad berated Linda for her many shortcomings. Linda responded with angry defensiveness, and Mom continued in the role Virginia Satir has called "the placator," until Dad muttered "I always promised myself I would be a better parent than my father was to me, and now it's obvious that I have failed and my Dad was right when he said I'd always be a loser at everything." Linda's response was a surprised — and gentle — "I never knew that Grandpa said things like that to you. That must have been tough for you."

This brief interchange was an important event. Linda was able to show some concern and empathy for her father, and with considerable support from his wife, his daughter, and me he was able to take it in. The dynamics had changed, and he became more able to express loving feelings, and to connect with Linda as she struggled with her own inner demons.

The developmental pull towards peers makes *group therapy* an attractive approach for many teenagers. However, they may be extremely sensitive about acknowledging as their peers other troubled youngsters (a.k.a. "weirdos.") I prefer group therapy to be adjunctive, not the sole modality Co-therapists provide needed consultation and emotional support, availability for emergencies, and additional insight and group interaction.

Counselors and therapists have the opportunity and responsibility to go beyond the confines of their consulting room or agency in dealing with the problem of youth suicide. By networking with schools, parent-teacher associations, community agencies, churches and synagogues, service clubs, hospitals, drug abuse centers — anyplace where there is interest in the welfare of young people — our profession can increase awareness and reduce the mystifying, or glamorous, or taboo aspects of suicide.

Availability of services is erratic; all too often crisis centers themselves don't enjoy a long life, requiring mental health workers to vigilantly keep current. I routinely call any mental health agency or center I haven't had recent contact with before giving the number out.

Peer pressure usually has a pejorative connotation; it can also be a powerful positive force. As noted above, group therapy utilizes this energy. If the school does not have a program of suicide prevention that includes rap groups, look to other agencies.

One of the most demystifying and deglamorizing presentations I've seen is *Sides,* (2000) a video made by and featuring high school students and described as "dark comedy. "Dark" it may be, and some adults might consider it offensively "flip," but it is also bursting with life, humor and energy. Eschewing anything sentimental or preachy, it employs a lightly satirical touch to make the viewer aware of such clinical issues as isolation, the shame of failure, the grief of survivors, the wish for immortality and fame, and the ambivalence. The final message portrays suicide as being totally un-cool.

Medication

When I wrote this for an audiotape tape in 1986, I noted that "Controversy continues over whether certain syndromes such as bi-polar affective disorder have organic etiology or involvement . . . perhaps biochemical imbalances are inherited in some cases."

Continuing medical research points more and more to organic etiology or involvement in the most serious mental disorders. And we have the rise of managed care to thank — or blame — for the growing practice of treating mental illnesses exclusively or primarily (and "cost-effectively") with medication. The consensus of researchers and clinicians seems to be that a combination of drugs and "talk therapy" is the most effective tool in working with severely depressed patients. What is still unclear is at what age, and in what dosage, medication is appropriate for young people. My own rule of thumb is to recommend that a chronically and/or severely depressed adolescent be evaluated by a psychiatrist who specializes in this age group. If, as frequently happens, the youngster is adamantly against this, I will have a personal consultation myself to help determine how best to proceed. In my experience very few people of any age *like* to be on medication, but if and when they are persuaded it is in their best interest they will give it serious consideration.

Personal Issues for Therapists and Counselors

There is no one kind of therapist or kind of therapy that is effective. An interest in and liking for adolescents is a necessary, but not sufficient, condition.

A valuable personal quality is *szits-fleish*, which roughly translated means the ability to remain patiently, even stoically, present over time. The work with depressed and suicidal young-sters is slow and often draining. Your youthful patient may whine, complain, and perceive everyone — including you — as unfair. Sometimes it will seem that no matter how much you give, it isn't enough to fill the aching, empty void. Like his parents, you may feel unappreciated, manipulated, and exhausted.

John Weeks reminds us in his classic "The Fragile Alliance" (1980) that these youngsters manipulate and demand because they don't know any other way to meet their needs. "They are convinced that no one will give them anything freely. They must blackmail, threaten, and coerce others . . . this manipulation is literally a matter of life-or-death. Only gradually can they come to see themselves as possessing any inherent strength and worth." (p. 261)

A support network for yourself is essential. If you are in private practice, your consultation sources should include professionals from various disciplines who can provide information and empathize and be supportive of your emotional needs. The responsibility of being involved with a young person who literally struggles with the conflict of living or dying is a heavy one. Don't try to bear it alone. As Weeks points out:

The objectivity of an uninvolved fellow therapist helps to prevent any mismanagement of the case, which might result from the primary therapist's emotional discomfort. Decisions of whether to hospitalize the patient . . . whether to allow the patient to take a trip or go away to college are better shared than made alone. The practical advantage of consultation in medico-legal terms is also readily apparent. There is an obvious additional dividend for the patient if consultation allows the therapist to be comfortable about his legal liability and his ethical responsibilit. (p. 261)

Don't include too many depressed and/or suicidal youngsters in your caseload. Most therapists find that two or three suicidal patients are the upper limit.

Therapists with depressive tendencies of their own may find it best to avoid working with suicidal youngsters. If tendencies you thought were worked through become activated, seek therapy for yourself.

Over time, and with some luck, your enduring belief in and regard for the youngster as she/he is can break through the bulwark of despair. You'll be tested, tried, and frustrated; the reward is when this I-Thou relationship flowers into a young person once again whole.

There is a poem, author unknown, which I often share with adolescents and with parents and professionals. I like it because it is a balance to the morbid poetry and song lyrics suicidal youngsters sometimes dwell on, and I like it because it is beautiful. I'll share it with you now.

Wait, for now.
Distrust everything if you have to
but trust the hours. Haven't they

carried you everywhere, up to now?
Personal events will become interesting again.
Hair will become interesting.
Pain will become interesting.
Buds that open out of season will become interesting.
Second-hand gloves will become lovely again;
Their memories are what give them the need for
  other hands.
And the desolation of lovers is the same: that
  enormous emptiness
carved out of such
tiny beings as we are
asks to be filled; the need
for the new love *is* faithfulness to the old.
Wait.
Don't go too early.
You're tired. But everyone's tired.
But no one is tired enough.
Only wait a little and listen:
music of hair,
music of pain,
music of looms weaving all our loves again.
Be there to hear it, it will be the only time,
most of all to hear
the flute of your whole existence.

References

Brokow, Tom (1999). *The Greatest Generation.* New York: Random House, Inc.

Centers for Disease Control. (1996). *Morbidity and Mortality Weekly Report.* (Vol. 45, No. 554-4; September 20/)

Center for Disease Control. (1995). *Youth Risk Behavior Surveillance Report.* California State Department of Education.

Centers for Disease Control. (1990). *Morbidity and Mortality Weekly Report* as cited in *Los Angeles Times* (1991)

Erickson, E.H. (1963). *Childhood and Society.* New York: W.W. Norton & Company.

Friday, J.C. (1995). "The Psychological Impact of Violence to Underserved Communities." *Journal of Health Care for the Poor and Underserved,* Vol 6, No. 4, 403-409

"Kids are People Too." (2000, July 11). *The Los Angeles Times.* pp 1, 18-21.

Klagsbrun, F. (1981). *Too Young to Die; Youth and Suicide.* New York: Pocket Book.

Lampert, Ruth (1986) audiotape. *Understanding Adolescent Depression and Suicide.* #MS 35, Seattle: MaxSound Tape Co.

Weeks, J. (1980). *The Fragile Alliance.* (2nd ed.) Malabar, FLA: Robert E. Krieger Publishing Company, Inc.

Mullen, P.E., et al. "The Long Term Impact of the Physical, Emotional, and Sexual Abuse of Children: A Community Study." *Child Abuse & Neglect,* Vol 20, No. 1. 7-21 (Pergamon).

Mussen, P.H.; Conger, J.J.; Kagan, J. and Huston, A.C. (1984). Chapter 7, "Cognitive Development." In *Child Development and Personality.* (6th ed). New York: Harper & Row, Publishers.

Pfeffer, C.R. (1986). *The Suicidal Child.* New York: the Guildford Press.

Ross, C.P. (1985). "Teaching Children the Facts of Life and Death: Suicide Prevention in the Schools." In M.L. Peck, N. Farberow, and R. Litman (eds.) *Youth Suicide.* Springer Publishing Company.

Sabbath, J.C.(1969). "The Suicidal Adolescent:The Expendable Child." *Journal of the American Academy of Child Psychiatry.* 8:272-85.

Schonberg, K. (1984). Cited in "Potential Suicides Often Give Warning Signals." (1984, August 19.) *Los Angeles Times,* Part VI, p.19.

"Some Things You Should Know about Preventing Teen Suicide." American Academy of Pediatrics. online AOL. Stepp, L.S. (1993) "Hope Springs Eternal? Not for Teen-agers." *Los Angeles Times*, p. E10.

Teicher, J. & Jacobs, J. (1966) "Adolescents Who Attempt Suicide: Preliminary Findings." *American Journal of Psychiatry*, 122 (11),1248-1257.

Thompsett, N.L. (Writer and Director). 2000. *Sides.* (Film).

Vernon, A. (1993). *Counseling Children and Adolescents.* Denver: Love Publishing Company

Woznica, J.G. and Shapiro, J.R. (1998). "An Analysis of Adolescent Suicide Attempts: A Validation of the Expendable Child Measures." In Schwartzberg, A.Z. (ed) *The Adolescent in Turmoil* (pp. 82-90) Westport, CT: Praeger.

Woznica, J.G. and Shapiro, J.R. (1990). An Analysis of Adolescent Suicide Attempts: The Expendable Child." *Journal of Pediatric Psychology,* 15 (6) 789-796.

10

—— THE RESILIENT CHILD ——

Resilient: "Capable of withstanding shock without permanent deformation or rupture."
—Webster's New Collegiate Dictionary

Why is it that some people who experience extreme trauma and misfortune early in life are able to emerge whole and well-functioning, while others, with equal or less severe trauma, suffer "permanent deformation?" And, more importantly for our purposes, what can we therapists do to foster and nurture this buoyancy, this ability to withstand?

Research, and clinical and personal observations, have teased out some of the attributes of resiliency. First of all, it seems reasonable to assume that heredity has something to do with it. Just as some infants appear to be physically hardier than others from the beginning of life, while others catch every cold and have a difficult time recovering from a myriad of ailments, it is likely that emotional hardiness too has genetic components. We know there are interventions which boost physical hardiness, and we know that nothing works all the time.

The presumption that emotional hardiness can also be enhanced meets the first criterion of the healing professions: It does no harm. Gestalt therapy, with its emphasis on organismic self-regulation and the I-Thou relationship, is a logical method to promote healing ability.

In a seminar on "The Invulnerable Child" Carl Hoppe, drawing on the work of Anthony and Cohler (1987), summarized attributes of resiliency, many of which can be encouraged in therapy:

1) *"Has a talent or special interest that brings pleasure and a sense of competency."*

The compensatory benefit of special talents is generally recognized; therapy provides an opportunity to bring into the foreground skills and abilities which have been minimized or overlooked.

For example, seven-year-old Judd, with two academically gifted older brothers and a history of being a "late talker" in a highly verbal family, was having trouble learning to read. His well-meaning parents told him they were sure he too could be an outstanding student if he just tried harder; they hoped therapy would motivate him to do so.

I noticed some interesting things about Judd. When working with clay his small hands seemed remarkably strong and adept. I mentioned that my pencil sharpener was broken; he fixed it in about three minutes. When I had trouble with the computer, he calmly said, "here, let me do that" and showed me where I was making a mistake.

These skills had gone unremarked on in this family of "idea and talk people" who looked down on things mechanical and electronic. Therapy soon centered on giving Judd opportunities to develop his talents and helping his family appreciate them.

As with some other attributes of resiliency, this one has a potential downside. If achievement deadens psychic pain, it can also be addictive — resulting in a workaholic personality. There is no free lunch, but sometimes a pricey one, especially if it is nourishing, is worth the cost.

2)*"Has one consistently good relationship with at least one adult."*
Although therapy is not a lasting relationship in the usual sense, its special quality — the I-Thou-ness of it — confers transcendency over the actual number of weeks or months it endures.

Being in a relationship with even one person, over even a relatively short time, who is consistent, respectful, and trustworthy carries a message: "If there is one person in the world like this, probably there is another one somewhere." And once it has been established that such persons exist, there is a tendency to find more of them.

3)*"The ability to distance"*
This is another double-edged sword. While distancing oneself from unpleasant events can be maladaptive. The child who can literally or figuratively leave the scene may be illustrating the proverb "He who fights and runs away lives to fight another day."

Two examples of behavior usually considered (but not always correctly) unhealthy or negative:

In family session a person begins to talk (again) about the child's misdeeds; the child goes into MEGO (My Eyes Glaze Over) mode.

A teacher reports that "when he likes the subject he's eager and alert; when he doesn't, he seems to fall asleep even if his eyes stay open."

In situations like this, the "helps/hurts list" is useful. Explore with the youngster the pros and cons of "tuning out." Some examples from the "helps" list might include "when Mom and Dad are having a really bad fight;" or "when kids tease me about being so short." The "hurts" list could include "when getting directions to go somewhere I really want to go" and "not listening to criticism which would help me."

Thirteen-year-old Roseanne's bi-polar mother periodically went on what Roseanne called "a word attack," viciously belittling every aspect of the girl's personality for fifteen minutes. Roseanne described to me how she taught herself to attend only enough to make periodic appropriate comments, while "sending most of my brain on a trip somewhere else." This was clearly a "helps" item.

On the "hurts" side of her list she wrote: "If I don't use my *whole* brain learning algebra I don't get it, and then I worry about my grades" and "tuning out my friends makes them angry at me."

By encouraging use of the sand tray or other equipment during family sessions we give the young child a legitimate and healthy way to distance during emotionally laden periods. The youngster who is forced to "sit and listen" will urgently need to pee, or get a drink, or do whatever necessary to escape the tension.

4) *"The ability to effectively ask for help from appropriate adults"*

I reinforce every instance, large and small, where this attribute is or could be used. When four-year-old Steven tells me he fell off the teeter-totter and ran to the teacher, I respond: "Good thinking. She's just the person who can help!" When eleven-year-old Janette says her science teacher humiliates her for not understanding, we explore whom in her world might she go to for assistance. We are talking about trust, and how to differentiate the trustworthy from the untrustworthy — even unto the therapist in his/her life.

Learning to recognize and reach out to those who can be trusted may be the best abuse prevention we can teach.

5. *"Plans rather than acts on impulse"*

Impulsiveness is one of the more common "traits" bringing kids into therapy, and a good candidate for a "helps/hurts" list. In the "helps" list we can reframe "Impulsiveness" as "spontaneity" and "enthusiasm;" thus it is an attribute which helps in social situations and in many creative endeavors. It hurts in those

situations calling for strategy, such as the game of checkers —
which is one of the many sweet uses of that remarkable game.

6. *"The fellow dissident"*
In the story of the emperor's new clothes, the boy who
insisted on the emperor's nakedness was alone in his (accurate)
perception. The youngster who realizes something is very strange
about mother's going to sleep every day at 5 P.M. but is told "Your
mother is just tired, don't ask any more stupid questions," feels
alone and crazy. When someone in the crowd agrees that the
emperor is naked, or when a sibling says, "I think it's weird too,
none of my friends' moms do that," an enormous burden is lifted.
Whether or not the situation changes, the child's perception of
reality is validated.

The therapist may be the only fellow dissident in a child's
life. Marlou was the rebel in her family, the only child who talked
back, argued, disagreed. She said to me: "This will probably sound
crazy Ruth, but sometimes I think they are glad I'm bad because
they can all get together and talk about me and they don't have to
notice that they don't really love each other as much as they
pretend." It didn't sound crazy to me, and I told her so, to her
enormous relief.

Incidentally, whenever anyone begins with "this will
probably sound crazy, but . . . " be prepared to hear something
singularly sane.

Julius Segal (1988) has suggestions for parents, which can be
equally useful for counselors:

1) *"Encourage a feeling of individuality."*
This may be difficult to achieve in families valuing confor-
mity; indeed, children with a strong sense of their own worth may
come across as haughty or naughty. Usually there is an adult in the
family with a streak of independence, giving you the opening of:

"It's easy to see who's been the model for this strength and personal integrity . . . " Or perhaps, "It must be in the genes."

2) *"Help your child to feel in command"*

Martin Seligman, (1975) developed the concept of "learned helplessness" — the inability to change a situation no matter how hard one tries — as an antecedent of depression. Therapy provides an opportunity for a child to be in command of and make changes in the immediate, present environment. Questions and comments such as: "Where is the best place for us to set this up?" "Choose the first activity." "Would you recommend this book for eight-year-olds?" "You're in charge of the sand scene world; you can change it if you want to" and so on, give appropriate control, and are wonderful esteem-enhancers.

The message is: "Even though *sometimes* you have no control — *sometimes* you do. Watch for those times; there will be more as you get older."

3) *"Provide a sense of order and stability."*

Resilient children seem to be able to find, somewhere in their chaotic environment, stabilizing anchors in a turbulent sea of stress." (Segal, p. 96.)

Steven J. Wolin, M.D., a psychiatrist, and Linda A. Bennett, Ph.D., an anthropologist, describe what they call "ritual protected" children. They observed homes where holiday celebrations, family celebrations and even mealtime rituals seemed to sustain children against the emotional ravages caused by heavy parental drinking. It seems they were " . . . better able to deal with the challenge if they feel that, despite the upheaval, the world retains at least a few reliable strands." (Segal, pp. 96-7.)

Sometimes the therapy room is the only orderly and stable place in the child's world. If he/she is lucky, school is another. Luckier still, there may be grandparents and/or other extended family members who provide steadfast oases. Luckiest of all, the parents will be able and willing to weave more "reliable strands."

4) *"Discourage inappropriate self-blame."*

Assuming responsibility for our mistakes and misdeeds is difficult and necessary if we are to be self-motivated to change, and to be well-functioning members of society. Some people seem unable to master this task. However, that is "quite different from a child's taking the rap for everything that goes wrong in her life because of *supposedly irremediable defects in her personality."* (italics mine.) (Segal, p. 97.)

Katie was doing poorly in high school. She did not blame the teachers or anyone else; neither did she understand where her studying and test taking methods needed improvement. She said: "I get bad grades because I'm lazy. I've always been lazy." Conceptualized in that way, there was nothing she could do to change the situation. It was simply a given.

About the loss of her first two jobs, she said, "I can't hold a job." Another given.

I saw the situation differently. Anxiety, perceptual problems, and poor working habits sapped the energy necessary to be a competent student. Her first job required clerical skills far beyond her present competence; she should not have applied, she should not have been hired. Her second job was boring; she didn't know what to do about that so she didn't show up for work for three days and got herself fired.

The therapeutic task was helping her change "I'm lazy" to "I need to do this and that and thus and so to achieve;" from "I can't hold a job" to "Learning to _____ and _____ and _____ will make me more employable."

Katie's belief system of "If bad things happen it's because I am inherently flawed" is an especially poignant aspect of the abused child syndrome.

5) *"Keeping the lines of communication open"*

When a child is really listened to, the resulting bond of trust and confidence provides a strong base for stress survival. Psychoanalyst Erik H. Erikson said that this " . . . communication link . . . helps the child absorb something that most individuals who survive stress take for granted most of the time. It is a feeling of basic security and trust" (Segal, pp. 97-98.). When we attend to the words, the play, the drawings, the sand-scenes, the entire process, we provide surcease and succor from psychic pain, and give resiliency more growing room.

We can also help parents to listen.

Five-year-old Trina seemed to be adjusting well to the divorce of her parents. On one of "Dad's days" she asked him, "Are you and Mommy going to get married again someday?" Dad told me this threw him for a loop and he was at a loss to find the right answer. I assured him that the "correctness" of his answer mattered far less than the trust Trina displayed by openly sharing her thoughts with him. By letting her know he understood that the divorce was painful for her and it was OK to talk about it, he was setting the stage for ongoing open communication.

6) *"Teach your child to care about others"*

I think it not a moment too soon in the Zeitgeist to encourage altruism as a legitimate goal of therapy. Noting that this capacity is found among resilient individuals of all ages, Segal (p. 98) suggests that reinforcing warmth and generosity "may be more important by far to the child's mental health than report card scores or athletic prowess." (p. 98)

Group therapy is one of the best ways to foster sharing and caring. Irvin Yalom (1975) in his classic "The Theory and Practice of Group Psychotherapy" lists altruism as one of the curative factors of group work. We need to take care that in the interest of self-awareness and self-care we not overlook or diminish this "capacity to turn outward, instead of becoming mired in hopeless preoccupations." (Segal, p. 98)

Most genetic conditions can be modified or even reversed by environmental considerations. Some, to date at least, cannot. In *The Broken Chord* Michael Dorris (1989) describes the heartbreaking experience of raising his adopted son Josh, a fetal alcohol syndrome baby. With deep reluctance Dorris changed from having total belief in the power of the environment to a painful realization that some conditions simply do not respond to even the most skillful and dedicated nurturing. Some interventions must happen before birth and/or conception to make a difference; in these cases, it is the parents who need to develop resiliency to keep their lives stable and satisfying.

This sad truth does not negate the fact that many childhood conditions — perhaps most — *do* respond to favorable environments.

Another important aspect of resiliency is what might be called the tincture of time. Segal (p. 98) notes that Emmy E. Werner and Ruth S. Smith found that about half the children in their longitudinal study of multiracial children who were considered vulnerable had apparently outgrown their previous problems by the time they were thirty. Recovery looks more promising when viewed in the long-term than when focus is limited to one traumatic time.

Werner and Smith's study also confirmed the conventional wisdom that some lucky children are born with personalities both robust and appealing, so that trauma is not only more easily withstood but more likely to be eased by the affection they evoke in others.

It will probably be a long time before we have a clear understanding of this intertwining of nature and nurture. In the meantime, we know that as therapists we impact the child's environment. We can help them develop social and coping skills. We recognize that there are clusters of strengths as well as of weaknesses.

We have the opportunity to develop the strengths, thus enhancing the capability of "withstanding shock without permanent deformation or rupture."

References

Anthony, E. and Cohler, B. (Eds.) (1987). *The Invulnerable Child.* New York: The Guilford Press.

Dorris, M. (1989). *The Broken Chord.* New York: Harper & Row, Publishers.

Hoppe, Carl. Seminar, "The Invulnerable Child," Oct-Nov, 1988. Beverly Hills, CA.

Segal, J. (1988, April.) Kids Who Bounce Back. *Parents* 95-99.

Seligman, M. (1975). *Helplessness.* San Francisco, W.H. Freeman and Company.

Wolf, H.B. et al. (1977). *Webster's New Collegiate Dictionary.* (5th ed.) Springfield, MA: G. & C. Merriam Co.

Werner, E. and Smith, R. (1982). *Vulnerable but Invincible: a Study of Resilient Children.* New York: McGraw-Hill.

Yalom, I. (1975). *The Theory and Practice of Group Psychotherapy.* (2nd ed.). New York, Basic Books, Inc.

11

—— WORKING WITH PARENTS ——
THE DIALOGIC CHALLENGE[*]

We do the same thing to parents that we do to children.
We insist that they are some kind of categorical abstrac-
tion because they produced a child.
　　　　　　　　　　　– Leontine Young

My professional entrée into the field of mental health, and my interest in working with the parents of children in therapy dates back to 1970 when I was a teacher in a pre-primary class of young children diagnosed with severe mental disorders, including autism. Bruno Bettleheim's *The Empty Fortress* had come out in 1967, and his view that autism was caused by cold, remote mothers was widely held.

The class was part of a center for educational therapy, and included mothers' groups as part of the program. The other professionals and I who met with the mothers and interacted with

---

[*] Based on a presentation at *The Gestalt Journal*'s Conference in honor of Erving and Miriam Polster, August 2 - 6th, 2000.

them informally when children were dropped off and picked up were skeptical of Bettleheim's theory. These women seemed in no way different than the mothers of children who were diagnosed as aphasic, or learning disabled, or in fact any of the moms we knew or were. Some were outgoing, some reserved, some more likeable than others, etc etc. etc. What they shared was the heightened anxiety common to parents of children with disabilities, and the burden of blame.

Our understanding of autism has changed. Although some controversy still exists as to exact causative factors and treatments of mental disorders, there is no longer a giant finger of reproach pointed at the mothers. Genetic factors are now considered at least contributory to mental illness and at most, *the* cause.

This is not to say that parenting is not a vital factor in children's well being. Prejudice against parents of troubled children is not always ill-founded. For better or worse, parents are *there:* our task is to help them be there in effective and loving ways.

Caveats and Disclaimers

In this presentation I assume that the child is the identified patient, and that his/her therapist also works with the parents. This is distinct from models where each person in the family has a separate therapist, from a purist family systems approach in which it is assumed that the child is the symptom bearer for the family's pathology, and to some extent from working with abusive parents. The last is the subject of another workshop, but we may touch on it today if there is time and interest.

Working with parents is part of the entity of therapy with children and while it rests on some major premises of Gestalt psychotherapy it is not precisely psychotherapy, nor is it precisely Gestalt. As a case in point, in Buber's model the other is not a means to an end; it this work it is, the end being the increased well-being of the child in and with the family.

I am primarily a practioner and not a theorist. My theorizing is rather simplistic, sort of "retro-Gestalt." I have great respect and appreciation for those who develop and teach theoretical foundations. I am indebted to them, and my final disclaimer is:

"In every case, when I discuss a theory or method, I will be telling you my personal understanding of theory or my own use of the method. Despite my immense gratitude for the teachers who gave me the knowledge, they are not responsible for this explanation of what I learned and used in my practice." (Helen D. Aronson, Ph.D., July 25, 2000, on the web.)

The I-Thou Relationship

Richard Hycner uses the term "dialogic" to refer to attitude and relationship. I will be using the terms interchangeably, referring to concepts such as the client always being worthy of respect and the relationship between therapist and client being horizontal, not vertical. These concepts are embodied in *inclusion,* that is, entering the phenomenological world of the other and accepting the person (though not necessarily the behavior to another (e.g., a child.)

Paths to dialogic relationship with parents are diverse. For example, being a parent oneself can help pave the way. I find that sharing (judiciously) some of my fears and failings and mistakes and general screw-ups as parent help in the joining process.

For therapists who are childless, (I can always recognize you, you look so rested and unwrinkled) conceding up front, as you would with any different culture, that you haven't been there replaces professional arrogance with informed sensitivity.

Acknowledging that styles in parenting change — indeed, that much of what "experts" sometimes put forth as scientific truth is a reflection of time and place — contributes to a working partnership.

Keeping babies on a rigid eating and sleeping schedule was once an absolute rule propelled by "fear of spoiling." More recently "fear of squelching" held sway. Today, we see a huge focus on cognitive development, with "fear of not getting into a good college" the driving force. (A recent magazine cartoon portrays a boy sitting on the couch next to his weeping mother who holds a letter in her hand. The boy says, "Don't cry, Mom, lots of people who are rejected from their first choice college go on to live normal lives.")

A trend I really like is the increased involvement of Dads, who now often bring the child to my office as part of their time together. I see fathers participating more actively in parent meetings and classes , and being more in touch with what goes on in their kids' emotional, social, and academic lives.

One of the favorites in my collection of old books is *Child Training: Suggestions for Parents and Teachers* by Mrs. Arthur H.D. Ackland, published in London in 1914 (MCMXIV) The chapter "Parent and Trainers: Their Duty to Themselves" is almost exclusively about mothers; near the end the author writes:

> It is far too easy to lose sight of the fact that fathers as well as mothers may have very valuable views about the bringing up of their children. One person must be the ultimate ruler, and of course the fathers, in the nature of things, sees much less of the children . . . but there may easily be too much of a tendency towards putting the father outside the life of the child, to portray him as a more or less clumsy interloper . . . it is a pity when this comes about, because the father is the very person who can view children both lovingly and from the outside.

Later she writes:

> Just what is it which is expected of parents and child trainers? I have a sense they may have to be as it were the road-makers for the next generation; but

inasmuch as the road is ever being made and never finished, it is foolish to clear every difficulty from the children's feet. What is wanted is to let them see how we work and to give them a share in the work themselves.

At the end of the chapter I'll share with you my conclusions on "How to be a "Perfect Parent."

OSR - Organismic Self-Regulation

Gary Yontef, (1993) Ph.D. says

Faith in OSR means accepting the patient as he is at present . . . and also confirming his 'becoming' — his inherent potential to grow and change from the way he is presently manifesting himself to a fuller manifestation of his potential. (p. 216, *Awareness, Dialogue, and Process)*

To illustrate this concept as it relates to working with children, I use the plant metaphor.
A plant knows how to grow. It knows which way to reach for the sun, where to send roots to get nourishment. If healthy development isn't occurring, perhaps it's too far from a window, or isn't getting enough moisture from the soil; corrective intervention can restore the necessary environmental balance.
In therapy, the therapist provides the intervention, with full appreciation of all that is healthy and resilient in the child.
When working with parents, the focus is on accepting the person as he/she is at *present*, and confirming the inherent *potential* to change and grow, which, in turn, has a positive effect on the child's environment. Parents once were kids themselves, and may have survived damaging environments by developing defenses which worked then, but which now are inappropriate and/or ineffective. Our understanding of their hopes, dreams, needs and

aspirations not only fosters their receptiveness to our recommendations/directives it also sharpens problem-solving skills. And surprisingly often their nurturing and their love emerges into the foreground to balance and offset all kinds s of what we consider "mistakes."

Awareness

Awareness, per Yontef,

> is accompanied by 'owning' — the process of knowing one's control over, choice of, responsibility for one's own behavior and feelings . . . the means whereby the individual can regulate himself by choice . . . our goal is to learn enough so that awareness can develop as needed for organismic self-regulation. (Yontef, G.M., 1993)

I have adapted the percept for the work with parents while remaining, I hope, true to its spirit. I'll say more about awareness in the coming section on "Barriers Within the Therapist."

Encouraging the growth of awareness in the parent can lead to an "AHA!" experience regarding his/her reaction to the child. As an illustration, here is a "success story" :

Eight-year-old Gerry (not his real name of course) was bright and likeable. The presenting issue was that although usually easy to get along with, he was given to occasional outbursts of anger during which he would hit his mother, younger brother, or classmates.

In parent and family sessions, we explored how Gerry's reactions reminded his parents of their own, as kids and now. Experiments with reliving early experiences helped Dad get in touch with his own process of converting anxiety to anger, and of the defusing power of piano playing, which was also one of Gerry's favorite diversions. Some practical anger management techniques were formulated and equally important, the father/son bond was strengthened.

The Paradoxical Theory of Change

We are indebted to the late Arnold Beisser for teaching us that we change not by pushing and exhorting ourselves to change, or by being pushed and exhorted by another, but by accepting more fully who and what we presently are. Only then are we truly free and capable of self-growth.

I use the following exercise with children/families/parents as an adaptation of this concept :

Begin with an attribute of the child that is considered a problem, such as anger, impulsivity, too slow, etc. On a large sheet of paper make three columns labeled "Helps," "Hurts," and "Goes Either Way." (It generally comes as a surprise that the "problem" could be anything but hurtful.)

For example, ten-year-old Lenora's slowness was maddening to her fast paced parents, and was a detriment to her in many school activities. Yet as we explored this quality together, we came up with a good-sized list, of which the following is a portion:

Slowness helps when:
> eating (digestion, weight management, savoring the flavors)
> strolling through gardens
> leaving phone numbers on answering machines
> playing pick-up sticks
> reacting when someone makes you mad

Slowness hurts when:
> taking a timed test
> getting ready for school
> interacting with other family members
> playing the card game "Spit"

Slowness can go either way when:
> crossing the street

reading

preparing for exams.

The important point made to Lenora and her parents was that there was nothing wrong with the basic, intrinsic Lenora. *Some* of her behaviors were not adaptable within the culture in which she lived, and we worked on modifying them. There is a world of difference between feeling like a damaged, unacceptable person and appreciating oneself as a worthy human being who needs to change some specific behaviors.

The moral applied equally to her parents. There was nothing basically wrong with their way of being. It was highly adaptable in the work world, and in their social lives they chose like-minded friends. As parents of Lenora — whom they loved — they needed to modify their way of interacting with her.

It should be noted that sometimes there seems to be a bad fit between parents and children. Maybe an artist is born into a family of engineers, or vice versa. It's as though the stork flying overhead with a baby intended for a certain family accidentally drops it over a very different family. As the baby floats down to its new home, the stork is heard to say: "Sorry about that, kid. Good luck in therapy."

For me, the heart and soul of the work lies in the overarching theory theme of the contactful, respectful relationship between therapist/teacher and client/learner, and the assumption that the individual has within him/her the necessary strength and health which, with empathetic and skillful encouragement, can effect change.

Barriers to Getting to the I-Thou with Parents

Barriers Within the Therapist:

1) Over-zealous advocacy of the child. At a Gestalt Educational Therapy presentation by my friend and colleague Cara Garcia of Pepperdine University a man in the audience vigorously

pronounced: "It's *always* the parents who are to blame if the kid isn't doing well in school."

My hand and my mouth were instantly activated, and for several minutes a hot debate ensued during which I tried to make the gentleman see the error of some of his ways. While his comments about children were sensitive and informed, his view of parents was, as it frequently is with professionals who work with kids, harsh and insensitive. Angry though I was, I am in his debt for providing a stimulus to preparing this workshop.

It is so easy to become frustrated with slow therapeutic progress, even easier to look for someone to blame, and easiest of all to dump the frustration on the parents. The fact that the blame may be at least partially deserved does not mitigate it's being a major barrier to facilitating change.

Following Our Internal Agenda Without Awareness

A highly tuned awareness of our own belief systems (or prejudices) and unhealed wounds, which inevitably will be twanged now and then by the parent, is a necessary attribute. The part of our role that is teacher may prompt us to leap over this sensitivity in the rush to correction.

For example, as therapists we value such things as openness, good eye contact, straightforward communication and non-violence. Comments such as "I'll give him something to cry about" may or may not be the same prelude to physical punishment as it was in the therapist's childhood. Lack of eye contact may signify not the pathology described in the textbooks but rather the accepted more of a different culture. Etc.

Barriers Within the Parent

The most obvious barrier is found in parents who have been mandated by the courts to counseling or parenting classes. In these cases, I like the venerable "choose to" approach:

Therapist: "I know you are angry at the judge for ordering counseling, but since you choose to be here, let's see how we can make it worthwhile for you."

Parent: "I didn't *choose* to be here, I *have* to be here."

T: "What would happen if you refuse?"

P: "I'd go to jail, that's what!"

T: "Since you choose to be here instead of in jail, let's see how we can make it worthwhile for you. "

Assume damaged pride in a parent deemed inadequate by him/herself, the school, or the courts. Shame is not conducive to good parenting. One way to help replace it with realistic self-confidence is to utilize skills and perspectives that have proved effective in other areas. For example, a tradesman who works with his hands understands patience and appreciation of the material (child). The marketing expert knows the value of friendly persuasion. A journalist can empathize with the difficulty of meeting deadlines. A gardener knows that enriching the soil helps the plant grow. And so forth.

I recall a physician in a parents anonymous group who liked to advise other parents on matters of physical health. She was asked about "preventative medicine" and this became a useful metaphor for averting family discord. In the same group a single mother who was something of a wizard at managing her limited finances was helped to bring this creativity to managing her children.

Another barrier is when the parental view/agenda/ex-pectation is that children in therapy are like adults clients. Young, even pre-verbal kids are dropped off with the admonition: "Be sure to talk to Ruth about that! You can tell her anything at all — she can't help you unless you talk to her — so talk to her!" I frequently interject: "Mom, it sounds like there is something *you* want me to know — why don't you tell me about it while Susie draws? At her age, she'll tell me things with the picture."

Sometimes it is necessary to correct the impression that the therapist serves a disciplinary, even punitive, function — something like a stern school principal. And on occasion I have had to disabuse a parent of the notion that counseling children is akin to obedience training for puppies.

Then there is the "I-pay-you-fix" parent. Whether because of denial or life-style or latent hostility this parent remains steadfastly aloof from the therapy process other than seeing that the child is delivered and the fee paid. I'll share a case history a little later to illustrate.

A common difficulty is when the parents disagree on the need for therapy for their child, and it becomes apparent that this disagreement is a manifestation of larger trouble in the relationship, whether they are divorced or technically "together." In such cases I find it best to ask for a commitment for a specified number of sessions — usually four to six — with half to be paid for in advance. I tell the child that we will be working together "probably for a month or two" to prepare for the possibility of abrupt termination. During that time, I do all I can to forge a trusting relationship with the parents, whether or not the decision is to continue. (And of course, short term may be sufficient.)

Unfortunately, sometimes a parent seems to be using counseling mainly or totally in "bad faith" — as a carrier of the parent's anger, a wish for revenge and/or a vehicle to contest custody arrangements. I routinely require that divorced or separated parents sign a form exempting me from being asked to testify in custody hearings. There is some question about whether such a form would hold up if challenged in court, but in my experience it has served its purpose.

Communication Aids

I encourage parents to use my private voice mail to tell me whatever seems helpful, such as family, school, or social issues which I can then weave into the session, thus building a working relationship between members of the same team.

I love to share the story of Gretchen, who at ten years of age was almost a direct opposite in personality from her single and struggling mother Sarah, and from her older sister whom I had seen the previous year. Where Sarah and older sister were perfectionist and reserved, with linear thinking styles, Gretchen was impulsive, creative, and expressive.

It was Gretchen who actually left the message on my answering machine: "We need help here! I got in trouble at school but it wasn't my fault and now my Mom won't let me go to Science Camp which doesn't make any sense because they teach the kind of stuff she wants me to learn." A talk with Mom resulted in her acknowledging that the punishment was too severe for the crime (a playground affray between peers) and a more suitable consequence was worked out. "Gretchen knows I sometimes leave you messages," Mom said, "At first I was angry at her for going behind my back but actually that kind of spunk is good, isn't it?" I assured her it was, and pointed out that Gretchen would not have done so if she hadn't known that Mom was basically fair, and could be trusted. (A comment Gretchen had made, and given me permission to share with Mom, only a week previously.)

The Waiting Room

The waiting room is another window of opportunity. Sometimes during the session I make an observation (such as "I appreciate how gracious you were when I bombed on that checker's game," or "you pick up new information very quickly") which I think would be helpful for the parent to also hear. If the child agrees, it provides a nice connection, giving me insight into parental reactions to praise, and if siblings are present, a mini family session.

Parents in Therapy

Parents being in therapy themselves usually, but not always, helps the work. Donald's mother and step-dad each had their own therapist, and everyone involved had opinions as to how parenting should proceed in order to transform the boy from an unhappy, argumentative, manipulative teenager desperately trying to hold his own in a chaotic family, into a respectful, well-mannered young gentleman. Obedience training indeed. This is not a "success story;" Donald was abruptly pulled from therapy, and I don't know what happened next. Likely it was miltary school.

Advice About Advice

Giving specific advice to parents is a two-edged sword. On the one hand, if the recommendation works, confidence in the counseling process increases and parental anxiety decreases. When it doesn't, it may be that the advice was a bad fit for that particular parent. Classic behavioral modification techniques such as earning rewards depend in large degree for their effectiveness on careful record keeping by the parent. The approach may be unsuccesful with a parent who is scattered and disorganized, or philosophically opposed to the concept, You may be able to work out an adaptation where you, or the teacher, are the actual record-keeper. Conversely, a different kind of parent may want and do well with very specific responses to specific behaviors.

To the parents of teenagers I say early on: "Once your youngster and I have a solid relationship going, be prepared to hear about the brilliant things I've said — things you have said many times only to reap the adolescent sigh-and-eye-roll. For example, 'Finish your homework first; you'll enjoy your other activities more with a free mind.' You'll need a sense of humor to keep your cool. In a funny way, this is actually a testament to your values — it's kind of a face-saving device. After all, what teenager can admit that sometimes Mom and Dad do know best?"

Here is some more "advice" I typically give to parents: If you formerly had a good relationship with this child, the probability is high that it can be regained. Keep the lines of communication open. Bad things sometimes happen in good families — being able to talk about them openly is at least half the battle. It's not always necessary to solve the problem; sometimes just knowing they have your love and support is enough.

And sometimes, as in marriage, it comes down to an ability to "muddle through." To wait. Maybe to pray. You don't need to be perfect, you just need to be "good enough." However, to keep my earlier promise, here is:

How to Be a Perfect Parent by Ruth Lampert

Anyone can be a perfect parent. All that is required is excellent physical and mental health; a good marriage; a support-ive extended family; loving friends; gratifying, well- paid, but not overly demanding work; a spacious home in a pleasant, safe neighborhood with good schools; no personal or professional emergencies; and cheerful, easy-going, low-maintenance children who are physically healthy and intellectually well-endowed.

Since you, Mr. and/or Mrs. Parent, don't meet the qualifica-tions, I'm afraid you must be diagnosed as "imperfect."

References

Yontef, G.M. (1993). *Awareness Dialogue & Process: Essays on Gestalt Therapy*. Highland, N.Y.: The Gestalt Journal Press

—— COUNSELING THE ABUSIVE PARENT ——

This chapter originally appeared as "Child Abuse: An EAP's Role in Breaking the Cycle," in the trade journal "Employee Assistance," Vol. 5, No. 12, July, 1993.

Most abusive parents are very much like you and me. Shocking though this statement may be at first reading, it contains the seeds of optimism. Most abusive parents are fairly ordinary people, trying to cope the best way they can, sometimes succeeding and sometimes making mistakes ranging from minor to serious — just like you and me.

There *are,* as we know only too well, physically abusive parents who maim, mutilate, and kill their children. Special expertise is called for in those rare cases. Fortunately, most physical abuse ranges from mild to moderately severe. The American Humane Association has estimated that minor physical abuse occurs approximately ten times more frequently than major physical injury.

Sexual abuse is another area beyond the scope of this article. What we can look at is the similarities of useful interventions, as far as they go, with sexually abusing parents, keeping in mind that there are important differences in dynamics and prognosis.

Emotional abuse, which may be as or more devastating, is difficult to objectively document, and less likely to come to the attention of mental health professionals. Let me introduce you to some composite abusive parents. They are not actual clients, but the situations are very real.

Samuel is a widowed aerospace engineer — highly controlled, ambitious. When the aerospace industry in Southern California shrank his professional future became uncertain.

He enjoyed being a parent to his only daughter until she reached a defiant adolescence. When she stayed out all night with her boyfriend and taunted Samuel with "I don't give a fuck what you think!" he lost his cool and slammed her into the wall. She ran screaming to a neighbor; now Child Protective Services says she can live at home if Samuel goes to counseling, where his anguished refrain was "How could I have done that? Why did I lose control?"

Marissa, thirty-seven, is an attractive, expressive ad writer. Her adopted daughter is slow-moving, inarticulate, with no interest in anything other than "hanging out with those stupid friends of hers at the stupid mall. She infuriates me to the point I've pulled her hair and slapped her so hard I left marks. I wish I hadn't adopted her, and that makes me even more ashamed I thought I was a much nicer person than I am."

Hector was raised in a family where physical punishment was the norm. When his divorced wife bought their ten-year-old son Arturo "cool" baggy pants, Hector saw the style as the signature of gang members, and remembered how *his* father had kept him on "the right side of the law." He forbade Arturo to wear the pants. When Arturo disobeyed him he responded with what he had learned was the right way to discipline kids — with a belt. Mandated to counseling, he continued to maintain that he had done the right thing.

A word here about the reporting process. While definitions vary from state to state on what constitutes physical abuse of a child, in general it means non-accidental, physical injury and/or neglect. Professionals working in any capacity where they might become reasonably suspicious of child abuse are among those mandated to report, and there are penalties for failure to do so.

In the case histories above, the parents were court mandated to attend counseling sessions or came voluntarily out of recognition of their potential to do harm. Frequently, however, it is the counselor (or teacher) who first notices "red flags," such as bruises on the back surface of the body; cigarette burns; unexplained injuries which the parent does not bring to medical attention; a child who is fearful, or very passive, or who frequently appears hungry or sleepy; and of course a child who reveals abuse to the counselor.

A counselor may note indicators of possible abuse in an adult client who states that he/she has punished a child severely, or drops hints, such as "my wife is too easy with our son; he doesn't *dare* disobey me, not anymore." The clinical dilemma is often how to proceed as you legally must and still keep the trust and confidence of your client. Even though you have explained, preferably in writing, the limits of confidentiality, you will have to explain again what your legal responsibilities are — in most states this is to report *reasonable suspicion.*

The client must be assured that although the counselor has no option and must make a report, this is not tantamount to an accusation, it is reporting a suspicion, which the agency in question will investigate. The counselor continues to care about the client's well-being and will work as part of a team to achieve a better family system; the client is part of that team.

I make every effort to have the client him/herself make the first telephone call from my office to Child Protective Services, thus establishing that there is already professional involvement with a motivated client. Failing this, I tell the parent exactly what I am going to say in my report and what will likely happen as a result. I assure the client of my concern for the well-being of the whole family and my commitment to work toward that end whether or not a formal investigation is made.

Only as a last resort do I call Children's Protective Services after the client has left.

Of course it doesn't always go that smoothly, and of course the system is flawed and agency intervention may be in itself abusive. That is another issue much beyond the scope of this article.

The history of child abuse in our country explains how and why the protective system developed; it also gives us clues as to how we can best intervene. Seeing the situation in historical perspective helps us to understand — *not to condone* — abusive behavior as something that is in fact as old as recorded time. Historically, it is barely a moment ago that challenges were first made to the concept of children being the property of their parents, and thus beyond society's sanctions.

The "cycle of abuse" is often interpreted to mean that children learn, and then repeat, the abusive behavior modeled by their parents. This is true to some extent, but as Alice Miller points out in *For Your Own Good*, the dynamics are far more complex (Miller, 1983). It's as though the psyche says, "I must persuade myself that my parents acted out of love for me; to think they did not love me is too painful to endure . . . I could not fight back when I small and helpless, but now I can get the relief of revenge by wreaking it on another small, helpless child . . . and all while maintaining that I am being a good parent, just as my parents were."

While child abuse knows no boundaries of class, culture, ethnicity, or occupation, there are some factors which seem related to higher risk. These are: large families with close spacing of children; single parenting; low socio-economic status with the accompanying high level of stress and isolation from support systems; and, most consistently, the parent having been abused as a child.

While men are more likely to sexually abuse, women are more likely to physically abuse, perhaps because typically they spend more time with their children.

Certain deficits in skills, knowledge, and attitude are suggestive of characteristics of abusive parents. These include parenting, coping, and interpersonal skills, and knowledge of child development. "Negative child rearing attitudes; inability to distinguish feelings of self and others, particularly the child, and inaccurate attributions about internal or personal responsibility for one's own actions" (Goldstein, Arnold et *al.*, 1985) to give us some guidelines for the treatment plan.

The mental health professional has a variety of effective interventions from which to choose, depending on the circumstances of each case, the characteristics of the abuser, the training of the therapist, and the practical considerations of availability and financial feasibility.

Based on those considerations the pyschodynamic model, while capable of effecting in-depth change, may be impractical. Aspects of it can be, and usually are, woven into most approaches.

The sociological model focuses on such factors as the attitudes toward violence and stress, including that related to familial and social isolation. The devastation wrought by life crises is often directly related to finances; business reversals in an affluent family with many resources for recouping does less damage to family functioning than does the loss of a job that is the only source of income in a large family without savings. A single mother with sufficient income to pay for respite via housekeepers, and a single mother with a supportive, extended family, will probably experience less stress than a single mother whose life is limited to going to work and caring for children.

An approach considered by many authorities to be the intervention of choice is the educational, or skill-building model. Strengthening such skills as anger control and communication are important components of parenting skill. Since behavior affects feelings and feelings affect behavior, a learning approach that integrates the cognitive, behavioral, and attitudinal aspects of parenting is adaptable to a wide range of individuals, as well as families and groups, in a wide range of provider settings.

My own conceptualization of this approach is Gestalt Educational Therapy. The "Gestalt" part refers to the overarching Gestalt theme of contactful, respectful relationship between counselor and client, and the assumption that the individual has within him/her the strength and health which, with skillful encouragement, can effect change. The "Educational Therapy" part refers to the careful attention to both the cognitive and affective modes to best promote learning, and is alert to psychodynamics and sociological concerns. This orientation underlies all the following issues and interventions.

Anger

Help the client separate this acceptable and important emotion from the unacceptable expression of it. "Brain-storm" together for alternatives to acting out, such as: go or a fast walk or run to cool down; call a good friend and talk about what happened; do some carpentry, or tear up newspapers.

Role-play with the client to increase his/her awareness of the individual "cues" for rage, which may turn out to be a tight stomach, or a dry mouth, or a fast heartbeat, or almost anything at all — what is important is for the client to recognize the cues in advance of acting out. Suggest keeping a journal of the different emotions experienced each day.

Teach stress reduction skills such as muscle relaxation, deep breathing, and imagery for self-care and diffusion of rage.

At each session, have the client report *one* instance since the last meeting in which an impulse to hit was successfully supplanted by an acceptable response.

At each session, have the client report *one* thing that pleased him/her about the child. Emphasize this can be something "tiny," such as — "said 'thank you' to grandma" or "brushed teeth without being reminded."

Self-Esteem

Abusive behavior tends to diminish as self-esteem increases. Realistically reframe negative self-perceptions. For example, to a client who says "I'm embarrassed because I'm the only one in the office who's never been to college," you might respond, "Sounds like you got where you are because of your ability. Nice going."

Artwork such as collages and sand-scenes remove the pressure to "perform," allowing for good feelings about oneself to emerge spontaneously.

As a model of the "good parent," the therapist does well to:

Be specific in praise ("You're coming up with more alternatives to hitting than I thought of").

Hold realistic expectations and give embedded suggestions for improvement ("You'll notice more and more good things about your son as we go along").

Remain consistent without being inflexible ("it's very important that we meet regularly; since you have a special work assignment next Tuesday let's reschedule for Monday or Wednesday.")

Display unconditional *regard* as distinct from unconditional *approval* and give permission to be imperfect but not abusive ("I understand the shame you feel when you lose your cool . . . true, yelling isn't the best way to go, but you have stopped hitting".)

Make judicious use of self-disclosure ("The part about parenting that's always been the hardest for me is_____" or "It took me years to figure out who in my family I could really trust."

Loneliness and Alienation

The therapeutic relationship ("I-Thou") in and of itself is a powerful healing phenomenon, as attested to by those who have experienced it.

The counselor is in an excellent position to enhance social, cognitive, and spiritual support systems; many people are unaware of what is actually available, and/or can benefit from the professional's support in overcoming timidity, suspicion, etc. Groups and classes on my list include Parents Without Partners; Sierra Club; Parents Anonymous; low-cost classes in a wide variety of subject such as music, photography, cooking, dancing, ad infinitum; local activities announced in newspapers; and spiritual/philosophical activities and organizations such as churches and synagogues, Yoga, reading/discussion groups, and Twelve-Step programs when appropriate.

Last but very far from least are the benefits to be gained from group therapy and family therapy. Although each of these modalities approaches the problem of abuse slightly differently, in general I use the same guidelines as I do in individual counseling.

Parenting Skills

Within the model of Gestalt Educational Therapy, classes and counseling for individuals and groups provide a learning setting. The understanding of basic developmental issues, which fosters realistic expectations, is easily integrated into dialogue. Guidelines for discipline, as opposed to punishment, are often more readily "heard" from a trusted counselor. I focus on certain main principles, such as suspension of privileges and fining; logical consequences of behavior; reinforcement of all "good" behavior (I'm very strong on this) and clear, congruent communication. I give many handouts on developmental stages and effective discipline.

Besides the behavior changes, there are enormous psychological gains to the parent who is able to acquire a new, workable, repertoire of skills, which brings further benefit to their children.

Counselor Attributes

It helps to be calm and "unflappable," both as an antidote to the chaos often characteristic of abusive families, and as a role model.

Being authoritative but not authoritarian is effective — just as research shows it is in raising children. The persona of a very human — and therefore imperfect — person who is in the process of personal growth is encouraging.

I am more directive than usual with this population. I don't have the luxury of fully following the client's pace when the safety of their children is at stake.

Being cross-culturally sensitive and informed means being better equipped to understand motivation, even while insisting upon adherence to certain standards of behavior.

Good self-care skills are necessary in all therapy and counseling; in the arena of child abuse they are imperative. Giving yourself loving permission to seek consultation, peer support, sufficient rest and relaxation and perhaps therapy (See "Transference Issues" below) will dramatically enhance your effectiveness, and your willingness to work with this difficult population.

Transference Issues

Expect a lot of anger to be projected onto you. At worst, your client has been dragged into a system which blames, punishes, and lacerates. You may very likely, albeit unfairly, represent that system.

Positive transference may cast you in the role of not just "good parent," but perfect, all-loving, all-knowing, all-forgiving.

All manifestations of transference are grist for the mill. Use the anger to explore all anger; use the admiration to effectively teach; use anything that comes your way to facilitate progress.

Remain self-aware and don't attribute every uncomfortable perception of you to transference. Maybe you *have* been blaming, maybe you *didn't* understand, and maybe you *are* terrific at your work.

As much as possible, work through your shock, horror, anger, dismay, pity, identification, etc. before beginning work in this field. Be prepared for and accepting of all resources available to deal with your own issues as they emerge — which they will. If you discover that your own issues are too raw, postpone or decide against this particular arena of mental health work.

There is more to good parenting than not being abusive. However, that will be your primary goal in working with abusive parents, so measure success in small increments. Remember that stopping or minimizing parental abuse sets in motion the kind of cycles we hope to perpetuate.

Nothing works all the time. Hard data is hard to come by. There is enough evidence indicating that intervention is effective to make the work well worth doing.

References

Child Abuse Prevention Handbook, Office of California Attorney General.

Goldstein, Arnold et al. (1985). *Changing the Abusive Parent.* Champaign, Ill: Research Press.

Miller, Alice. (1983). *For Your Own Good: Hidden Cruelties in Child Rearing and the Roots of Violence*. New York: Farrar, Straus & Giroux.

13

— QUATERNARY —

FAMILY THERAPY WITH FOUR GENERATIONS

This originally appeared as a chapter in A Living Legacy of Fritz and Laura Perls: Contemporary Case Studies *edited and published by Bud Feder and Ruth Ronall, Montclair, NJ, 1996.*

Forward: In the thick of therapy, theoretical constructs are, as they should be, in the background. During the course of my work with this fascinating and difficult family, I found even more than the usual need for consultative support, whether face to face, phone to phone, or eye to page. Some of the concepts which emerged from that support are periodically indicated in italics. Many voices blended in this "voice of the consultant in my head," especially those of Bud Feder, Gary Yontef, Miriam and Erv Polster, John O. Stevens, Claudio Naranjo, Liv Estrup and Arnold Beisser.

Fifty-six-year old Delila was a strikingly elegant woman. Her appearance suggested a quiet, well-bred manner with softly modulated voice and speech. This was not the case.

"You know how it is with second marriages well this is my third and I don't know *why* I married Stan well I guess I do it was because of my daughter Bette who is really almost the real reason I am here."

This, and much more, was delivered in a brassy staccato broken by frequent short bursts of nervous laughter. I wondered as I listened whether and when I should interrupt. When she got to "my daughter always was *gorgeous* and to tell you the truth I never knew how to handle her so I mostly just let her alone and I never have interfered with anything she does except that now I just can't sit by and see her mistreat that poor girl Nikki who if you ask me wouldn't be half bad-looking if she would fix her hair a little, but of course she'll never be beautiful like her mother — " I wedged in with, "Was it concern for your granddaughter Nikki that prompted your call to me?"

Her voice slowed a little.

"Yes. Bette got your name from a friend of hers and suggested I see you for marriage counseling. I decided to use the chance to get some help for Nikki although God knows I could use help with my marriage. Actually sometime I'd like to talk to you about my mother too, I just can't keep driving all the way down there to take her to her doctor's appointments but who else is going to do it if I don't?"

Verbosity is one of the many ways to deflect, to avoid contact; it can become addictive.

I told her that if Bette called I would be happy to set up an appointment; meanwhile, her own marriage issues sounded pressing. Delila agreed, saying "Stan probably won't come in though, he thinks he's perfect and everything is my fault." In the next few sessions Delila proved agile in darting from descriptions of how the people in her life took advantage of her to denial that she was being taken advantage of. For example, she cancelled her third appointment a few days before the deadline for filing income tax returns, saying she needed the time to work on "all these returns." "All these returns" turned out to be hers and Stan's ("I've *begged* him to get an accountant to do it but he refuses, and of course I guess he's right, it only takes me a couple of hours and we never do anything at night except watch T.V. anyway") and a co-worker's who simply couldn't figure out the forms ("I feel so sorry for the poor little thing, she just sits and answers the phone all day, she only makes $6.00 an hour, that boss of ours is even meaner to her than to me") and her mother's ("she doesn't trust anyone except me to do it right, and really it's not that hard to do.")

"And your daughter Bette?" I asked. "When do you do hers?"

"Oh no," she replied, "Bette never asks for help from anyone."

"I wonder where she gets that . . . "

For the first time Delila paused a long time before responding, looked directly at me, and quietly said, "Maybe she's like me and thinks she doesn't deserve help?"

"Maybe," I answered, feeling my heart lift with the hopefulness contact brings.

However . . . useful interventions, exercises, experiments, all eluded me. When I interrupted her monologue/litany, she switched to another topic; when I asked for clarification she assured me she was getting to that in a minute; and so on and so forth. I put my trust in the trusting relationship we were establishing, reminding myself that the root meaning of the word therapy is "to wait."

Include yourself in her field through respectful listening. Establish contact at the only boundary possible with this client at this time, supporting her resistance.

She talked about her early life in a small New England town, with an alcoholic father who beat her mother and her until she was old enough to escape, taking Mom with her. Her eight-year first marriage was to another abusive alcoholic; this time she escaped to California with her baby daughter, Bette, and Mom.

"I still hadn't learned, and got married again, to another son-of-a-bitch, but this time I got smart sooner and left after six months. Now I'm married to Stan, who doesn't drink, doesn't hit me, but does what I think you call emotional abuse."

At the fourth session she said she had persuaded Stan to come in with her. "I told him you weren't like what he probably thought therapists were like. I told him you paid attention and made a person feel that what they said was important."

"Thank you," I replied. Transference and/or reality, it was good to hear.

By making contact foremost, we are free of the rule that every interaction in therapy is a distortion of the past. Consider what is and is not valid in the here and now.

Naturally I expected Stan to be quiet, withdrawn, obsessive-compulsive. Wrong again.

Big, bluff, and hearty, he did most of the talking at the first conjoint session, while Delila sat quietly and demurely as he explained to me what Delila's problems were:

"I don't know if she told you, but her first two husbands really abused her something awful, besides what happened with her father. Is it O.K. if I talk about this honey?"

"Say anything you want, darling," she replied, adding sweetly, "you always do."

"Tell me about *you,* Stan." I suggested/invited/directed.

"Yes sweetheart," came the poisonously sweet voice of Delilia, "tell her about your last two wives and how they and your children left you and you never hear from any of them. You see," she said turning that sugary smile in my direction, "I'm not the only one who has problems although that's what he'd like you to think."

The hearty salesman's smile left Stan's now purpling face, and he shouted, "Jesus Christ, you are something else, I thought you wanted me to come here to help you!"

I heard myself saying silently to myself, "You goofed, seeing them conjointly after seeing her one-on-one. You're in for it now."

I also re-heard Delila's "you make a person feel that what they say is important." Stan needed respectful attention too. I suspected part of the trouble was not with what he said, but the way he said it — in what I termed New York volume, very different from New England restraint.

Put yourself as fully as possible, without judgement or interpretation, into the experience of the other. That's a prime characteristic of the essential element of dialogue.

I pursued this a bit, reframing Stan's bellow into a statement of frustration at being misunderstood, and conjecturing that Stan's way of expressing feelings might make Delila think he was a lot angrier than he really was, and in fact, sometimes what she heard as anger might be worry.

Another point of contact as the purple left Stan's face and he said, "Bingo! You got it! Where I come from, if you got something on your mind you just say it!"

"Where I come from," Delila answered, "people speak in a considerate tone of voice."

"Yeah, and you never know what they really think."

Words used for reasons other than direct communication are another way to deflect, to isolate oneself from contact with others, to reduce awareness of one's own experience.

The way was paved for some classic communication exercises such as changing "but" to "and," speaking in "telegrams," giving voice to gestures and substituting words with body language, and reframing questions as statements. The increase in understanding of how their different backgrounds and personality styles impacted interactions was followed by awareness of some similarities they had not recognized, such as each of them being terrified of the prospect of becoming "a third time loser" in marriage. From fear of failure per se they moved to the fear of loss and abandonment.

Stan: "I married my first wife because she was pregnant, and I felt guilty when she left; I married my second wife because I hated living alone but ended up alone again; I married you because there is just something about you that makes my heart lift, and losing that would be God awful."

Delila: "I've always gotten along on my own and I could again, but life without you would be like having only black and white T.V. after getting used to color. I guess I need you more than I want to admit; I'd rather be the one who is needed."

Ruth: "You are saying your lives are richer and fuller with each other than without. That's promising."

Then eleven-year-old Nikki ran away from home, showing up two days later at the apartment of Delila's mother, Nanny Ellen. Nikki, who had been her Grandma Delila's ticket of admission to therapy, now came in with her mom, the beautiful Bette.

Bette looked very much like Delila but she didn't sound like her. She opened the interview by saying in crisply perfect enunciation,

"I wish to express my recognition of your professional excellence. Since entering treatment with you the level of compatibility between my mother and her husband has markedly increased."

Good grief. What next with this family?

Next was Nikki, whose thin little pinch-featured face was spotted with zits and whose nails were bitten almost to the quick. There was, however, quite a sparkle in her eyes and a pride in her bearing as she chose to sit in the chair furthest from her mother. In answer to my question about what she hoped would happen by coming to see me, she responded,

"I want to live with Nanny Ellen. Can you make that happen?"

"If I can't, would you settle for you and your Mom getting along better?"

"Why bother? I already get along with Nanny Ellen. And with Grandma Delila and Stan. It's just my mom who can't stand me."

I thought I heard a little desperation in Bette's "I personally would welcome increased rapport between us. I do try. I am non-plussed by her attitude. She cares nothing for her appearance, or for our lovely home. She does not utilize any of the advantages with which I provide her including a fine private school."

"What about Dad? Is he in the picture?"

At the mention of her father Nikki got up and walked over to the sand-tray and began examining the objects. Bette gestured as though to say, "See what I mean about her?" and I gestured back "That's O.K., leave her be."

Contact interruptions may be healthy or unhealthy depending on context and field; here you have a nice example of how deflection can be a healthy response.

Bette's voice dipped a degree further into chill. "My ex-husband chose to distance himself from all responsibilities, believing that to be the prerogative of artists, which he considers himself to be."

Nikki agreed to return the following week to "fool around with these paints and clay and stuff you've got." Three individual sessions revealed a youngster who coped valiantly with the pain of abandonment, using her considerable artistic talent both to bolster her low sense of self-worth and to keep hope alive. She had a dim memory of her father, drawing him as tall and thin, with long blonde hair in a pony-tail. She said she suspected he had left because of a mysterious ailment, possibly amnesia.

A favorite fantasy was that he would come to her opening at the County Art Museum where, seeing her artistic style so similar to his own, he would recognizes her as the daughter he had left long ago. She concluded with, "Course that's all bullshit but it's better than nothing, right?"

Interrupt the introject in the service of awareness!

"You bet it is," I replied. "Actually I think it's more imagination than bullshit, and imagination gets you further than bullshit. What does Nanny Ellen think about your dreams of becoming an artist?"

"She thinks I should become a lawyer, but she'll go along with whatever I want. She says the reason she is still alive is because she wants to go to my graduation from law school, or, if I insist, art school!"

"She sounds like quite a woman. I'd sure like to meet her."

That was the overt reason for my requesting a family session including child, mother, grandmother and step-grand-father, and great-grandmother. My covert agenda was to demonstrate in vivo to Nikki how many people there were who cared about her, since it seemed unlikely she would ever receive warm, loving affection from her mother. I wanted to avert the familiar pattern of a child desperately and vainly trying to coax warmth from an emotionally distant parent. Every therapist is familiar with the syndrome: lonely middle- aged clients, locked into the belief that the only mothering that counts is that which comes from the actual mother, shutting out the nurturance that is available. Nikki already had a loving relationship with her great-grandmother; Delila and Stan, with a longer life-expectancy, had expressed affection and concern. Perhaps "improved rapport" with Mom could happen too, but first on my agenda was to spotlight the love that was already there.

Help her scan the environment and introject an image of an extended family.

My office was crowded that first family meeting, and was to become more so, though I didn't know it at the time. Nanny Ellen arrived with Bette and Nikki. At eighty-seven her beauty was fragile and weathered but still elegant. She sat in the room's only straight-backed wooden chair, commenting "Those couches look tempting, but I've been fooled before; once down I may not be able to get up and Nikki here would have to help me, which she is good at doing, bless her."

"Bless *you* Nanny Ellen," I thought. It was hard to imagine this forthright, forthcoming woman having ever been a "victim" of abuse; the word "survivor" seemed made for her. She quickly dispelled the notion of over-dependence on Delila, as she demonstrated a nice grasp of free services available to senior citizens, including taxi voucher systems, ("why Delila thinks I can't get to the doctor on my own is a mystery to me") income tax preparation ("Delila doesn't trust them to do it properly, as if my estate were so complicated!") and counseling ("They won't see the whole family though, and it's the rest of this family who needs it, so here I am, at whatever you charge which is probably plenty.")

"You're pretty peppery, aren't you? I responded. "I think I'll take some lessons from you, I'd hate to become one of those boring sweet old ladies."

"You're not exactly a spring chicken now," she returned, creating an I-Thou relationship on the spot. She remained the star of this and many sessions, with a talent for speaking her mind so artlessly and directly that the sting was more stimulating than painful. Even Bette warmed to her scolding about "it's time you stopped organizing your closets and paid more mind to that nice young man Carl who doesn't seem to care that you are such a fuss-budget about everything. I'd be real happy to stay with Nikki while you go out and enjoy yourselves." For her part, Nikki was mostly silent until I suggested that everyone say something they wished to change, and something they especially liked, about their family.

The broader the range of possible responses, the greater the possibility of creative solutions.

Nikki burst forth with, "I wish I could change how my Mom treats me, I don't want to live with her, I'd like to change my looks and be grown-up and able to have my own apartment and have a lot of money and a car and a boyfriend. What I like is that Nanny Ellen and Grandma Delila are cool, and that Grandpa Stan lets me help him with his computer stuff."

Bette wanted, predictably, for Nikki to be more responsible and neat and so forth; she liked that Delila and she had lunch together twice a month.

Delila's wish for change was that everyone would get along together; she too liked the lunches with Bette, and liked Nikki's coming over to visit her and Stan.

Stan wanted to change the way Delila would get sarcastic; he liked the way Nikki helped him with his business records.

Nanny Ellen wished Bette would get married again and have a regular family; she liked that no one bugged her to move to a nursing home as did the families of most of her remaining friends.

Applying "The Paradoxical Theory of Change"[Arnie Beisser] to family work permits each member to honor his/her basic way of being; certain behavioral adaptations may make it easier and more fulfilling to live in the world, and the family, as it is.

We agreed to meet in family session every other week, with Stan and Delila continuing their work on a weekly basis and Nikki seeing me individually every other week with regular parent contact with Bette. Nanny Ellen said, "Looks like this family will be paying your rent for awhile. Well, it's better than more divorcing and running away." Joining this family on their divergent and convergent paths was often unsettling for me. I felt miles away from the well-planned and structured approaches of some current schools of family therapy, and self-doubts frequently assailed me.

Remember that inclusion — putting oneself into the other's experience without either judgement or confluence — is the highest form of validation.

Self-examination, as well as professional consultation, was crucial to my staying on the course of commitment to the process, to facilitating awareness and growth, to illuminating choices and midwifing healing.

It seemed to be working. Delila and Stan's relationship was becoming more fulfilling to both; Nikki did not move in with Nanny Ellen, but she spent weekends with her, and worked, for pay, at Grandpa Stan's two afternoons a week; Nanny Ellen maintained her important role in family sessions, sharing reminiscences of both Delila's and Bette's girlhoods, which was bonding for the three other female family members and fascinating to the one male.

Then, just in time to avert any complacency on my part, Bette called to say that she was pregnant, Carl wanted her to marry him and have the baby, she didn't want to do either, and could they make an appointment to "explore, in an atmosphere of objectivity and reason, our differing stances." I learned that Carl and Bette worked in the same computer software company, she as the office manager, he as an outside salesman. He had a boyish enthusiasm that went well with his freckles and shock of blond hair. His position was very simple:

"I'm twenty-nine years old. I've dated a million women, fell in love with Bette the first day I saw her in the office. She thinks that because she's ten years older than me I'll get tired of her, but that's a bunch of bunk. That baby she's carrying is mine too and I want it. Nikkie and I can learn to get along. What's the problem?"

Consider shame, the handmaiden of a sense of inferiority, which often accompanies unrealistically high standards of competency.

With the chink in her fortress now revealed, I said, "Bette, do you think you can let Carl know, without any words, how frightened you are of his someday leaving you?"

As though we had rehearsed it, she curled up into a fetal position, put her thumb in her mouth, and looked at him with sorrowing eyes.

During six more conjoint sessions her fears of entrapment/abandonment and his legitimate concerns of being a step-father were explored.

She agreed to let Carl move in, to have the baby, and consider marriage if "one year from the date of birth we find our family relationship sufficiently harmonious to formalize it with marriage."

They announced these plans at the following family session, which now included Carl. He and Nanny Ellen agreed they would prefer marriage to precede parenthood but saw Bette's point of view; Stan and Delila thought the "kids" were smart to not rush into marriage; Nikki rolled her eyes heavenward in the classic adolescent expression of giving up on adults, and said, "I won't have to share my room with the baby, will I?"

There had been subtle changes in Nikki's appearance over the months as her thin scrawniness evolved into a gamine delicacy, not unlike Nanny Ellen's. In an individual session, she commented on the new living arrangements: "Carl is a dweeb, but Mom is so busy trying to whip him into some kind of shape she is staying off my back."

Bette found two occasions during family sessions to express appreciation and praise for Nikki:

1) "I realize my standards of housekeeping are probably too exacting. I want you to know I appreciate your doing the dishes last night even though at the time my only comment was that the job isn't done until the sink is bleached. Thank you."

2) "I think having a pregnant mother may present some social difficulties for a girl your age. You seem to be handling it rather gracefully."

On both occasions Nikki flushed and responded: "No big problem."

Progress. A flush is an example of contact expressed in body language. Be careful not to interpret; rather, observe and utilize.

Fourteen months after the first phone call from Delila, we had our "stopping place." Delila and Stan's marriage was still full of problems, but they now saw these problems as difficulties to either be worked through or lived with, rather than as propulsions to flee. Nikki's awareness of how much her extended family cared for her, plus her social skills with peers and her artistic talent, eased the pain of her mother's emotional distance. For her part, Bette conscientiously worked on looking for points of contact with this daughter with whom she had never really bonded. Her work was cognitive, and she was not motivated to explore deep feelings.

She did recognize that her holding Carl at arm's length was a protective maneuver, and she was willing to risk letting him closer. Nanny Ellen, in sharing her reminiscences of the past, was doing what the elderly need to do for themselves at the late stage of their life journey, while providing connecting lore-links to the family saga.

Baby Joshua was present at this session, and Grandpa Stan observed, "I've gone from being the only man in the family to being one of three. Terrific stuff, this family therapy."

It *is* terrific stuff.

If I could re-do it all in this case, I would have a co- therapist during the family sessions. What did I miss that someone else would have caught, as five and eventually seven family members inter-acted? Do I really need to put so much pressure on myself?

Another thing I would change is that time and money would be of little consideration (I would say "no consideration" but have learned that some cost serves the process well) so that more in-depth, long-term work could have been done on individual bases.

What I liked was that in fact so much was accomplished in a relatively short time within the realities of this family's resources. The pervasive fear of abandonment that ran through the system was not fully allayed but was, with the support of awareness, manage-able.

Of special personal gain to me (besides all those fees Nanny Ellen mentioned) was the broadening of my own experiences, and my deeper understanding and appreciation of the forces that move families and thus individuals — including mine and me.

I continue to work with different configurations of this family from time to time.

Stan and Delila periodically come in for a couple of sessions when strain and pain threaten to overshadow the gain of their mar-ried life.

After extending the decision deadline to two years, Bette and Carl did marry. In a recent phone message she told me "I realize I have unfinished emotional business. When Joshua starts pre-kindergarten I will address myself to individual therapy. Nikki and I still have our troubles but she is quite loving with Joshua, who is, and I say this objectively, remarkably lovable. He adores her. Her art is going well and she has many friends."

Deflection by intellectualization continues to defuse her intense emotions. Honor her need for the defense; support her awareness.

Nikkie sent me the following note last year on a Christmas card:

"Nanny Ellen died and I think my heart will break. Mom says if I want to see you I can make an appointment." She did, and we laughed and cried together as we remembered Nanny Ellen. "I want to be like her when I grow up," Nikki said.

"So do I," I answered.

14

—— NOTES FROM ALONG THE WAY ——

This chapter originally appeared as an article in Journal of Couples Therapy, *Vol. 1, Nos. 3-4, 1990, Haworth Press, Inc.,NY and then as a chapter in the book* Intimate Autonomy/Autonomous Intimacy, *edited by Barbara Jo Brothers, 1991, Haworth Press, Inc., NY.*

As a Gestalt therapist, the I-Thou relationship is my most powerful "intervention." It is in developing a contactful therapeutic relationship, through the use of self, that I am most effective in enhancing my clients' abilities to problem-solve and effect change.

As a woman, issues of intimacy and of autonomy are tightly woven into the fabric of my personal life. I have struggled, sometimes successfully, sometimes not, to gracefully integrate these two needs. I am pleased by some of the resultant patterns, dismayed by others.

Never is the line between I-Thou use of self, and counter-transference, more delicate than when I am involved in the intricate work of exploring with a couple their particular route to integrating inter-personal intimacy and personal autonomy.

Does such a destination exist in reality, or is the whole notion of "Intimate Autonomy" an oxymoron? One part of my consciousness ponders this conundrum during the session with Frederick and Susan. They talk and argue and mis-communicate about wanting closeness, wanting personal space, feeling isolated, feeling smothered, needing more of the other, needing less, considering ending the relationship, and rejecting that consideration in panic.

The "Go for consultation!" light flashes in my mind as I become aware of an urge to burst into tears and cry out: "Oh, this conflict is exactly what destroyed my first love"! (Or was it my third? Or both?)

Revelation of this urge clearly would not be in the best interests of Susan and Frederick. I bracket it off as my own unfinished business, to be dealt with on my time, with my money.

What I do is interrupt their speeches with,

"You two have got to be fantastic in your work as attorneys. But to tell you the truth, all those words are making me feel like my head is in a food processor. Please, try this experiment. Pretend that there are no telephones or fax machines or e-mails available and you can only communicate by telegram. Every word costs $5,000. Now talk to each other." They frown, looking bewildered and a little annoyed. Then they begin repeating to *me* what they were saying to each other.

"No you don't!" I insist. "Talk to *each other* — at $5,000 a word."

Their mouths open, close, and then form into smiles. They begin to laugh and I laugh with them and the tension is broken. Actually, this isn't what I expected to happen, but that's the way it goes with experiments. They have moved a jot closer to each other on the couch, and I ask if they are aware of this.

"I can fully appreciate here how the concept of body language is useful . . . " Frederick begins to pontificate. Susan interrupts with "Oh, can that crap, will you?"

"That was terrific Susan — so good I'm going to discount the price to $3,750!" I say in what I hope is not a patronizing tone.

Apparently it isn't, because they leave looking pretty happy. As for me, I am delighted to have experienced, finally, some genuine contact between these two bright and over-intellectualized lovers.

When they began working with me I explained my position on conjoint therapy:

"I don't have a bias either in favor of saving a relationship, or in favor of ending it. I think you both know, down deep, which will be best for you. I can help you clarify the issues that trouble you. If you are committed to continuing the relationship, I will do all I can to help you continue it in a way that is good for both of you. If you decide to end the relationship, I will do all I can to help you do so in a way that is as non-destructive as possible to both of you."

Doesn't that sound terrific?

Is it true?

Is my objectivity that pure?

On a day when my own personal relationship is going particularly well, do I lean toward keeping a couple together? Confess now. Haven't I sometimes thought that, well, sure, Frederick and Susan are having their struggles . . . but if they only knew the sweet warmth and comfort that can be theirs if they just hang in a little longer, work a little harder . . .

And on a morning when I drive to my office full of angry sorrow for my lost singularity? Perhaps I will see Susan and Frederick a little differently then; perhaps what will emerge as foreground for me is how vitally and fiercely independent each one is, and how really beautiful that independent spirit is.

I am reassured by the fact that I am worrying about all this. It tells me I'm aware of my own process as well as theirs. If I ever completely stop worrying about it I'd better find another way to make a living.

I have a session alone with Frederick. Sitting in that particular posture, with that particular ray of light falling across his hair, he suddenly looks very much like someone I once loved and lost. Sounds like him, too.

"The thing is, I'm not sure I'm really in love with her. I usually have a great time when we're together — she has this incredible sense of humour that turns the most mundane situations into sparkling events. I laugh more when I'm with her than at any other time in my life. And I trust her more than I trust anyone. Sex is great. But somehow . . . I keep thinking something is missing in the way I feel about her. Sometimes I think I want more."

Lost Love said that to me, just before he left. (I heard from mutual friends that he regretted it later. Haa!) From that old ache in my heart I hear a silent voice muttering to Frederick-cum-Lost Love:

"Don't be a damn fool. There isn't any 'more'. You want to still be looking for 'more' when you're ninety and in a nursing home?"

I bring myself back in contact with Frederick-Here-and-Now, who says with a rueful smile, "I don't suppose you have a formula for determining if it's the real thing?"

"Frederick, I don't even know what the 'real thing' is! What I do know is that you are going through a painful struggle. And I'm getting a feeling that there's something else beyond what you are saying . . . "

I put this out very tentatively, because I'm not entirely sure if this "feeling" is coming completely from Frederick's present being, or if it's some leftover of *my* wanting 'more' of what I wanted, back then, from Lost Love.

Apparently, I am on target. Frederick looks at me with the most direct, in-touch, gaze I've received from him and says, "All the way here today I was wondering if I should tell you this other thing that's bothering me. 'No,' I said to myself, 'that doesn't have any-thing to do with why Susan and I are seeing Ruth, it's a separate matter . . . ' . . . but it keeps coming to my mind . . . and I think you'll understand . . . " He then tells me that Susan had an abortion a year ago, and he is not entirely sure the baby really *was* his. More than that . . . if it was his, he has some regrets . . .

"I'm very touched that you risked telling me about that. Right now you look very soft . . . and vulnerable..I wonder — does that softness and vulnerability trouble you?"

We explore this a little further. I wonder to myself if he will be able to transfer that trust and vulnerability to Susan. Probably he will, given support, and time.

Susan has her individual session with me. She goes deeper into memories of her family of origin than she has done in conjoint sessions. I hear a story of a favored child, a princess, whose father adored her — as long as she remained "Daddy's little girl."

"When my brother brought home A's, Dad would say, 'Good job, Arthur!' and pound him on the back. When I brought home A's, he'd say, 'That's nice, honey. You're looking mighty pretty today.'"

"Ouch, that hurts my feminist soul," I say, "and I'm imagining the struggle it must have been for you to not only go through college, but law school! You must be very brave." "Yes, well, but you see . . . I did lose my father's adoration."

She cries softly for a moment, then straightens up, wipes her eyes, and asks briskly,

"So is that the reason I resist trusting Frederick? Am I afraid that if he finds out how really smart I am he'll withhold his love and my experience with my father will be recapitulated?"

"That's a good interpretation," I say, "but what I'm really interested in is what you are afraid would happen if you told Frederick what you just told me?"

Our conjoint sessions continue. Little by little they risk letting each other in to more of their heart's domain. They gradually become more comfortable with the understanding that sometimes that essential "letting in" is manifested as "go away now."

I can only be effective if I connect with them intimately and personally. Therefore I too must risk pain and confusion.

At times, a wave of panic washes over me, and I wonder, "Why are you bringing these problems to *me*? Me, of all people? Do you really think I know anything about relationships, let alone *intimacy*? My God, can't you see I'm a fraud?"

As the three of us valiantly wrestle with the awesome business of being alone in the world and being with another, we sometimes get bruised, often get tired, but always, we grow.

It occurs to me (how the obvious does get obscured!) that therein lies the secret of why this work is a no-lose proposition. It's in the very process of working on the integration of these disparate parts that we become more whole. Whether or not we will reach our desired destination is always uncertain. We flourish by taking the journey.

VOLUME II

RUTH LAMPERT'S
FAMILY THERAPY WORKBOOK

*Exercises and Experiments for Working
with Children, Adolescents
and their Families*

VOLUME II

RUTH LAMPERT'S FAMILY THERAPY WORKBOOK

Exercises and Experiments for Working with Children, Adolescents and their Families

INTRODUCTION

Working with families, in all their various permutations, is among the most gratifying avenues the mental health professional can travel.

It can also be frustrating, emotionally draining, and fraught with periods of "I don't know what to do! Help!" Exercises and activities can provide needed relief during these periods, as well as offering dynamic ways to access emotions and providing fresh perspectives.

My training as a Gestalt therapist underlies and informs all my work. My training as a family therapist keeps family dynamics in focus whether I am working at the moment with an individual, a couple, or a family. Those threads provide the basic material of the exercises and activities in this workbook.

I considered arranging the workbook into categories, such as "Self-Esteem," "Expressing Feelings," "SelfCare," and so forth. However, the activities not only overlap categories, they take on different meanings under differing circumstances and times. Approach the book as if it were a buffet table, and decide what dish would nourish you and your client for this particular meal.

If you are metaphor minded, I think you will find rich veins to mine in these pages.

If you are creative, I'm sure these activities will act as a stimulus to your own inventiveness.

In whatever way you use them, I hope they make your work with children, couples, families, groups, and individuals more productive and satisfying.

— Ruth Lampert, M.A., MFCC

MY ARRIVAL

    This exercise, appropriate for children ages about six through ten, is a wonderful way to encourage parent-child interaction.

    I usually start by asking a few questions about what the child knows about how things were in the family when he/she was born or adopted, and then suggest doing an interview (like on television) to "get all the facts." I briefly explain the plan to the parent(s) so that about fifteen minutes can be set aside for quiet, uninterrupted time.

    Kids are usually pleased, and sometimes surprised, to learn how meaningful the event of their birth or adoption was; most parents also enjoy the experience. If the child isn't old enough to write, the adult can be the "secretary."

    It's perfectly OK for a stepparent, foster parent, grandparent, etc., to be the "interviewee" if neither parent is available, or, sadly, willing.

    I have used this exercise with very positive results in individual work, family therapy, group therapy, and classroom settings.

    On the following page is one example of an interview. As always, adapt for the specific purpose as you see fit.

Name_____

Date_____

AN INTERVIEW WITH MY PARENTS ABOUT MY ARRIVAL

1. Mom, how did you feel when:
   (For biological Mother) you were aware labor was starting?
   (For adoptive Mother) you knew I would be coming to you soon?

2. Dad, how did you feel when:
   (For biological Father) labor started and you knew I was on the way?
   (For adoptive Father) you knew I would be coming to you soon?

3. What do you remember about the reaction of other family members or friends when they learned you were expecting me?

4. Is there any special meaning to my name?

5. Please tell me the following about my arrival:
   Arrival time, day of the week, date:
   Where I was born:
   My weight:
   My length:
   Color of my hair:
   Color of my eyes:
6. Mom, how did you feel when you first saw me?

7. Dad, how did you feel when you first saw me?

8. Mom, is there anything else about my arrival that you especially remember?

9. Dad, is there anything else about my arrival that you especially remember?

_____

WHAT'S MY ADJECTIVE?

Hand out three by five cards. Have each family member write down five adjectives that describe him/herself. Some examples: funny; sensitive; gorgeous; anxious; shy; etc etc. Young children can tell you the words, and you write them down.

Collect them, and read aloud one at a time. Family members try to guess who it is. The person who wrote the card needs to "fake it" and pretend to be guessing too — this adds a little fun to the proceedings.

Some things to talk about:

Do others see us as we see ourselves?
Are we shy about using "boastful" adjectives?
Was it hard to think of five descriptive words?
Was it hard to stop at five?

Consider participating yourself. How do you feel about that?

BROWN BAGGING IT

This activity is an excellent way to encourage the awareness of feelings about oneself; the structure allows the participant to decide how much and how soon he/she wishes to share with others.

As with collages and montages, collect in advance a large, diverse number of pictures cut from magazines. Put them in baskets in the middle of the room, with individual bottles of paste or glue (one for each person).

Give a brown paper bag to each member of the family (or the couple, or the group) with these instructions:

"This brown bag represents you . . . your Self. Look through the pictures, and choose some that represent how you feel about yourself INSIDE. Put those pictures inside the bag. You can staple it shut . . . or fold it closed . . . or leave it open. Any way you choose is correct.

"Next, choose pictures that represent how you present yourself on the OUTSIDE. Paste these pictures on the outside of your bag."

Things you will be observing in the process include the degree to which each person honors the privacy of the others; facial expressions and body language as they choose pictures; hesitancy or eager involvement; etc.

When everyone has completed their brown bag, ask what they experienced as they did the choosing, putting inside, and pasting outside; how they felt about others' "secrets;" what new things each person learned about him/herself and the other participants; etc. Usually a lively discussion ensues, often with surprises for everyone, including the therapist.

CHANGES

This sentence completion exercise is easily adaptable for children, families, and couples.

I especially like to use it when there is a great deal of pressure on a person to change in order to satisfy someone else (frequently a parent or a spouse). When used with couples and families, each person fills it out privately, then shares it with everyone present. Their reactions are often the most significant aspects of this activity.

Here is one example that "fits" for most persons, individually and/or in conjoint and family sessions.

The person (people) who is (are) always on my case to change something about myself is [are]:

They think I should change the way I:

I think [name of person(s)] want(s) me to change because:

Actually, there are some things about myself *I'd* like to change, such as:

There are many things about myself that I think are just fine, such as my: and the way I:

When other people try to change me, I feel:

I usually say to them:

What I don't tell them is:

If I don't change at all, I will be a [insert quality here] person, and that will make . . . [insert name(s) here] . . . feel

All in all, I think that the way I am now is:

CINQUAINS

Suggest to the average person the exercise of writing a poem, and the response will probably be a loud groan, accompanied by protestations of no-talent.

Make the suggestion to the average teenage boy, and the reaction will probably be even more strongly negative, possibly verging on panic.

Suggest instead that the individual, family, class, or group experiment with a Cinquain. These are the instructions:

First, a noun is chosen from several possibilities to be the one-word title. You suggest some possibilities the first time around to demonstrate the process. Four good titles to choose from are:

VACATIONS
FAMILIES
FRIENDSHIP
DATING

You'll notice that the degree of emotional intensity of these topics differs; usually the first choice is less intense, such as Vacations.[*]

When the Cinquain is written by more than one person, an exercise in democratic process is a secondary gain. You can vote, take turns, work toward consensus, or. . . . ?

---

[*]   However, students in my psychotherapy classes and professional workshops usually choose "Families;" Sixth graders in my sexuality classes usually choose "Puberty."

The next step is to actually write the Cinquain, and in fact, the first line has already been composed — it is the one-word title, which is a noun.

The second line is two adjectives that describe the noun.

The third line is three verbs that are related to the noun.

The fourth line is a four-word sentence fragment. It cannot be a complete sentence.

The fifth and last line is again one word. It can be a synonym for the title noun, or the first word that comes to mind in connection with the title.

Here are some examples of Cinquains that will give an idea of how they can work out.

●

FAMILIES
FUN NOISY
FIGHTING TALKING
HURRY UP NOW, KIDS
GROWING

●

PUBERTY
SCARY INTERESTING
DATING CRYING GROWING
BODIES CHANGE MINE TOO
WHEN?

●

DIVORCE
LONELY NECESSARY
TALKING TRYING RUNNING
NO FLOWERS ANY MORE
APART

Following a specific structure of grammar and format helps lessen the anxiety of "being creative," and of "opening up," and makes both those processes safer.

Creating the fourth line often takes the longest and carries the most impact. If it proves frustrating, I facilitate by saying: "pretend I am from Mars, and until I came to Earth I never heard this word: (family, or puberty, or whatever). Just tell me what it's about, please. I'll tell you when I hear a possible four-word fragment, and you can decide if you want to use that one, or keep explaining."

For future Cinquains, either in the same session or at a later time, the poet (now called by that name) may well have a number of suggestions, and you can include your own to move toward a therapeutic issue you consider important. For instance, I may include such choices as adoption, pregnancy, unemployment, marriage, arguments, drugs, graduation, and so on through the endless list of human experiences.

CLAPPING

You don't need any kind of musical instrument, or record player, or radio for this exercise in using rhythm as a means of expressing a wide range of feelings. You need only hands and hearts.

If you have already compiled a list of feeling words (see FEELING SILLY) you can draw from them, and/or generate feelings relevant to the moment. Have each particpant (including yourself) draw one and then demonstrate that feeling by clapping.

You can make the game more complex by having the feeling card drawn secretly, with the other person/s guessing what feeling is represented; you can make a tape recording if you have the equipment; you can use your imagination to make up new games.

Whatever you do, at the end give a big round of applause to all the players.

THE CLUB

Remember what clubs were like when you were growing up?

Your answer to that probably depends on many things, such as: Were you included or excluded? What were your special interests? And so forth.

The following sentence-stem activity is useful in helping youngsters become aware of many things about themselves. I usually do it in individual sessions, but it could be adapted for couples or families; and it would be interesting for adults (including the therapist) to speculate on whether things have changed much, club-wise.

I'd like to start a new club, called:

To get into the club, kids would have to:

The decision to accept or reject new members would be made by:

Just to be *considered* for membership, kids would have to be age(s):_____and interested in:

We would definitely not accept (names) or (names) unless they agreed to:

Meetings would be held every:

Dues would be:

We would discuss:

The first president would be:
      Vice-president would be:
      and the other officers would be:

We would hold elections every :

The best place to build the clubhouse would be:

We would paint it the club colors, which are:

The sign outside the door would say:

Our secret club motto/password would be:

The Clubhouse

COLORED SALT–SAND

Many — very many — of the arts-and-crafts exercises used by teachers in all grade levels are easily adaptable for use in counseling and psychotherapy, where the primary importance is the *process*, rather than the *product*. The therapist is primarily interested in *how* the youngster goes about creating, and what happens as a result.

For instance, what is the affect, and how does it change (if it changes) during the process? Is the youngster restrained or freely involved? Is he/she a careful worker, or disorganized, or distracted, or fully engaged, and/or?

The following activity is a departure from my usual approach of not having a specific product in mind at all. It is fine for groups and individuals, and for kids as young as three years. The process is very relaxing; the collecting of pretty jars is something parents can be involved in.

I save the small individual serving jars of apple juice which I always have available in my office. The finished products can be used as paperweights, or "objets d'art" to be given as gifts. With imagination they can become animals or persons to be used in the sand tray. You and the children will think of other uses. Be sure to avoid a sense of competitiveness, or pressure for perfection.

Directions

All that is needed is colored chalk (broken pieces are great) and table salt which can be purchased reasonably in large quantities at discount houses.

Put some salt into a small container such as an empty yogurt cup or margarine tub. Rub a piece of colored chalk into the salt until the chalk disappears and the salt is colored.

Pour the colored salt-sand into small jars or bottles; it can be layered, different colors can be swished around for different effects, etc.

For more vivid colors, powdered tempera paint can be used instead of chalk. However, use care in preparation that the mixture is not inhaled; after adding the paint powder to the salt, close the lid tightly before shaking.

WHAT COLOR DO YOU FEEL?

Children who are relatively nonverbal, either by virtue of their developmental stage or by temperament, enjoy using the following method of identifying their feelings by color. This identification is made not by an "expert," but by the individual child determining which colors represent her/his feelings.

I sometimes start with a chart. With the child's help, I make a list of feelings, with the child drawing "matching" colors next to each word. It's best to start with simple, unambiguous feeling words, such as:

HAPPY
SLEEPY
SAD
ANGRY
PROUD

At this or later sessions add more complex or subtle feeling words, such as:

AMBIVALENT
SERENE
ECSTATIC
ALOOF

I personally think it's fine to use slang words, such as "bummed,"and so-called swear-words, such as "shitty."

In the process of making up this chart, we are talking about feelings in a nonthreatening way, thus gently encouraging the child to be able to label, and honor, a wide range of feeling.

At the beginning of the session I ask, "What color do you feel today?" and the child responds by making a color mark on that day's process notes.

Of course we often have to go over the chart, at least in the beginning, and especially with children who are just learning to read.

The child may choose to talk about the feeling, or may make no response other than the color mark. Either way is perfectly acceptable.

A variation is the following sentence completion exercise:

Colors and feelings often seem to go together. For example, when I see or imagine the color red, I feel:

or sometimes,

If red had a sound, it would sound like:

if it had a taste, it would taste like:

For me, the color blue is like the feeling:

If it had a smell, it would smell like:

I think that for my (parent; teacher; friend; sibling) blue might be like the feeling:

Yellow goes with:

If I could hug yellow, I think it would feel like:

This is a lot like the color :

The color green matches the feeling or feelings: (   ) for me.

The time of year it reminds me of is:

The color that goes with morning is:

The color that goes with evening is:

And so on and so on as far as you want to go. Add sentences and variations.

THE COMEDY HOUR

In addition to being one of the most delightful of human experiences, laughter has benefits including but not limited to stress and anxiety reduction, pain management, and improved digestion. "A sense of humor" or lack of it correlates with abstract and divergent reasoning ability. The class clown should be channeled, not squelched. Here's an activity that can be used with individuals, groups, or in some cases, families:

Tell an ancient joke, such as: "Why did the chicken cross the road?" and have the group generate as many punch lines as possible, such as:

"To flirt with the cute chick who lives there"
"To get to _____(name a favorite local chicken take-out place) before the rest of the flock;"
Etc. etc., as well as the venerable "to get to the other side."

Let the group vote on the funniest punch line, and share more joke beginnings.

Comic strips can be utilized in various ways, such as remediation of some learning difficulties. First, cut a strip into its individual frames, numbering the correct order on the backs, and mix them up.

For practice in sequencing, have the youngster put them in the correct order.

Have him/her deliberately put them in some other order and make up a different story to go with the new strip.

Prepare a set of "balloons" with words,to be matched to the characters instead of the ones in the strip.

Let a young child do the cutting-up to practice with eye-hand skills.

Observing whether the youngster arranges the frames according to a story line, or matches the edges like a puzzle, tells you something about his/her learning style.

DRAW WHAT YOU HEAR

(And Listen to Your Picture)

This is a popular activity for individuals ranging in age from about seven to seventy-eight. The outer reaches of clients I have used it with.) It's easily adaptable for groups and families.

I especially like to use this with "tight," perfectionistic folks; the small amount of structure seems to provide a safe means to experience the freeing effect.

Buy, or tape from the radio, an audiotape with a variety of songs and musical selections. The greater the variety (classical, rock, rap, folk, etc.) the more interesting the results.

Divide a sheet of paper into eight sections. Have plenty of crayons and felt pens available.

The directions are:

"I'm going to play some music. While listening, draw, or scribble, or doodle, anything you like, using any color or colors you choose, in one of the boxes. After about two minutes I'll move ahead to another selection; you will move to another box, and again draw whatever seems to you to fit with the music you are hearing."

It's interesting to experiment a week or two later with bringing out the sheet of "musical pictures" and asking the client if he/she remembers the name, or the melody, that evoked the individual picture. Be careful with this: some people perceive it as a kind of test. Try it with one picture first, and if your client seems to enjoy the process, continue; otherwise, move on to something else.

EGGS HAVE FEELINGS TOO

For this game, which is most fun when played with a small group, you will need a variety of colored plastic take-apart eggs, sold just about everywhere at Easter time, and a variety of small objects that will fit inside each one.

The children assign a feeling equivalent to each color, e.g. yellow = happy; green = proud; orange = angry; blue = frustrated; pink = curious; or whatever. This is written down on a chalkboard, or large sheet of paper, visible to all.

With eyes closed, each child in turn chooses an egg from a basket, and then talks about the feeling represented by the color of the chosen egg. If all agree the response is "egg worthy," the youngster opens the egg and takes the prize. Any honest response is "egg worthy."

Some small objects that fit inside these eggs are nuts or small candies; inexpensive rings or charms; stickers and gummed stars; quarters; micro-machines; unusual marbles; whatever you can find.

THE FAMILY BANK

     The Dow goes up, the Dow goes down. Does anybody put money in the bank anymore? The Family Bank is the depository of assets even more valuable than money, such as affection, trust, support, understanding and shared history. Here are some banking matters to be considered:

Who makes deposits?

Who makes withdrawals?

Who keeps the records?

What happens if there is an overdraft?

How late is the bank open?

Is it insured?

What happens if it fails?

What if there is a merger?

Does everyone have a passbook?

Can everyone reach the ATM machine?

Draw a picture of it.

FAMILY BULLETIN BOARDS

Keeping the family members involved in the therapy process between sessions; adding to the interest and pleasure in that process; encouraging their creativity as a problem solving intervention; increasing awareness of their individual and family personalities — these are some of the benefits of family bulletin boards.

As "homework" after the first or second family session, assign the family the task of making a family bulletin board and placing it in a room where the whole family congregates, such as the kitchen or family room.

If space permits, the board should measure about 3 feet by 5 feet. Larger is fine; smaller OK if space is limited.

Say that the purpose of the board will be discussed at the next session. (Obviously this creates a therapeutic double-bind, since if they "disobey" you and decide among them how they want to use it, they will have communicated and bonded.)

At the next session, explore the process with the family, asking:

How did you decide who would be in charge of making or buying the board?
How did you decide where it would be hung?
Was everyone satisfied with that decision?
How long did the process take?

As with all exercises, it is important that the family members (and you) are absolutely clear that there are no right or wrong answers, and the purpose of asking the questions is to facilitate growing awareness and *not* to analyze.

Here are some ideas for what can go on the Family Bulletin Board. You and your clients will think of more.

Family Sculptures

Using Virginia Satir's sculpting exercise, have each member in turn (not necessarily in the same session) position the family in the way he/she would most like it to be.

Take a Polaroid photograph of each sculpture. After talking about the experience, give the family the photograph.

Choosing the person you actually hand the photograph to can depend on many factors. For example:

• Hand it to the youngest child, or the one considered inadequate or unworthy, as a silent message that this person can handle responsibility.

• Put it on a table without indicating who will take it; note who remembers at the end of the session, and who takes it.

• If Dad is seen (by you, the other family members, or himself) as an "absent father," hand it to him.

Having all the photographs displayed in one place is a vivid (and often touching) presentation of the many ways a family can be.

You may want to also take photographs for yourself to keep in the family's file for future reference.

Cartoon of the Week

Family members take turns selecting cartoons for the Bulletin Board. (My personal favorite sources are "Calvin and Hobbes,"[now retired, but available in anthologies], "For Better or for Worse," "Jump-Start," "Zits," "Agnes," "Shirley & Son," and "Committed.")

Humor reminds us of the universality of many of those trials and tribulations we think of as our exclusive miseries. There may be veiled hostility in humor; the therapist can safely midwife anger into constructive being. And a hearty laugh helps promote physical and emotional well-being (See "The Comedy Hour").

TRADITIONS AND RITUALS

This is especially useful for stepfamilies, where the loss of former traditions and rituals is a significant but often unrecognized source of pain. In addition to dealing with the loss of the old, family therapy can help the rebuilding process by gently encouraging new traditions and rituals for this new blended family, such as:

Trophy Display

Giving awards and certificates to be placed on the Bulletin Board. Some my clients have shared include:

From one sibling to another: "In recognition of leaving my stuff alone for three whole weeks. Keep up the good work."

From husband to wife: "In appreciation of your being supportive of my going to visit my sister — who you dislike — to be polite about it."

From wife to husband: "In appreciation of your understanding that I needed to work long hours last week, requiring that you do much more than your share of household chores."

From a parent to a child: "In recognition of your improved grades this semester in two important subjects, after I said you were too lazy to try. Sorry, and mazeltov."

From a child to a parent: "In appreciation of your not freaking out when I *slightly* dented the fender."

Using this method, verbal strokes that are shared during sessions can be put into certificates at home, and certificates granted during the week can be discussed in session, thus doubling the shelf-life of good feelings.

The Memory Board

Mount photographs and/or mementos of pleasurable family activities — and *only* those which all members agree they remember with pleasure! This activity has the useful side-benefit of encouraging honest communication. (How many times have you heard a parent describe an activity as having been "beautiful," etc., while the youngster has privately told you "I hated every minute of it but didn't want to hurt their feelings"?

THE FAMILY STORY

Use as many of the following sentences as there are family members; add more or make changes as necessary for the particular family.

Put each sentence on a three by five index card and have family members pick from a hat.

When everyone has completed their sentence, collect them and, in numerical order, read the completed story. It's best to use this exercise when all children are old enough to write; if only one cannot, you can privately read the question and write the answer. It gets confusing if there are several young pre-literate kids.

1. Families can really be:

2. If I didn't have a family, I would:

3. Some families seem to think that:

4. What most families need to learn is that:

5. One thing a family should always do is:

6. If this family were a television show, it would be called:

After the story is read, I sometimes ask members to guess who wrote what. Be careful, though; highly critical parents may use that information against the child, labeling the response "stupid" or "silly," etc.

I type the completed story and give a printout to be kept on the family bulletin board.

FEELING SILLY

I began doing this activity many years ago, first using three by five cards, and then a chalkboard. Although I still use those low-tech methods, I have added a computer to my resources. Whichever method you use, begin by generating, with the youngster's participation, a long list of "feeling words," such as:

happy.........sad.........embarrassed.......delighted........sleepy........ bummed........thrilled........relaxed........bored........uptight........ grossed out........and so on.

The advantage to having the words on individual three by five cards, or on the computer, is that the list can be saved for future reference.

Next, compose a sentence stem, with four choices of feeling words to complete it. For example:

Jason finally got the bike he had been wanting for three years. He felt:

SLEEPY HAPPY MISERABLE FRUSTRATED

The youngster then deletes on the computer, or puts back in the pile of three by fives, or erases from the chalkboard, words that "don't fit," i.e., "sleepy," "miserable," and "frustrated." Now the sentence would read:

Jason finally got the bike he had been wanting for three years. He felt happy.

That makes good sense . . . which isn't what we are after in this activity. We are looking for non-sense. So the next step is to again write a sentence, this time with all *logical* choices to be deleted/put back/erased, so that we will end up with a silly sentence.

For example:

Mary wanted to stay overnight at her favorite aunt's house but her aunt invited her older sister instead.

Mary felt:

ANGRY   DISAPPOINTED   JEALOUS   POWERFUL

After getting rid of the logical words, the silly sentence will read:

"Mary wanted to stay overnight at her favorite aunt's house but her aunt invited her older sister instead. Mary felt powerful."

The silliness provides some distance from the emotionally charged issue of sibling rivalry, and opens up avenues for discussion (if the child so wishes.)

The next step in this game is for the child to make up a sentence stem, with possible conclusions, for you the therapist. Now, the youngster can consider various emotions, their good or bad fit to the situation, and have the fun of watching you struggle with, and hear you express, concerns that he/she may have had but needed to avoid.

For example, here are some stems kids have put on the computer for me to complete:

Steven's parents made him give away his cat because his little sister is supposedly allergic to everything in the world, including cats. Steven felt:

TERRIFIC   AWFUL   BUMMED OUT   NOTHING

There was this really cute guy and Nicole really liked him and she thought he liked her friend but it turned out he liked her. Nicole felt:

FANTASTIC   LONELY   FRUSTRATED   AWESOME

Her friend felt:

HAPPY   JEALOUS   PISSED   BORED

Ruth was driving too fast and she got a ticket — again. She felt:

PROUD   STUPID   MAD   DELIGHTED

TO FORGIVE

This sentence completion exercise is especially useful in working with couples who wish to improve their relationship, and/or to reconcile after a separation. I use it also in premarital counseling.

Note that all the sentence stems are "I" or "me" statements. It is possible to convert some of them to "accusatory you" statements; for example, #3, "I find it easier to forgive when" *could* be answered *"he* hasn't been acting so mean and stingy." Therefore, your instructions should be: "your completion should only refer to yourself, and not to your husband (girlfriend, fiancee, etc.)."

Of course, this instruction will sometimes be ignored . . . challenging your expertise even more.

1. To me, forgiving means . . .

2. Forgiving is hard for me when . . .

3. I find it easier to forgive when . . .

4. To be forgiven makes me feel . . .

5. I first learned about forgiving when . . .

6. What I don't understand about forgiving is . . .

7 The most forgiving person I have ever known is . . .

8. Forgiving myself is . . .

HOW TO BE A CRAZY MAKER

This all started when a youngster began telling me all the ways she knew to bug her mom. We made a list, which included:

— When she says "Sit down young lady" I plunk down in the middle of the floor and when she hollers about that I say innocently: "You didn't say to sit on a CHAIR."

— When I brush my hair I leave a really big wad of hair in the brush.

— When I do something I know I shouldn't do and she hollers "I did NOT give you permission to do that," I say sweetly "But you never said I COULDN'T."

Turning this into a family exercise provides laughter and insight. Give everyone a chance to tell ways they know to drive others crazy, such as:

"The easiest way to bug my brother is borrow his stuff without asking. "

"It's so easy to get a rise out of my daughter — I just put classical music on the radio."

"Leaving my socks laying around works on my wife, especially if she has had a hard day at work."

You can include teachers in the target list. And don't forget to invite instructions on "How to Drive My/Our Therapist Crazy."

LADIES WHO LUNCH

This is a nice activity to use with little girls labeled "rude," "rowdy," "disruptive." From a small decorated chest I take a pretty china service (it looks more expensive than it actually is). I explain that we are going to have a pretend fancy luncheon (or tea party) and we must be on our best behavior. No grabbing or pushing or shoving. Lots of "please"s and "thank you"s.

"Whom do you wish to invite?" I ask, in my best British accent. Guests are chosen from among the dolls and stuffed animals in the room; names are made up, or chosen to represent real people: we talk about the reasons for inclusion or rejection and what the unchosen would have to do to be invited. Her decisions and reasons are honored, and are grist for the therapy mill.

We write invitations on pretty paper, or call on the toy phone. We might create a recipe and/or think about appropriate attire for this special occasion.

By demonstrating that she is valued, respected and deserving of the finest, she is encouraged to respect and value others, and to enjoy doing so. At the same time she is permitted to express honest feelings about others, such as: "Allie will never be invited; she's mean, and makes fun of me because I live in the trailer park;" "Maybe next time Mattie can come if she learns to not hit." and so forth.

LET THE GAMES EXPAND

Standard board games offer many opportunities for creative adaptations and therapeutic extras.

For example, with "Concentration" (sometimes called "Memory") with picture cards you can:

•Note the child's preferred arrangement of cards(haphazard or ordered) as clues to learning process.

•Note the developmental level of strategies used, and model effective ones.

•Use the opportunity for naming concepts such as colors, shapes, etc according to the child's developmental level.

•At the end of the game add a "Gestalt Spin" by utilizing the picture cards for a story telling exercise which provides practice in sequencing, expressive language, vocabulary, and divergent thinking, and also provides a vehicle to deal with social/emotional issues.

•Some games are grown from the therapeutic issues. I call these "Organic Games."

For example, one ten-year-old had the idea to make a game she called "To the Rescue." On a piece of cardboard she drew paths going to and from a "scene of disaster," including a fire, an automobile wreck, and an earthquake. (My office is in Los Angeles).

We color coded the markers from another game as green for ambulance, red for police car, and blue for helicopter. Players chose their markers from a hat, and the throw of the dice determined the number of moves to make. Along the route were squares with typical instructions such as "go forward two spaces," "out of gas, go back one space" etc.

The winner was the vehicle first completing the trip to and from the disaster bringing the injured back to "hospital."

Conversation was about the factors of luck, time, available rescuers, and other splendid metaphors.

Some common issues emerging from the therapy which can be utilized are debt; moving day; dating. It will quickly become apparent that whether or how often the game is actually played is not as important as the process of creating it.

Once when a board game was started near the end of the session I speeded up the process by multiplying each throw of the dice by two. Voila! An educational side benefit. Now I sometimes suggest multiplying by larger numbers, or by adding or multiplying the number of one die against the other.

THE LONG AND SHORT OF IT

The detailed, circumstantial verbal style of adult clients we label obsessive-compulsive is often apparent in children at an early age. The anxiety caused by the possibility of leaving something out is reduced by including more than the reader or listener needs or wants to know, at the expense of being tiresome.

When I hear kids getting anxiously bogged down in the details of their stories (whether Children's Apperception Test responses, Gestalt Story Starters, or whatever) I suggest (with a smile) that we experiment with *really* omitting nothing, making *absolutely* sure that the reader is informed of *everything.*

For example, the child begins a story, "What We Found at the Beach":

"Saturday morning my sister and I decided to go to the beach." I interrupt: "Wait, wait! What *time* Saturday morning?"

"It was 9:30."

"Exactly?"

"Yes! So my mom drove us there . . . "

"Wait, wait! Did you just jump out of bed and into the car? Aren't you leaving something out?"

"We had breakfast first . . . "

"Did you eat in your pajamas or get dressed first?"

"We got dressed and then we ate break . . . ."

"You mean to say you didn't brush your teeth first? Or pee?"

By this point I am getting some reactions from the story teller, such as:

Laughter.

"I want to get to the part where we found the wallet!"

"They don't need to know all that, Ruth!"

"This is getting really boring."

Enough said.

One variation is the short long story, useful for the youngster who rushes through everything:

"Last Saturday my sister and I decided to go the beach . . . "

Interruption: "Never mind all that, just tell me you found a wallet!"

"But that isn't the whole story, there's the part about our exploring the cave, and me falling down, and . . . ."

Point made.

And for the tangential teller: "Last Saturday my sister and I decided to go to the beach . . . "

Interruption: "Didn't you have a fight last week with your sister, and she said you were a pile of poop, and she wasn't going to talk to you ever again, so how come you were talking to her Saturday, what happened, did you make up — like the last time when you had a fight about her borrowing your clothes, which she has been doing since you were three . . . .?"

"Yeah, yeah, but that doesn't having anything to do with this story and now I forgot how it goes!"

Yes indeed.

It is important that you come across not as mocking, but rather as playful, perhaps affectionately teasing, and in fact laughing at yourself for being so ridiculous.

MARTIANS

This activity is appropriate for children from about six to 11 years old.

A good beginning is to "wonder" if indeed there is life on Mars (you may prefer a different planet) and if so, what the people there might be like. Go on to speculate about issues in the life of the child you are working with, e.g.:

> "Do you suppose they have brothers and sisters?"
> "How do they get along?"
> "Do Martians ever go to therapy?"
> "Do Martians have birthday parties?"

and so forth.

Suggest that the child write a letter(or e-mail) to his/her Martian "counterpart;" offer sentence stems, with the child making the completion. When appropriate, the child can dictate his/her answer for you to write in; you or the child can use a computer if available. I also have an imaginary fax machine in my office.

On the next page is an example of a "Letter to a Martian Pen Pal;" add, delete, revise as seems right for the individual child.

Frequently I ask the child to write back as the Martian; as with all projective activities, this is usually highly imaginative, and safely revealing.

A sample letter is on the next page:

Dear Martian Pen Pal,

Do you have to go to school? I do, and I think it is:

My teacher reminds me of:

The smartest person in my class is

The one who has the most trouble is:

We have to go to school for at least 12 years. I think that plan is:

If it were up to me, school would start at:

and end at:

The rule about vacations would be:

To get to be a teacher, a person would have to:

Every class would:

Report cards would:

Please write soon and tell me all about school on Mars.

Your friend from Earth,

MUSIC HATH CHARMS

And not just to soothe the savage breast. It has the ability to promote relaxation and "loosening up" and to improve concentration and imagination. With a small, inexpensive piano keyboard (mine cost ten dollars at a chain electronic store) you can :

Do a variation of the exercise "Draw What you Hear."

Use it as a prop in "Today's Famous Guest is:"

Compose a theme song for the session.

Just have it available in individual, group, and family sessions for whatever uses emerge.

MY NAME FEELS

This activity is simple, fun, and an effective "loosener." The ability to print or write is the only skill necessary.

If you and your client have already compiled a list of feeling words (see the exercise: FEELING SILLY) you can draw from them, and/or you can generate feelings relevant to the moment.

The instruction is:
Write your name as if it were feeling: (silly, sad, tired, etc.).

Now write it as: (another feeling) and so on for anywhere from five to ten renditions.

Below is an example of some of the ways my name can feel:

RUTH (strong)

Ruth (silly)

RUTH (nervous)

Truth (confused)

Ruth (shy)

NEW STORE IN TOWN

I was working with a depressed fourteen-year-old who simply could not think of anything good to say about herself. One day we got into a conversation about a new mall opening nearby. The metaphor presented itself, and I have used it in a variety of ways ever since.

This can be used in individual sessions with a child, or in family counseling. It can be a drawing, or a collage.

The instruction is:

Pretend that you (or your family) is opening a new store. Create the advertising copy and artwork by informing the public all about the new store, using both pictures and words.

Be sure to include:

The name of the new store.

The owner/owners.

Location, including any branches.

Specialty. Indicate such things as small boutique, department store, etc.

Date of the grand opening.

Special attractive features, such as "All major credit cards accepted;" "Open seven days a week;" etc.

If positions are still open, indicate what they are and what makes this store a good place to work.

In other words — by word and picture — "sell" your store to the public in such a way they will want to come in.

THE FANTASY ORGANIZER

Most youngsters are urged at least sometime in their lives by parents and teachers to "get organized," usually in the service of completing and turning in homework promptly. This is a laudable goal. However, in therapy an issue being nagged about can sometimes be slyly transformed into an expression of personal issues important to the youngster, though not necessarily to the adults in his/her life.

There can be a fascinating paradoxical result when the youngster enjoys the control and the expression of fantasies, and without any direct pressure, also makes progress in the direction of the "acceptable" goal, e.g., prompt completion and return of homework.

I use it mostly with adolescents.

Give the youngster an inexpensive appointment book with the instruction to "organize" his/her wishes and fantasies by entering them into the book as though they are actually going to happen.

The reminders can be somewhat terse, or explicit as to where, when, with whom, and other pertinent information such as what will be worn, who else needs to be notified, etc.

Here are some entries from some "organizers":

JULIE, age twelve:
January 3: Audition for lead role in new musical.
February 14: Begin rehearsals.
December 25: Open on Broadway.

JASON, age fourteen:
May 1:   Get Susie's phone number from Jennifer.

May 2: Call Susie.

May 3: Call Mike, tell him you talked to Susie and ask advice about what to do next.

MOLLY, age sixteen:

September 4: Write to birth mother.

September 30: Make plane reservations to meet her as per her response.

October 7: Shop for clothes for trip. Ask Heather to come with me.

October 12: Have lunch with Mom at Veggie Cafe to make sure she really is O.K. with my meeting birth mother. Tell her I will call her by first name, not "Mom."
Wear blue sweater and leggings Mom got me for birthday.
Go to movie with Heather in evening to tell her what happened.

PERFECT CHILD/PERFECT PARENTS

This guided fantasy is especially useful when parents bring their child to be "fixed," and don't really expect to be part of the family therapy process themselves.

Use any guided fantasy or relaxation opening (see "RELAX"). You can start with either the parents or the child; explain that each generation will have a turn, and all will discuss the experiences.

Here is the parental script:

"You know your child better than anyone else in the whole world . . . so now, sitting comfortably, let your eyes close . . . let your mind wander . . . think of what (child's name) would be like —both of you, Mom and Dad, imagine this, if you will — imagine him/her at his/her best . . . imagine him/her at home first . . . place your fantasy in v-e-r-y slow motion . . . really get into this . . . let yourself know how you feel with such a good kid . . . stay with your good feelings for a little while . . . enjoy them . . . give yourself permission to get into this . . . you know nothing need interrupt this fantasy."

Afterward, discuss the fantasy. If the parents say they can't imagine this, ask them to go back in time to the days before the problem which brought them here. When they agree on a time when things were o.k, encourage them to relive that time. For example, if the child is currently skipping school, parents may remember a time when he/she was happy to attend.

"All those memories are stored in your mind . . . .isn't that amazing . . . you can bring them back to life just by relaxing for a moment and letting yourselves go back in time to those days . . . get in touch with the feelings you had then about your child . . . those feelings are still there, in your memory file . . . you can bring them back to life now, and enjoy them now, once again . . . you can be there as if you had gone back in time."

If the parents say the child was *never* good, ask them to imagine how good he/she *could* be. They may realize that their expectations are unreasonable, or that they need to be more consistent, or cooperative, or?

Next, do the exercise with the child. Ask him/her to pretend, to imagine, that his/her parents are just right, the best possible parents in the world, etc.

In the follow-up discussion, ask each to describe the experience, and what they discovered about themselves, about each other.

Surprisingly often the child becomes quite realistic, recognizing parental limitations and realizing his/her own responsibility. For example "I imagined they trusted me more, and I would like that, but if I didn't stay away from home without letting them know where I was, it would help."

SUPER SURPRISE PARTY

As a therapist, you probably do a lot of self-esteem work with your clients. When family members learn to do this for one another, they will be on the road to a more satisfying family life. However, it can be frustrating to encourage this practice, as there is a tendency for negative mind-sets to take over.[*]

Begin this exercise by putting slips of paper bearing each family member's name in a basket, and then having everyone draw a name.

The instructions are to plan a surprise party for the person whose name you have drawn in order to honor something special about that person. For instance, a party could be given in honor of Mary's handwriting; or Jim's patience; or Mom's great back rubs; or Dad's help with homework; etc. etc. The party *cannot* be in honor of an event usually noted, such as retirement, birthdays, anniversaries, graduation, sports achievement, etc.

The party plans should include:
> A guest list
> Where the party will be held
> The hours it will last
> The color scheme
> What music should be played
> Who will be the host/hostess?
> Who will be in charge of the clean-up? (*Not* the guest of honor!)

---

[*] For example, I once asked a critical father to watch carefully during the week for something his son did that was praise worthy, and to report that at the next family meeting. Here is what the father said in praise of his son:

"We went out for dinner last Sunday, and his table manners weren't quite as disgusting as they usually are."

Allow about ten minutes before collecting the plans. To be sure that everything about the party *honors* the person, explain that you are the "professional organizer" and will look over the plans and makes any necessary changes before giving your approval.

When you are satisfied that each person will be sincerely honored, distribute the plans to the honoree to be read and shared.

I like to put in my two-cents worth at the end of the reading and ask, "Since this is a surprise party, what do you think you will be wearing when you arrive? What will you say?"

WORLD'S BEST PIZZA
(OR SOUP....OR STEW ....
OR SANDWICH....OR....)

I usually use this with individual children, but it can easily be adapted to use in family or group sessions. The "restaurant" could be for a single specialty; full service; a franchised chain; or ???

To make the world's best pizza, I would start with

Then I would add a little

      a lot of

      and some

Depending on what was in the refrigerator,
      I might decide to add

      or

      or even

If I didn't want to make it by myself, I would ask...........to help me. I would *not* want.............to be involved.

I'd probably make enough to serve (#) people.

I could make it for (name(s))'s party, or I could bring it to

Maybe I would go into business and open a pizza restaurant. I would call it .... and I would advertise the World's Best Pizza. Maybe my picture would be in the ads.

People who ate it would say:

      Some might even say:

When they asked me for my recipe, I would reply:

My first month in business, I would make . . . $

If I decided to sell the restaurant, I would ask . . . $

I think I would stay in the business until:

FEELING PROUD

The concept of "improved self-esteem" has become something of an article of faith in therapy. Simply heaping praise on kids for anything and everything isn't very effective; as they learn to experience realistic self-pride, for realistic achievements, self-esteem becomes more than a catchword.

This exercise is good for kids up to about age ten, and lends itself to variations for adolescents, especially in groups.

The things that make me proud of myself are:

and

and sometimes even:

At school I felt proud when I was able to:

One of my proudest moments at home was when:

My friend (...name...) is proud of me when:

My teacher is proud of me when:

My mother/father is/are proud of me when:

A time when everyone thought I would be proud of myself but I wasn't was when:

I wasn't proud because:

When I am a grown-up, I will say "Good for you!" to children when:

or when:

or maybe when:

When I feel proud of myself, it's as though the weather had:

Then I feel as though I could:

and even . . .

THE FAMILY PUZZLE

This activity is a powerful way for family members to increase their awareness of their individual, and group, dynamics when involved in problem solving through cooperation.

Five or more people are necessary; if there are four family or group members, the therapist can be the fifth.

If there are more than five family or group members, the "extra" members are to silently observe. They may not comment, hint, or help in any way, verbally or otherwise.

If the therapist is the fifth player, he/she plays as though it were the first time — which, as you will see when you try this exercise, isn't terribly difficult!

You will need five envelopes, marked one through five, each to contain pieces of cardboard cut into patterns forming six inch squares, as shown below. Cut the squares into parts, lightly penciling them "a" through "j" as noted. Distribute the pieces into the marked envelopes as follows:

> Envelope 1 - j, h, e
> Envelope 2 - a, a, a,c
> Envelope 3 - a, i
> Envelope 4 - d, f
> Envelope 5 - g, b, f, c

Write the envelope numbers on the pieces, erasing the penciled letters. This will allow the pieces to be returned to the envelopes after the game is finished.

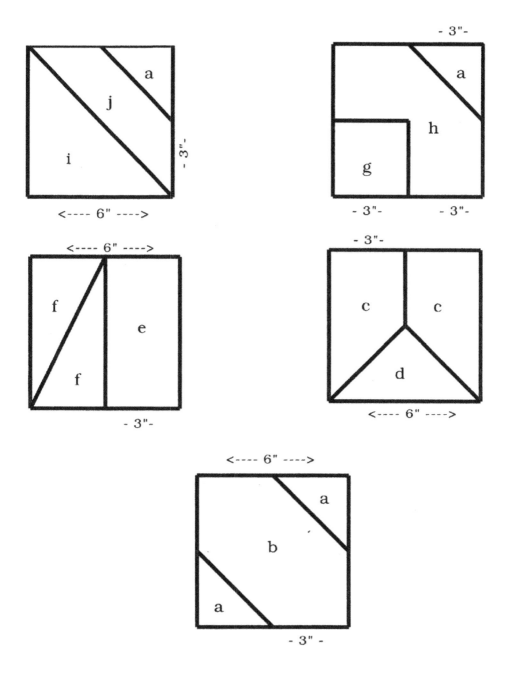

Instruct the players to take out the contents of the envelope when you give the signal. The task is to form five squares of equal size. The task is not complete until each person has constructed a perfect square, and all squares are the same size. (Note that several combinations of the pieces will form one or two squares, but only one combination will form five squares.)

The rules are:
No one may speak.
No one may signal in any way that he/she wants a certain card.
Anyone may give a card to anyone else.

At some point the therapist will have the uneasy feeling that something has gone wrong. . . . that in fact this task cannot be completed. (The players think that from the beginning.) I have observed/participated in this exercise countless times; each time I become convinced, at some point, that I actually lost one of the pieces.

When the task is completed (as it will be!) everyone, including the observers, shares what was experienced in the process. Some typical responses are:

"I figured out what we needed to do, and wanted to take over and get the job done already!"
"I felt stupid . . . I thought I was the one who was keeping back the others."
"It was hard to just watch, and not participate."
"It was really a challenge. I enjoyed it."
"I was surprised that we seemed to catch on quickly."

My reaction the first time I played was: "This is a game for engineers. It's like geometry. I hate this. When will it end?"

RELAX

When everyone in the family is intense and overactive.

When intellectualizing and talking . . . talking . . . talking is turning the session into an exercise in going nowhere.

When family members have had to rush even more than usual to make the appointment after answering urgent phone calls at the office just at quitting time, or after a soccer game that ran late, or a traffic jams on the freeway, or a plumber who showed up late to fix the overflowing toilet . . .

Instead of proceeding with the agenda, try having the family do one of the following five-to-ten minute stress-reduction exercises before proceeding with the session.

The simple fact of everyone doing something *relaxing* together is in itself a curative experience.

I sometimes follow the exercise with a discussion of what other activities the family does together that are of a quiet, meditative nature. (Watching TV doesn't count!) Some responses have been prayer and church or synagogue attendance, family walks, and sitting around the fire before bedtime on camping trips. It is significant how few activities actually fall into this category.

A variation is to ask the members to jot down what they think are the issues for the session before beginning the stress-reduction exercise, and then again after the exercise.

Following are some simple relaxation exercises you can use. You might also want to play portions of relaxation audiotapes.

Stress-reduction exercises are also helpful for the therapist at the end of a long day, which is frequently when family sessions are scheduled.

Basic Relaxation

Begin by closing your eyes . . . notice how cool and comfortable they feel . . . relax all around your eyes . . . .let your forehead become soft . . . smooth . . . feel the relaxation spread across your cheeks . . . and nose . . . relaxing around your mouth . . . relaxing your jaw . . . maybe you'll want to swallow . . . maybe not . . . it's not important . . . let your scalp . . . and your ears . . . and all of your face and head relax . . .

Relax the muscles of your neck . . . maybe you'll feel a tingling down the back of the neck . . . maybe not . . . it doesn't matter . . .

Feel yourself relaxing across your shoulders . . . and down your right arm . . . and down your left arm . . . your wrists relax . . . your hands let go . . . maybe one arm is more relaxed than the other . . . that's fine . . . it really doesn't matter . . . all that matters is the relaxation . . . feel it move down your back . . . from the upper back . . . to the middle back . . . to the lower back . . . to the buttocks . . . everything so relaxed . . .

Let go of the muscles of your chest . . . let go of the muscles of your abdomen . . . feel all the muscles of your abdomen relax and let go . . . you are more and more comfortable . . .

Relax from the hips . . . down the left leg . . . down the right leg . . . letting the thighs relax . . . and the knees . . .

and the calves.. .and the ankles . . . the feet . . . the toes . . .
as you let comfort and relaxation smooth over . . . all that
matters . . . is the endless comfort . . . .

Now you have let your whole body be relaxed and
comfortable . . . your head . . . the trunk of your body . . .
your arms . . . legs . . . all the organs of the body . . . even the
heart . . . as the mind..and the body . . . work together to
bring you relaxation . . . and comfort.

Relaxing Imagery

"Well, here you are, relaxing in just the way you most
like . . . Knowing that you don't have to keep your eyes open,
it's o.k. to let them close . . . and this seems like a good time
. . . to take a trip in your imagination . . . to a lovely place you
really like . . . . . . warm and sunny . . . the ocean . . . or
maybe a quiet lake . . . or a meadow . . . whatever appeals to
you . . . perhaps there's a rose garden nearby . . . it smells so
nice . . . and you can hear lots of pleasant things, too . . .
maybe your favorite music . . . clouds are drifting overhead
. . . there's a gentle breeze . . . the breeze sounds as though
it's dancing in the trees, making sweet little swishing sounds
. . . it's so wonderful just being there . . . and you know that
any time you see . . . or smell . . . or hear anything that
wouldn't be good for you, you'll know exactly what to do to
take good care of yourself . . . and all the wonderful things

you see . . . And feel . . . and smell . . . and hear . . . seem even more delightful than usual . . . and maybe you've decided to be alone in this lovely special place . . . or maybe you want company . . . That's easy too . . . people are right across that little path there, any time you want to see them . . . either way . . . at this time . . . it's so restful . . . and quiet . . . and comfortable . . . to just relax and think whatever you want to think . . . .

And you know you can come to this wonderful place any time you want to . . . it's your special place . . . you can always add anything or anyone to it you want . . . and if you don't like something you can just send it faaaar away . . . you can give yourself any suggestions you like that will make you feel good and strong . . .

My suggestion now is . . . that in a moment or two now . . . you'll come back to this room . . . and . . . you'll remember whatever it helps to remember of this fantasy trip . . . and now you're ready to come back . . . And stretch your legs a little . . . and move your fingers about . . . And you're probably noticing the sound of my voice . . . as you come back . . . to this time and place . . . feeling refreshed . . . And wide awake . . . and feeling great . . . full of serene energy.

Brick Pile

Let yourself be comfortable . . . take a few easy, natural breaths . . . and as you relax comfortably . . . take a moment to think about all your concerns and worries . . . all the things you will need to do this coming week . . . all the errands you'll need to run . . . the homework assignments you'll have to finish . . . the chores you'll be expected to do . . . the deadlines you'll need to meet . . . and now . . . as you think about all these concerns . . . let yourself feel their weight . . . like a huge stack of bricks . . . bricks are good things to have when you are building . . . and . . . . .you don't need to carry them with you . . . all the time . . . you don't need them right now . . . so think about each task and take a brick off your shoulders . . . and little by little . . . build a stack . . . each time you think of another chore . . . another responsibility . . . place it on the stack . . . as the stack becomes larger and heavier . . . your mind feels more and more free . . . and relieved . . . each time you think of an appointment . . . or an assignment . . . place another brick on the stack . . . watch the stack become larger . . . and . . . higher . . . . .heavier . . . each time you think of another task place another brick on the stack . . . watching it become larger and heavier. ..feeling yourself becoming more . . . and more . . . relieved . . . piling up the bricks one by one . . . taking the weight of those responsibilities off your shoulders . . . laying them aside for right now . . . feeling free . . . feeling relaxed.

STORY STARTERS

I first used story starters in my work as an educational therapist. This method of giving youngsters a "start" to read, write, and use their imagination is a wonderful way to integrate the cognitive and affective domains of learning. After training as a Gestalt psychotherapist, I continued to use story starters, but with an added twist.

Story starter activities are sold at educational supply stores, and/or you can make your own. All you need is 8 ½ by 11 sheets of sturdy paper or cardboard; a variety of pictures cut from magazines, or, if you have artistic ability, hand-drawn; and some creativity. (If you supply the first, kids can help with the second and third.)

Under the picture are a few open-ended sentences to "get started." For example, you might have a picture of a wall and/or the title: "The Mysterious Wall." Here are the sentences:

"You pass this wall on your way to school every day. Today, you notice there is a door in it, which is partially open. You walk through the door. What do you find on the other side of the door?"

Another example:

The Dream Store

"You go to the mall to shop and hang out with some friends. You see a new store, with a sign "Make Your Dreams Come True, Inc." You go inside. Who is in the store? What is being sold? What do you do?"

The Gestalt therapy twist comes after the story is completed. Choose one character or object in the child's story, and ask that the story be told again from the point of view of that character or object. It helps to give a starter here too, i.e., "I am the bear in the story. Here is what happened" or "I am the sign on the store . . . ." And so forth.

It is this twist that brings forth rich and revealing projections. You will also note that the pictures aren't really necessary for the activity, especially with adolescents.

In psychotherapy sessions I usually have the younger kids dictate their story to me, as I want to encourage their free flow of ideas and feelings without being concerned about handwriting, grammar, or spelling. If kids are adept with a word processor, they do their own.

Here are more suggestions for evocative beginnings.

The Garage Sale
You are helping your grandparents prepare for a yard sale. In the garage, you come across an old trunk, hidden from view by boards and tools. You open the trunk. What do you find?

Animal Conversations
You awake one morning to hear your cat meowing, and realize you can understand cat language. You soon discover you can also understand, and speak, the language of any animal. What do you say and what do you hear?

The Magic Garden
Imagine you are a flower growing in a magic garden. What kind of flower are you? Describe yourself and your life in the garden.

The Mysterious Tunnel
While on a hiking trip with your family, you see the opening of a tunnel in the mountain. What happens when you go through the tunnel?

A Dream Come True
One night you have an incredibly wonderful dream. You awake in the morning to discover your dream has come true. What is the dream? How does your life change?

SUDS

No, it isn't the laundry list!

"SUDS" is the acronym for "Subjective Units of Distress," a way of measuring the amount of stress caused by events that range from annoying to devastating. Each person has a unique hierarchy; an important aspect of stress reduction is creating a list of stressors and assigning "SUDS" ranging from 1 to 100 in units of 5.

Thus, for one individual the lowest ranking stressful situation might be "missing a bus," with a SUDS of 5, with the highest SUDS, 100, going to "giving an oral presentation."

This variation of subjective perception between couples and/or family members can be a significant, but overlooked, cause of tension. Once so identified, tension begins to lessen.

In family therapy sessions all members work together on making up a list of stressors. If this proves to be slow going, you can suggest some common examples from everyday life, such as being put "on hold" on the telephone; not having quarters for the parking meter; meeting deadlines; entertaining friends; having out-of-town-guests; going to the dentist; having a spouse go out of town on business; having to go out of town yourself on business; and so on, drawing from your knowledge of this family.

During the time between sessions, make enough copies of the completed list to go around, and prepare a chart for each:

RANK	ITEM	SUDS
1		5
2		10
3		15
4		20
(up to 20)		(up to 100)

In session, each family member independently completes the hierarchy chart. Sharing the results may evoke surprise, laughter, and hopefully, conversation and contact.

Well, maybe it *is* a laundry list at that.

TALKING SQUIGGLES

This is a favorite even among reality-bound kids who resist most imaginative activities.

Therapist and client take turns. The first player quickly scrawls a scribble; the other turns it into an object or creature. Then the first player gives that object or creature words.

In the following examples, created by Ruth and Sandy, the dotted lines represent the original squiggle (in actuality the lines are unbroken) the unbroken lines represent the completion, and the attributed words are in a balloon. We put our initials on the side to represent the order of starter, completer, and speaker.

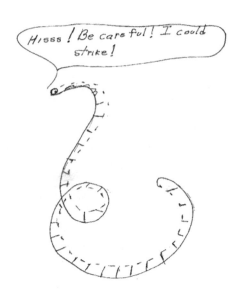

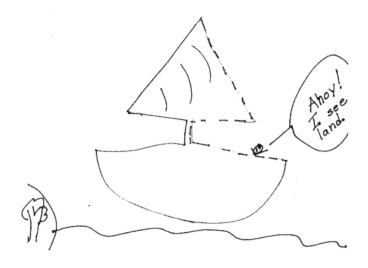

I am often surprised by the ability of youngsters to "see" much more in a scribble than appears, just as I am a bit dismayed by own lack of such ability. I seem to see Snoopy everywhere.

BRAIN TEASERS

I first used brain teasers in educational therapy, as a way of encouraging abstract thinking and reasoning. I avoided teasers with trick endings, using only those that can be solved with some form of logic, or by careful listening.

I follow this same format in psychotherapy, using the technique more in groups than with individuals. I choose those I think will be springboards to discussion.

I have not used them with families, because I sense they could become vehicles of scoldings and putdowns. But perhaps that is *my* problem, and you will put them to good use in this setting too.

Listed below some which have proven particularly effective as discussion generators. When I make them into little booklets, I have the answer upside down, or on an answer page in the back.

1. Question: What is always in front of you, but you can't see it?

Answer: Your future

Possible discussions: Whether it would be good to be able to see your future; Can you "see" your past?

2. Question: What do you call a boomerang that doesn't come back?

Answer: A stick

Possible discussions: Which is more fun? Is this a trick question?

3. Q: A man had seventeen sheep. All but nine died. How many were left?

Answer: Nine

Possible discussions: How easy it is to misunderstand something simple; how often we make things harder than they are; how we miss the obvious.

4. Q: If a plane crashed on the borderline of the United States and Canada where would the survivors be buried?

Answer: Survivors don't need to be buried anywhere.

Possible discussions: Same as No. 3; does the subject matter (death) make any difference to getting the answer? If so, how come?

5. Q. I can touch you, but you will never see me. When all is still and quiet I am never about, but everyone knows when I am on the move. Then I feel strong and you know I am coming. What am I?

Answer: The wind.

Possible discussions: Does the part of the country you live in, or the season of the year, make a difference as to how easy or hard this is? How did you go about figuring it out?

And the following, which, I am happy to report, is "caught on to" much more quickly these days than formerly. I know you know the answer, and the possibilities for discussion.

6. Q. A father and son were in an automobile accident. The father was killed and the son was injured. He was rushed to the nearest hospital for surgery. When the surgeon was called in to see the boy, the operation had to be postponed because the surgeon said, "I can't operate on that boy, he is my own son!" How could that be?

TODAY'S FAMOUS GUEST IS:

For this "talk show" you'll need a real tape recorder[*] and a toy microphone. You can buy the latter in a toy store, or improvise with a ball of clay stuck atop a ruler. Begin by explaining that the recorder will be on during the interview; but either of you can hit the pause button if you want to say something "off mike." Some youngsters like to have a copy of the tape; your copy will be afforded the same confidentiality protection as everything else.

As the famous guest to be interviewed by you, the youngster chooses an occupation he/she would like to be famous for. Singers, rock groups, and sports stars are favorites; I've also hosted artists, writers, veterinarians, rocket scientists, and chefs in my "studio."

The youngster can use his/her own name, or make one up. A station name could be the letters of your name, the child's, or anything that pleases both your fancies. Decide who your sponsors are, and after a brief commercial and the usual introduction: "We are privileged today to have as our guest the famous_____ "

Start the interview with questions such as:

When did you decide you wanted to be a_____?

What attracted you to the profession?

Who helped you to achieve your ambition?

In what way(s)?

What difficulties did you have reaching your goal?

What advice do you have for others who want to be a famous_____?

----

*For a fuller explanation of uses of the tape recorder, see the chapter "Releasing Creativity."

What special talents are necessary?

Knowing what you know now, what would you have done differently to prepare for this career?

Slant your questions to the child's situation. Responses may reflect projections, imagination, biographical information about a real famous person, and any or all combinations. They are sure to be illuminating and usually entertaining.

Next time, your client might want to interview you. What would you like to be famous for?

UNFAIR[*]

Even though I am only.................... years old, a lot has happened to me already. Here are some things that happened when I was younger that I think were really unfair:

These are things that are happening in my life now that I think are unfair:

Things I used to think were unfair but now consider fair are:

On the other hand, what I once thought was fair but now consider unfair is:

All in all, I'd say that I've had (circle one):

> more
> less
> about the same

unfair treatment than most people I know.

---

[*] Although this is slanted to children, it can be adapted for use wtih couples and families.

THE WORRIER'S ALPHABET

Every family has at least one worrier; youngsters as well as adults can be kept awake at night by obsessive and unwelcome thoughts. Here are instructions for a trick that often works:

Rather than try to turn off the obsessing, turn it to your advantage.

Work your way up the alphabet, thinking of one or more words for each letter that, for you, evokes relaxation, cheerfulness, optimism, or a smile. If you get stuck, think of places, colors, food, people, sings — anything at all, as you KEEP OBSESSING until you come up with at least one word for each letter.

Here is the first part of a sample list:

A	Apple pie. Aloha. Auntie Anna.
B	Bubbles. Butterflies.
C	Calm. Contented.
D	Delightful
E	Even. Equal.
F	Float. Flow. Fuchsia.

Should the worrier fall asleep before the alphabet is completed (a wonderfully common experience) the process must be picked up where left off at next bedtime. If the worrier doesn't remember at what point sleep took over, he/she must begin again with A.

For future lists, the same words can be re-used as necessary. The only rule is that the words have positive connotations for the individual worrier. As with guided imagery, one person's peaceful pond may evoke someone else's worst childhood memories.

The process of family members sharing their words and reactions can be revelatory and bonding. As one mother who was criticized for worrying so much pointed out:

"It only takes two letters to change a worrier into a warrior."

BETWEEN GENERATIONS

Some of my most productive and memorable family sessions have been with three — and occasionally four — generations. Grandparents and great-grandparents add dimensions of continuity, and sometimes surprise.

One way to break away from age stereotypes is to do a role reversal between the youngest and oldest generations. Since nostalgia is traditionally the province of older people, give that role to the youngest generation. Ask them to look back to "the good old days," or share early hardships, such as:

The first day of school
Before I had a little sister
Favorite meals grandma cooked
The time grandpa
When my allowance was only $

and so forth.

Then ask the seniors to do what kids do a lot of: look to the future. This can be a poignant experience if the elders respond, as they sometimes do, "I don't have a future." Take that as a cue to inquire:

"What about tomorrow? That's the future."
"Didn't you say earlier you were going shopping for a birthday gift? Is there going to be a party?"
"I wonder why you are taking those computer lessons," etc., etc., etc.

The "sandwich generation" is then asked to share what they learned about their children, and their parents, during the exercise. This is frequently the most moving part.

A CHILD'S EYE VIEW OF PROCESS NOTES

Children often inquire about what is in their folder. Usually I explain that it contains their drawings and stories, and use this opportunity to go through the material together as we reminisce, talk about changes and growth, and so forth. If they inquire about my written notes, I explain that I jot down a few things to help me remember what we did and when we did it. One curious youngster wanted to know in greater detail about what I wrote and why. I explained about "process notes," and the usefulness of noting what was helpful about that session, what issues were especially important, etc. etc.

"Would *you* like to make process notes also at the end of the session?" I asked and of course she very much likes to. We each follow the following outline, and then share and compare, which is the best and most contactful part of the activity.

An important thing that happened in our therapy session today is:

It is important because now I understand more about:

What I enjoyed most about today is:

I felt uncomfortable when:

I think (the other person's name) didn't like it when:

What I want to remember to do/say/ask next time is:

On a scale of one to ten, I'd rate today's session as a:

INDEX
FOR VOLUME I AND VOLUME II

Index for Volume I and Volume II

Index for Volume I and Volume II

Index for Volume I and Volume II

Index for Volume I and Volume II

Printed in Great Britain
by Amazon

82165212R00192